THE FIGHTER ACES OF THE R.A.F.

The Fighter Aces of the R.A.F.

E. C. R. Baker

NEW ENGLISH LIBRARY

TIMES MIRROR

First published in Great Britain by William Kimber & Co. Ltd., 1962
© William Kimber & Co. Ltd., 1962

*

FIRST NEL PAPERBACK EDITION JANUARY 1974
Reprinted April 1975

*

NEL Books are published by
New English Library Limited from Barnard's Inn, Holborn, London, E.C.1.
Made and printed in Great Britain by
Hazell Watson & Viney Ltd., Aylesbury, Bucks

45001710 9

AUTHOR'S FOREWORD

ALTHOUGH it has never been the official policy of the Air Ministry to publicise the exploits of its ace pilots, from time to time stories have been told of these knights of the air, some so fantastic that they are almost unbelievable. But a number of these tales are merely fiction, and one of the aims of this book is to put on record the true personal histories of these ace pilots.

During the Second World War more than forty Royal Air Force pilots were each credited with the destruction of at least twenty hostile aircraft in air combat. Some of these airmen are already well-known and very little need be said about their valiant deeds. Many are still unknown to the general public, and it is the intention of this book to give these pilots some of the publicity they so richly deserve. In these pages you will read of pilots from the Commonwealth, from Poland, France, Czechoslovakia and America, as well as from our own native shores, all of whom had one thing in common – they were all ace pilots of the Royal Air Force. You will meet the forgotten aces of the campaigns in the Western Desert, Greece, and Burma, the gallant pilots who defended Malta, the 'Few' who won the Battle of Britain, the aces who scored their first victories in the battles over Dunkirk, the hunters who pursued and fought the Luftwaffe over their own territory in the latter part of the war, and last, but by no means least, the intrepid band of fighters who went out in their Hurricanes, Beaufighters and Mosquitoes to take on the might of the Luftwaffe in the quiet stillness of the night.

I have taken the yardstick of twenty victories as the basis for my book purely in order to limit the number of personal histories that could be included. This does not mean that a score of twenty or more victories denotes greatness, and that a smaller score does not. I could quote a number of cases where a pilot is credited with a much lower total of victories, and yet is recognised by experts in the field of aerial warfare as being a truly great exponent of the art of shooting down enemy aeroplanes. Names which spring readily to mind are Victor Beamish, John Peel, Basil Embry, Richard Stevens, Peter Townsend and Desmond Mac-Mullen. No one could deny these the right to be called great fighter aces. The victories credited to the pilots have been verified with Air Ministry records and/or with the pilots themselves, and are as authentic as any list yet published. Even though the Royal Air Force was proved to have claimed more victories than could finally be substantiated from post-war evidence, close examination of their records proves that there was no intention to mislead and that official figures given after a battle were as accurate as could possibly be ascertained at the time.

The following story throws an interesting light on the Air Ministry's method of assessing the veracity of claims. In August, 1941, Flight Lieutenant H. M. Stephen was a member of a long-range Spitfire Wing detailed to give protection to Number Two Group daylight bombers who were being sent to attack the power station at Cologne. Whilst waiting to rendezvous with the bombers near Amsterdam, Stephen spotted a Junkers 88 night fighter which he attacked and left smoking. Before he could finish it off the bombers appeared, so Stephen rejoined the Spitfires to escort the bombers home. On landing he claimed one Ju. 88 damaged.

In February, 1942, Stephen was reading the confidential reports (circulated to fighter pilots about captured German pilots) when he found that a German Wing Commander of a Night Fighter Squadron, having been interrogated at great length due to his rank and experience, admitted that he had been shot down whilst on a leisurely morning flight in his Junkers 88 over the estuary of the Scheldt the previous August. There was no doubt about his being the pilot of the 88 claimed as damaged by Stephen. As a result of the report Stephen wrote through Fighter Command to the Air Ministry claiming an additional victory, confirmed by the evidence of the pilot-victim himself. After two or three months a polite note came back from the Air Ministry saying that since the aircraft had fallen on German soil the Air Council could not see their way to granting a confirmed victory, but were agreeable to having it raised from one damaged to one probably destroyed.

I think this is a true reflection of the conservativeness of Air Ministry policy and the caution with which it dealt with pilots' claims. It is a policy I do not choose to criticise in any way.

A book such as this would be impossible to write without the help and goodwill of many people. In the years I have taken in compiling it, my enquiries have led me to contact many people in all parts of the world, to whom I should like to record my gratitude.

I am indebted to the Air Ministry and, in particular, to the staff of the Air Historical Branch and of Department A.R.8. Much of the manuscript could not have been compiled without their generous help.

My thanks are also due to the staff of the Imperial War Museum, and in particular to Miss R. E. B. Coombs, who not only supplied valuable information, but was also a source of constant encouragement.

I also gratefully acknowledge the assistance of the Minister of Air, Melbourne, Australia; Royal Canadian Air Force Headquarters, Ottawa, Canada; the Air Department, Wellington, New Zealand; and *Service Historique de l'Armée de l'Air, Versailles*.

In addition I am grateful to Group Captain D. R. S. Bader; Wing Commander R. Bannock; Group Captain C. R. Caldwell; Group Captain F. R. Carey; Group Captain J. Cunningham; Group Captain A. C. Deere; Group Captain B. Drake; Squadron Leader N. F. Duke; Squadron Leader R. B. Hesselyn; Group Captain P. H. Hugo and his daughter Petrina; Air Commodore J. E. Johnson; Group Captain D. E. Kingaby; Squadron Leader J. H. Lacey; Wing Commander D. A. Oxby; Wing Commander H. M. Stephen; Group Captain M. M. Stephens; Wing Commander R. R. S. Tuck; and Wing Commander V. C. Woodward.

There are many others who have given freely of their time, and to all these I express my sincere thanks.

E. C. R. BAKER.

CONTENTS

THE FIGHTER ACES OF THE R.A.F.

1

THE PRIDE OF 85

Flight Lieutenant G. Allard
D.F.C., D.F.M. and Bar

'HERE THEY COME,' yelled the Flight Sergeant.

The R.A.F. ground crews sprinted across the windswept grass of the airfield as the Hurricanes of 85 Squadron came in over the trees that marked the boundary of the French airfield. One by one the Hurricanes touched down and rolled to a stop, to be met by their respective servicing crews, who swarmed over the aircraft to perform their various duties – rearming, refuelling, and repairing damaged fabric and metal, which had received the full fury of the Luftwaffe's cannon shells and machine-gun bullets.

The last Hurricane rolled to a standstill and a young, oil-stained leading aircraftman jumped on to the wing to push back the cockpit canopy.

Excitedly he exclaimed: 'How many this morning, sergeant?'

There was no answer. Puzzled, the fitter stared into the cockpit – and almost fell off the wing in surprise, as he was greeted by a snore. The pilot of the Hurricane was fast asleep.

He was Geoffrey Allard, 'Sammy' to his fellow-pilots, a sandy-haired sergeant from Yorkshire, who was so worn out by the countless sorties he had flown during the last few days, that he had not enough energy left to climb out of his fighter plane. It was May, 1940, and the Royal Air Force in France were flying as many as four or even five sorties in a single day. For day after day the fighter pilots' normal routine was to get up at dawn, make four or five patrols of an hour and a half each, and tumble into bed well after dark – only to be kept awake half the night by the rumbling of the anti-aircraft guns.

It was a welcome relief for Sammy when he was sent back to England on the 17th May for a short rest period. He had certainly deserved it, since in seven days he had shot down ten enemy aircraft for certain in addition to several probably destroyed or damaged. When the squadron left France three days later, having destroyed eighty-nine enemy planes in eleven days, it had only three Hurricanes left which were fit to fly, but very soon new Hurricanes arrived and new pilots, also, to replace those lost or wounded in action.

By the beginning of July the squadron was fully operational again and, under the command of Squadron Leader Peter Townsend, won further glory in the Battle of Britain. Its ace pilot Sammy Allard, newly commissioned, and fighting with renewed vigour, went on adding to his successes. On the 8th July he shot down a Heinkel 111, which crashed into the sea six miles south-east of Felixstowe; the following day he sent another Heinkel vertically down into a layer of cloud 3,000 feet over Harwich, but he did not see it actually crash, so he only claimed a 'probable'. On the 29th July Sammy was decorated with the D.F.M. at an investiture held at Debden Aerodrome; two days after this he helped Flight Lieutenant Hamilton to shoot an Me. 110 into the sea, and to knock pieces off a second.

On the 19th August, Number 85 Squadron was transferred to Croydon to join Number Eleven Group; here the tempo of the battle was increased as the Hurricanes were scrambled time after time to intercept the gigantic formations of bombers and escorting fighters sent over by Goering. In a few days the squadron destroyed over forty enemy planes and Allard in nine days from the 24th August to the 1st September shot down ten Huns, and probably destroyed a further three enemy machines.

The first of these successes took place over Ramsgate soon after breakfast on the 24th August when he attacked two Me. 109's which were climbing to join another twenty flying higher. He pulled up under one of the Messerschmitts, fired two short bursts and then dodged into some friendly-looking clouds, as the hostile fighters above dived towards him. He came out of the clouds a few seconds later to see the bunch of 109's heading south; the one he had fired at was just about to crash into the sea three miles from Ramsgate.

Two days later, in the afternoon, the squadron sighted eighteen Dornier 215's over Eastchurch with an escort of about thirty Me. 109's. The Hurricanes made a head-on attack on the bombers, Sammy selecting a trio of Dorniers who had detached themselves from the main formation. After his first onslaught the starboard Dornier broke away, so Sammy climbed up into the sun and then came diving down for another shot at the bomber. He repeated

14

this manoeuvre and as he broke away he saw that both the engines of the Dornier had stopped; he turned to attack another Dornier which had just come through the clouds. This time one three-second burst from directly astern of the bomber was sufficient to cause it to glide down and land on the aerodrome at Rochford.

The following day the squadron failed to make contact with the Luftwaffe, but during the afternoon of the 28th, Sammy was leading the squadron when he sighted twenty Me. 109's at 18,000 feet near to Dungeness. Allard led his ten Hurricanes in a diving attack out of the sun and, as usual when surprised, the enemy fighters broke up. Sammy picked out a 109 two hundred yards ahead and, as he closed to twenty yards' range, pressed the firing button. Eight guns belched forth flame and destruction. The German fighter caught fire and plunged vertically into the sea, just outside Folkestone Harbour. By the time the 109 had reached the sea, Sammy had already chosen a second victim, another 109 which had turned towards France. He fired several short bursts from 250 yards and the 109 dived down to level out about twenty feet from the sea. Allard fired again, and this time black smoke poured from the Messerschmitt's engine. It crashed about five miles north of St Inglevert. When Allard returned to Croydon after this fight, he was told that the squadron as a whole had shot down six Me. 109's without loss, and that the Prime Minister, who was visiting the south-eastern coastal defences, had witnessed the whole of the action.

Two days later Sammy destroyed two Heinkel 111's. The first one had both engines set on fire and was seen to crash by his Number Two, Pilot Officer English. The second he attacked burst into flames and dived straight down to crash in a field about thirty miles south west of Croydon.

On the last day of August, Sammy flew on three sorties, each time leading the squadron. He failed to score on his first outing, but during the late afternoon he claimed two Dornier 215's probably destroyed and on his last sortie of the day shot down a Messerschmitt 109 which crashed near Folkestone.

Sammy again led the squadron on the 1st September, just before lunch. He attacked twelve Me. 109's in a dive from out of the sun and chased the last aircraft in the formation out to sea, but as he found he could not get any nearer than 300 yards he opened fire in very short one-second bursts. Soon white smoke appeared and he was able to close to a hundred yards, where he gave a longer burst of bullets which sent the 109 into the sea ten miles from Cap Gris Nez. Up again after lunch, he led the squadron against a vast armada of almost 200 Dorniers and Messerschmitts. Three times he took his Hurricanes down in scorching attacks out of the sun. He succeeded in breaking up the enemy formation and shooting down a Dornier 17, in spite of fierce opposition from the 109's who managed to shoot away his starboard aileron and damage his engine. However, he made a forced landing at Lympne with a dead engine and asked some mechanics to have a look at it. Whilst they were doing so an Me. 110 dived out of the clouds and dropped two bombs near the Hurricane. One of the mechanics was killed and the plane was holed by shrapnel in several places, but next day Allard was able to fly it back to Croydon.

The squadron moved to Church Fenton a few days later and became an advanced training unit, Allard being promoted to Acting Flight Lieutenant and taking command of 'A' Flight on the 8th September. On the 14th September he was awarded a Bar to his D.F.M. and, only two days later, he was notified that he had been awarded the D.F.C. The citations credited him with the destruction of seventeen enemy aircraft, although he had at this time nineteen confirmed kills plus a share in others, according to the squadron's operations' book; his score as shown in his combat reports added up to twenty-one enemy aircraft destroyed plus a share in the destruction of two others.

In October, 1940, the squadron moved to Kirton-in-Lindsay to specialise in night fighting operations and within a few months were exchanging their Hurricanes for the new American Havoc aircraft. It was whilst taking off from Debden on the 13th March, 1941, to collect another Havoc that Allard and two companions were killed in a most unfortunate accident. Their plane stalled and spun into the ground; a piece of the front gun panel had become detached and lodged in the fin. The same day a signal was received by the squadron from the Air Officer Commanding (then Air Vice-Marshal Leigh Mallory, C.B., D.S.O.):

> Deeply regret to hear of Allard's death which is a very great loss to the service.

2

THE LEGLESS WONDER

Group Captain D. R. S. Bader
D.S.O. and Bar, D.F.C. and Bar,
Légion d'Honneur, Croix de Guerre

THE youngest son of Frederick and Jessie Bader, Douglas Robert Steuart Bader was born in St. John's Wood, London, on 21st February, 1910 and his early years were spent in India, where his father was in the Indian Civil Service. When his parents returned to England, Douglas was sent to a preparatory school at Temple Grove, where he soon shone both in the classroom and on the playing fields. He won a scholarship to St Edward's School, Oxford, and by the time he was eighteen he had captained the school at rugger and cricket, and won a prize cadetship to the Royal Air Force College at Cranwell. He studied and played hard whilst at Cranwell, and when he finally left there in June, 1930, he was posted to Number 23 Squadron at Kenley as a Pilot Officer. He continued his sporting activities and that summer he was chosen for the Royal Air Force Cricket Team. In the winter he played rugby for the Air Force, the Harlequins and Surrey, and the Combined Services against the Springboks' Touring Team. Suddenly, on the 14th December, 1931, he was involved in a terrible aircraft crash. He was so badly injured that both his legs had to be amputated and for weeks his life was in the balance. Slowly, however, he recovered and with the aid of artificial legs learned to walk again, to drive a car, and eventually to pilot an aeroplane. He was considered unfit for service flying, unfortunately, and in May, 1933, was invalided out of the Royal Air Force.

Bader joined the staff of the Asiatic Petroleum Company and remained with this firm until November, 1939, when after a medical and flying test he was accepted to rejoin the Royal Air Force. He was then posted to the Central Flying School at Upavon for a refresher course on single-engined aircraft. On completion of the course in February, 1940, he was posted to Number 19 Squadron with the rank of Flying Officer. Within a few weeks he had been promoted to Flight Commander with Number 222 Squadron. He flew a number of convoy patrols at this time but did not see any German aircraft until the end of May, 1940, when his squadron made several sorties over the Dunkirk area. During one of these, on the 31st May, Bader shot down his first Hun, an Me. 109 which fell in flames to crash near Dunkirk. The same afternoon he flew back to Dunkirk and found a Heinkel 111 diving on a destroyer. He scored hits on the fuselage and killed the enemy rear-gunner, before two more fighters jumped in and finished it off.

Soon after this Number 222 Squadron moved to Kirton-in-Lindsay and Bader was promoted to command Number 242 Squadron. This was a Canadian Hurricane Squadron which had been in the thick of the fighting in France, and which was now at Coltishall near Norwich, resting and reorganising. Whilst still in the middle of this reorganising period, Bader shot down his second Hun. It was the 11th July and the weather was so bad that all flying had been cancelled for the day; then a message came through that an enemy raider was heading for Cromer. Bader took off immediately and eventually found a lone Dornier. He closed in, lined up the enemy bomber in his sights and opened fire. The enemy rear-gunner stopped firing and then the Dornier plunged into the dense cloud. Bader returned to base prepared to claim only a damaged, but was delighted when he was told by the Duty Officer that a member of the Observer Corps had seen the Dornier dive out of the clouds and go straight into the sea.

By the end of August, 1940, Squadron Leader Bader had moulded his squadron into a first-class fighter unit and on the 30th they were ordered to take off for their first patrol during the Battle of Britain. South-west of North Weald they found about twenty bombers and thirty fighters. Bader led the Hurricanes in to attack. He himself dived right into the middle of the bombers and then found himself with three Messerschmitt 110's directly in front of him. He pressed the gun button and instantly pieces flew off one of the 110's. To the right he saw another 110 slowly circling, and he went after it, closing fast. A hundred yards behind he fired a sharp three-second burst. The German plane wobbled, pieces flew off the wing and flames burst forth. Another 110 had crept up behind Bader and was just about to open fire when the Hurricane swung round in a very tight turn. The Hun dived away with Bader following, but gradually losing ground to the much faster German fighter. Bader fired several bursts, in the forlorn hope of being able to slow down the Messerschmitt,

18

but observed no hits and a few minutes later gave up the chase.

On the 7th September, the Luftwaffe began an onslaught on London and Bader had a narrow escape. He led three squadrons of Hurricanes to intercept over seventy raiders heading for the capital. He fired at several Dorniers with no apparent effect, before a Messerschmitt 110 filled his sights. He fired a couple of bursts and saw smoke pour out of the 110, before he had to break away as cannon shells from a 109 knocked holes in his Hurricane. He slid away from the danger and then saw another 110 a few hundred feet below. Rolling over, he came down on the unsuspecting fighter from the rear. One burst was all that was necessary to send the 110 down to crash near a railway line. Bader, realising his damaged Hurricane had taken enough punishment for one battle, nursed his plane back to Coltishall for repairs.

Two days later Bader again led three squadrons to intercept sixty raiders, and on this occasion destroyed a Dornier 17 without any damage to his own aircraft.

Soon after this Bader was awarded his first decoration, the Distinguished Service Order for 'displaying gallantry and leadership of the highest order'; at the same time he was told that he was getting two more squadrons, Numbers 302 and 611, to fly with his formation, which was now to be called 'Twelve Group Wing'.

On September 15th, at the head of his sixty fighters, Bader gave the order to attack forty Junkers 88's and Dorniers. Two hours later he had them against another large bunch of bombers escorted by Messerschmitt 109's. His pilots had a field day and claimed fifty-two aircraft destroyed and eight probably destroyed. Bader's own share was one Dornier 17 destroyed and one other damaged.

Three days later his wing again met up with the enemy and this time shot down thirty Huns without loss. Bader accounted for one Junkers 88 and one Dornier 17 to bring his own personal score to eleven confirmed victories. He claimed his twelfth victim, a Messerschmitt 109, on the 27th September, but by this time the mass dog-fights of the Battle of Britain were over and in October, 1940, Bader's wing was disbanded. He remained Commanding Officer of Number 242 Squadron which in November, 1940, began re-equipping with new Hurricane II's.

In 1941, Fighter Command went over to the offensive and Bader was in the forefront of it. Promoted Wing Commander of the Tangmere Wing, consisting of three Spitfire Squadrons, Numbers 145, 610 and 616, he led them on several sweeps across the Channel, expecting any moment to be set upon by hordes of Messerschmitts, but never meeting a single one. He had to wait until the 21st June before the 109's eventually summoned up enough guts to attack the Spitfires. Bader soon showed his skill had not deserted him after his long interlude by sending one of them down to crash on the French coast. Five days later he shared a 109 with his wingman before lunch and, his appetite whetted, claimed another 109 during the afternoon sweep to St Omer. By this time the Messerschmitts were beginning to show interest in the Spitfires which were virtually flying regular daily trips to the Luftwaffe airfields and, during the month of July, Fighter Command found them most willing to join in the fighting. This suited Bader perfectly and in the first nine days of the month he added four more 109's destroyed, two probables and two damaged to his score. On the 12th he claimed a 109 destroyed and three damaged and a week later sent a 109 into the Channel, shot pieces off a second and scored hits on a third. The weather prevented any sweep on the 23rd, so taking Squadron Leader Burton of 616 Squadron as wingman, Bader flew to Dunkirk where he found an Me. 109 which splashed into the sea after a well-aimed burst.

Bader now received a new Spitfire V fitted with cannons, but he quickly had these removed and replaced by eight Browning machine-guns, since he had a particular preference for this type of armament. In fact, throughout the whole of his fighting career Bader only once used cannons and that was because his own Spitfire was unserviceable. He had done more sweeps now than anyone else in Fighter Command, but still he insisted on leading his wing on every raid. In seven days he did ten sweeps and then at the end of July was told that he had better have a spell off operations. He argued so vehemently against this that he was allowed to continue for a few more sorties. He was now fifth on the list of Fighter Command aces with twenty and a half confirmed victories, but was determined to add to this before he was taken off operations.

On the 9th August he made his last sortie. Leading his wing, he soon spotted a dozen Me. 109's near Le Touquet; they were flying slightly below the Spitfires. Leaving 610 Squadron to act as top-cover he led the rest of the Spitfires down. Misjudging his distance he sped right through the German pack, to find another six 109's flying placidly along unaware of the presence of Bader's Spitfire. He sneaked up behind them and from a hundred yards' range poured a burst into the middle fighter which fell away with flames trailing behind it. Bader veered slightly to bring his guns to bear on the next 109, which began to stream white smoke as Bader's bullets poured into its glycol tank. The next instant there was a terrific bang behind Bader and before he realised what was happening his Spitfire had fallen into a spin. Looking back Bader saw that the whole of his tail unit was missing. One of the Messerschmitts had run into him and sliced the tail off with its propeller.

Tearing off his helmet and mask, Bader struggled to get out of the cockpit of his doomed fighter, but somehow his right leg had become stuck fast. It seemed ages before he fell out, without his leg, and pulled the ripcord of his parachute. He landed in a cornfield and was immediately captured by three German soldiers, who handed him over to the hospital authorities at St Omer.

Several days later a new artificial leg was dropped for him by the R.A.F. and, fully mobile again, Bader was transferred to a prisoner of war camp. He remained a prisoner until he was released on the 14th April, 1945. He took two months leave and then, promoted Group Captain, took command of the Fighter Leader School at Tangmere. Later on he commanded the North Weald Fighter Sector and on the 15th September, 1945, he led the victory fly-past over London, to celebrate peace and the fifth anniversary of the greatest day in the Battle of Britain.

He was offered his old job with the Shell Petroleum Company, together with his own plane to fly anywhere in the world, and in February, 1946, Bader resigned his commission in the Royal Air Force and rejoined the Shell Company.

3

'SCREWBALL'

Squadron Leader G. F. Beurling
D.S.O., D.F.C., D.F.M. and Bar

As A youngster George Frederick Beurling spent all his spare time watching aircraft at the airport a few miles from his home in Verdun, a suburb of Montreal in Canada. His father, a commercial artist, would have liked his son to train for his own profession, but after George's first flight in an aeroplane, when he was ten years old, there was no doubt as to what his future would be. Beurling wrote in his autobiography *Malta Spitfire* – 'I was a flyer for the rest of time, no matter what happened.' All his spare time and money were spent on flying lessons, and eventually he passed the flying and written examinations for his pilot's certificate – only to learn that he was then too young to be licensed.

The Second World War broke out and immediately young Beurling volunteered as a pilot in the Royal Canadian Air Force, but was told that his educational standard was insufficient to meet the extremely high demands of this service. Still determined to fly, George volunteered for the Finnish Air Force and was accepted, but his father refused to give his consent. Undismayed, George kept on flying and by the spring of 1940 had logged 250 hours solo flying. Wisely he also studied hard at academic subjects.

His next objective was to join the Royal Air Force. One day in May, 1940, he sailed to England, made his application at an R.A.F. Recruiting Centre and was told that he must produce his birth certificate. George did not have it, so back to Canada he sailed to fetch it. He returned to Britain on the same ship, working as a deckhand, produced the document to the recruiting officer and on September 7th, 1940, he was accepted for flying duties with the Royal Air Force.

From the time he enlisted Beurling's one and only ambition was to follow in the footsteps of the famous aces of the First World War. He trained with all his heart and soul, puzzled over the problems of aerial combat, absorbed all the knowledge possible, and when not on duty read and studied the life stories of Ball, McCudden, Mannock, Bishop and other ace pilots of the 1914–18 war. Every minute of his training period was devoted to making himself into a first-class fighter pilot. He excelled at shooting and each day would spend some considerable time at target practice, until he had become a magnificent marksman with all kinds of weapons and at all distances, both in the air and on the ground. He realised early on that eyesight was very important to a fighter pilot, and he spent hours on training his eyes to pick out tiny articles at great distances. He became so good at this that when he subsequently went into action he was nearly always the first member of his squadron to sight the enemy.

By December, 1941, Beurling had completed his training,

which had been done under the expert guidance of that great Battle of Britain veteran, 'Ginger' Lacey, and was immediately posted to Number 403 Squadron. He took part in many fighter sweeps over the Channel and Northern France in the early part of 1942, but had to wait until May 1st before he shot down his first enemy plane, a Focke-Wulf 190 which exploded over Calais. Two days later Beurling repeated the feat. This proved to be his last victory in this theatre of war for some time, since shortly afterwards he was ordered to join Number 249 Squadron, which was stationed at Takali in Malta. This was already one of the crack Spitfire squadrons, having a total of 180 enemy planes to its credit, when Sergeant Beurling joined it on the 8th June, 1942.

Four days later Beurling had his first real taste of action in Malta, when he and three other pilots encountered fifteen Me. 109's. In a few minutes the enemy had been routed and were on their way back to their bases in Sicily, but not before young Beurling had badly damaged one of them.

'Screwball' – the nickname was given to him by the squadron, because he had a peculiar habit of calling everything and every-one by this unusual name – had to wait nearly a month after this before he had another chance to meet the Germans, for a spell of bad weather followed and the gallant defenders of Malta had a period of rest, whilst the bombers of the Luftwaffe and the Regia Aeronautica were grounded in Sicily. On July 6th the lull ended and the enemy bombers started to raid the island again. Early in the morning eight Spitfires of 249 Squadron intercepted three Cant bombers and thirty fighters heading for Luqa. The Spitfires charged into the enemy formation, Beurling selecting one of the leading Huns as his target. He peppered its fuselage with cannon shells and machine-gun bullets, before he whizzed past and climbed to attack a Macchi 202, one of Italy's best fighters at this time. A slight touch on the gun button was all that was necessary to send the Italian fighter down towards the sea, burning fur-iously. Looking round Screwball saw one of his comrades in trouble with a Macchi on his tail, so he swung across to help. The Italian dived away, closely followed by the Canadian. When the two planes pulled out of the dive 5,000 feet lower down Screw-ball fired a long burst of cannon shells. The Macchi broke up into small pieces to make Beurling's score two destroyed and one damaged in that fight. Returning to Takali, Screwball quickly refuelled and took off again to meet two Me. 109's heading for Malta. The Messerschmitts split up and tried to climb away, but Beurling was after one of them in a flash. He gave it a three-second burst after which it streamed a trail of white smoke until it dived into the Mediterranean Sea. The other Messerschmitt made off as quickly as possible in the direction of Sicily.

The Squadron was again up early on the 10th July to intercept four Junkers 88's escorted by about thirty Me. 109's. Beurling headed for the fighter escort and fastened on to a 109 which was about to open fire on a Spitfire. Screwball pulled up sharply under the tail of the Messerschmitt and fired into its belly. The enemy fighter turned completely over and then went straight down into the sea. On a second patrol later in the day Beurling found a solitary Spitfire being attacked by seven Macchi 202s. He dived into the middle of the fighters, scattering them in all directions. He followed one of them, which twisted away to escape the clutches of this fearless fighter, but Beurling stuck to it as if he were tied to it. For several minutes the combat went on, with Beurling just not able to keep the Macchi in his sights for more than a split second, until the Italian suddenly went into a loop. Beurling held off until it straightened out and then gave it a burst into the front of its fuselage. The next second the Italian pilot baled out. The rest of the enemy fighters had disappeared so Beurling joined up with the other Spitfire to fly back to Takali.

The next day Beurling and three other pilots met another group of bombers on their way to Malta. Again Sergeant Beurling attacked the fighter escort, this time diving on a Macchi and opening fire from a range of 300 yards. His aim must have been very accurate for immediately the Macchi fell away streaming glycol. As he closed in for another attack Beurling saw the cockpit cover of the Macci slide back and then its pilot baled out. Ninety minutes later Beurling and another pilot on a second patrol found two more Macchi's. The Canadian caught up with the rearward of the pair, gave it a short burst and it went down in flames. Whipping round behind the other one, Screwball also gave this a short burst and it dived down to join its mate below the waves of the deep blue Mediterranean Sea. Two victories inside ten seconds brought Beurling's score to ten, eight of which he had destroyed in three days of fighting over Malta, which explains why he was awarded the Distinguished Flying Medal shortly afterwards for 'displaying great skill and courage in the face of the enemy'.

A fortnight later Beurling shot down four enemy fighters in a single day. On the early morning patrol, on the 27th July, the squadron intercepted seven Junkers 88's with an escort of about forty fighters. Screwball spotted a group of four Macchi 202's in line astern and headed for the nearest one. The Italian saw him coming and pulled away. Beurling tightened his turn and allowing for the deflection aimed in front of the Macchi. It flew right into the deadly stream of hot lead and next instant went down to crash-land on the beach near Kalafrana. In the meantime Beurling had caught the next Macchi, which exploded in mid-air. The other two Macchi's, their pilots thoroughly scared by the deadly marksmanship of the young Canadian ace, zoomed and skidded all over the sky in an attempt to avoid their pursuer, but they need not have worried, for Sergeant Beurling had already spotted two Me. 109's directly beneath him, and instead of pressing his attack on the Italians, he rolled and pulled up underneath the 109's. He caught the first one with a burst into the petrol tank and, as it went down in flames, used up the rest of his ammunition on its companion. Beurling then broke off the combat in order to refuel and rearm.

An hour or so later Beurling and three others climbed back into the battle to find twenty Me. 109's circling round four Junkers 88's. Beurling got on the tail of one of the Messerschmitt's and started to chase it round in ever diminishing circles, until the 109 finally stalled and fell away, with the determined Canadian hot on its heels. He opened fire, hit the Messerschmitt in the glycol tank, and a few moments later saw it dive vertically into the sea. This was Screwball's sixteenth confirmed kill. Not long after this Beurling shot down another 109, and was rewarded for his almost unbelievable run of victories by being awarded a Bar to his D.F.M. and a few days later was granted a commission.

During the next six or seven weeks there was a great lull in the fighting over Malta. The enemy stayed at home to lick their wounds after their enormous losses in the great air battles of June and July and only a few bombers came over to try to bomb targets in Malta and these came mostly at night. During the same period the squadron's Spitfires were completely overhauled and there were also many changes in the personnel of the squadron. Squadron Leader Bob Grant, Flight Lieutenant 'Laddie' Lucas, and Flight Lieutenant 'Buck' McNair, who had been with the squadron for some time, were all decorated and then repatriated to the Mother Country. A new Station Commander, Wing Commander Donaldson, arrived and the squadron had a new Commanding Officer, Squadron Leader 'Timber' Woods, who had won his D.F.C. in the Battle of Britain.

Towards the end of September the lull ended and once more

the Nazis sent over swarms of bombers and fighters in another attempt to wipe out the heroic defenders of Malta. But the Spitfires were ready for them and made the aggressors pay dearly for the attacks. Beurling and Flight Lieutenant Eric Hetherington by this time had formed a partnership which met with great success. The two of them would attack an enemy formation, pick out a victim, and Hetherington would make dummy attacks causing the enemy plane to come within range of Beurling's guns. A short burst from this expert marksman and he would be able to claim another victory. The Canadian was so good with his shooting that it was very rare for an enemy plane to escape once it had entered his sights. In this way Screwball soon became the top-scoring pilot on the Island and before the end of September had added the Distinguished Flying Cross to his decorations.

During the month of October Beurling was only in action for two days before he was repatriated, but in those two days he packed enough excitement to fill a lifetime. On the first of them, the 13th October, he was out with the squadron on the dawn patrol when they encountered fifteen Junkers 88's escorted by almost a hundred fighters. Immediately Timber Woods gave the order to attack and the Spitfires roared down in line abreast with guns blazing. Beurling fired at one of the bombers, but was himself attacked by about twenty Me. 109's, so he wheeled round and charged head-on into the group. He went straight through the Messerschmitts, banked steeply and came in directly astern of one of the 109's. He gave it a short burst, saw his shells striking the fuselage of the enemy fighter, and then the 109 exploded and fell to earth in small pieces. A slight turn now brought Beurling on to the tail of another 109, so he pressed the gun button once more. The cockpit hood of the enemy machine flew off and the German pilot baled out. The Canadian then turned his attention to the bombers, one of which he caught just as it was about to release its bombs. Beurling gave it a long deflection burst which caused black smoke to stream from its engines. Another short burst and the Junkers dived right into the ground. The rest of the enemy formation turned and fled towards Sicily before this resolute young airman had a chance to do any more damage.

The next day Screwball gave the Germans another lesson in marksmanship. It was his last day in action over Malta, but what a glorious day it turned out to be. Shortly after noon the whole squadron scrambled to meet eight Junkers 88's with an escort of about fifty Me. 109's. As usual Beurling was off first and met the enemy formation just off the east coast of the island. He picked out a Junkers 88, gave it a two-second burst, and the raider, blazing from end to end, plunged headlong into the sea. At the same time a Spitfire shot past Beurling with eight Me. 109's on its tail. Beurling tore after the Huns and fired a long deflection shot into the leading 109, which immediately dived into the sea streaming smoke and shedding pieces. As the Canadian veered slightly to bring his sights to bear on another Messerschmitt, bullets and cannon shells from an enemy bomber tore into his cockpit and Beurling was hit in the hand and forearm. Yanking hurriedly on the control column, Screwball climbed quickly out of range of the bomber's guns and then saw another Spitfire in trouble just below him. He went down vertically and pulled up underneath a Messerschmitt 109. He pressed the firing button as he closed rapidly on the German, saw the port wing of the 109 break away from the rest of the aircraft and then watched the remains of the fighter as it spiralled down into the sea.

It was a bad mistake.

He did not see the next 109 as it came in from astern, but he certainly knew it was there a split second later, when a hail of bullets and cannon shells smashed into his Spitfire. The controls were shot to pieces, and Screwball himself was hit in the leg, heel and arm, but he managed to struggle out of the cockpit and fall headlong into space. He pulled the ripcord of his parachute and thankfully breathed a sigh of relief as the large white mushroom billowed out above his head. He looked up and saw the Messerschmitt which had shot him down being chased by a Spitfire, and then he fell with a splash into the cool, blue waves of the Mediterranean. In a few minutes an Air/Sea Rescue launch picked him up and thirty minutes later he was in hospital, being treated for his wounds. He was still in hospital a week later when he heard that he had been awarded the Distinguished Service Order for his gallant action on the 14th October. He also heard, much to his annoyance and regret, that he was being taken off operational duties and sent back to Canada.

Early in November he was flown back to his home country, where he received a tremendous reception, being hailed as the greatest Canadian ace since the days of Billy Bishop in the 1914–18 War. The Canadians now wanted him back in the Royal Canadian Air Force and in 1943 Beurling was transferred as a Flight Lieutenant to Number 403 (R.C.A.F.) Squadron. He returned to operations with the squadron when it came to England, and on the 24th September, 1943, shot down a Focke-Wulf 190 during a sweep over Northern France. He shot down his last victim, another F.W. 190, over South-west Germany on the 30th December to bring his final score to thirty-one and a third confirmed victories. Soon after this he was taken off operations and spent the rest of the war as a gunnery instructor at Catfoss.

When the war ended Beurling decided to leave the Royal Canadian Air Force and for a time became a pilot with a civil air line in Canada. This was not exciting enough for Beurling and in May, 1948, he decided to join the Israeli Air Force, where he hoped once more to indulge in the art of aerial combat. His wish was never fulfilled for this remarkable man was killed in an air accident near Rome on the 20th May, 1948, whilst ferrying his aircraft to Israel. So died Screwball Beurling, the greatest fighter ace produced by Canada during the Second World War.

4

ACE INTRUDER PILOT

Wing Commander J. R. D. Braham
D.S.O. and Two Bars, D.F.C. and Two Bars, A.F.C.,
Croix de Guerre Belge

THE Blenheim night fighter had been patrolling back and forth over the River Humber for more than an hour, and its young blond-haired pilot was bored. It was August 24th, 1940, the Battle of Britain was in full swing, the day fighters were shooting down the Luftwaffe planes by the score and here he was, after nearly a year of operational flying as a night fighter pilot, still waiting to fire his guns at an enemy plane. His thoughts were suddenly interrupted as the voice of the Operations Controller came over the radio-telephone, informing him of the presence of an enemy aircraft. Instantly, the pilot was alert, scanning the dark skies about him for some sign of the raider. A few moments later he spotted an aircraft caught in a cone of searchlights. He opened the throttle and, as he closed rapidly, he identified the raider as a Dornier 17. A short burst from the Blenheim's forward-firing guns caused smoke to billow out behind the Dornier, and then another burst from the gunner's turret settled the issue; flames leaped from the Dornier, and it fell away to explode as it hit the ground. 'Bob' Braham, destined to become the top-scoring intruder ace of the R.A.F., was at last able to claim his first confirmed victory.

The son of a vicar, John Randall Daniel Braham was born at Bath on the 6th April, 1920 and was educated at Taunton Grammar School. He joined the Royal Air Force on a short service commission in December, 1937, and a year later after completing his period of training successfully was posted to Number 29 Squadron stationed at Debden. In September, 1939, the squadron was re-equipped with Blenheims and spent the next few months in training for night fighting. At this particular period of the war, the night fighter pilot had none of the radar aids which subsequently proved of such great value. He had to rely on his eyes to find the German night raiders and, since visibility in the air at night was so poor, he seldom even caught a glimpse of an enemy plane. Consequently night fighter victories were rare occurrences, and Bob Braham had to wait until March, 1941, before shooting down his second victim. In the meantime the squadron had been re-equipped with Beaufighters and this change undoubtedly had a lot to do with Braham's subsequent run of successes. Another factor which helped considerably was the transfer of 29 Squadron to West Malling, which meant that they were now responsible for guarding the approaches to London.

On the 8th May, Braham scored his third night fighting success. This time, with the help of his radar operator, he sighted two Heinkel 111's over Croydon. He fired at one which dived away, so Bob dived after it and gave it a longer burst of cannon shells and machine gun bullets. This time flames appeared, so Braham left the stricken bomber and tried to find its companion. It was miles away by this time, however, so Braham gave up the chase and returned to West Malling.

A few weeks after this victory, Braham teamed up with Sergeant 'Sticks' Gregory as his radar operator and together they set up a thriving partnership, which ultimately became one of the most successful of all night fighting crews. Their first success together took place early in July, 1941, when they sighted, engaged and shot down a Junkers 88. It fell in flames into the River Thames.

The Luftwaffe gave up its mass night attacks during the rest of the summer months in favour of small low-level hit and run raids, which our night fighters found extremely difficult to engage because of the ineffectiveness of their radar apparatus at low altitudes. Braham and Gregory therefore were unable to add to their victories until the 12th September, when they caught a Heinkel 111 returning from a raid on the Midlands. With one short burst which only used up 72 rounds of ammunition Braham sent down the Heinkel in flames. The following month Braham and Gregory shot down another night raider, but this was to be their last success for some time, since in December, 1941, both of them were rested from operations and posted to Number 51 Night Fighter Operational Training Unit near Bedford. At the same time Braham was awarded a Bar to the D.F.C., which he had won in the previous April, and Gregory received the D.F.M. and a recommendation for a commission which came through two months later.

Whilst they were still officially 'not on active operations against the enemy', Braham and Gregory shot down a Dornier 217. They were paying a visit to their old squadron, Number 29, in June, 1942, and managed to persuade the Commanding Officer to lend them a Beaufighter, during a night raid on Canterbury. They took off and very quickly Gregory with the aid of his radar equipment led Braham towards an aircraft, which turned out to be a Dornier 217. One short burst was all that was necessary to send the Dornier down into the sea.

The following month, Braham and Gregory began their second tour of operations when they rejoined Number 29 Squadron at West Malling, Braham being made flight commander of 'A' Flight. Bob quickly proved he had lost none of his old skill during his rest from operations, for within a few weeks he destroyed three Huns, and damaged three more. The last of this run of victories occurred on the 28th August when he shot down a Junkers 88. On a second patrol in the early hours of the morning, Braham made contact with another Ju. 88, whose rear-gunner put a long burst of cannon shells into the Beaufighter, causing one of its engines to catch fire. Braham, making a hurried retreat, managed to put out the fire and then flew back on one engine to the first airfield he saw, where he put the Beaufighter down in a belly landing.

Braham was awarded an immediate D.S.O. in October, 1942, and celebrated by adding a Junkers 88 and a Dornier 17 to his confirmed victories before the month had ended. In November he was promoted to Acting Wing Commander and given command of Number 141 Squadron who were stationed near Chichester. There was very little night activity for several weeks because of the bad weather, but during one patrol in December, Braham managed to shoot down a Dornier 217 into the sea.

The squadron moved to Predannock in Cornwall in February, 1943, for a spell on convoy patrol duties, and within a few days Braham was making an attack on a U-boat in the Bay of Biscay. He scored several hits and caused it to make a hurried crash-dive. Shortly afterwards he found a motor torpedo boat in the same area and after a couple of low level strafing attacks left the boat burning furiously and its crew floundering in the sea. Soon after this Braham was awarded a second Bar to his D.F.C.

The Air Ministry 'back room boys' now produced a new type of radar equipment that would enable the night fighters to penetrate deep into enemy territory to search for German night fighter aircraft. Night bomber escort missions were introduced therefore and Number 141 Squadron was one of several units entrusted with this operation. They moved to Wittering and in June, 1943, Braham and his colleagues had their first taste of this type of mission. It did not take Braham long to prove the capabilities of the equipment, for on his very first escort mission, on the 14th June, he intercepted and destroyed an Me. 110 night fighter over the Zuyder Zee.

In three months, six more enemy night fighters were shot out of the dark skies of Germany by Bob Braham, and on the night of 29th September, when he destroyed another Me. 110, he brought his total of kills to twenty, nineteen of which he had shot down at night, thus equalling the night fighter record score set up by Group Captain John 'Cat's Eyes' Cunningham. This led to the award of a Bar to Braham's D.S.O. at the end of his second tour of operations in October, 1943. He relinquished command of Number 141 Squadron and was posted to the Army Staff College at Camberley, where he remained until February, 1944, when he became Wing Commander (Night Operations) at Number Two Group Headquarters. He was now allowed to do only a limited amount of operational flying, but he was lucky, for although he flew an average of only one mission per week he nearly always managed to find a victim. He was flying a Mosquito now, on another type of sortie: low-level daylight intruder missions deep into the heart of enemy territory.

He made six of these trips during March and April, 1944, and only on one of these missions did he fail to claim a success. During the other five sorties he shot down seven enemy aircraft, one of them a large four-engined Heinkel 177. His first mission

31

in May, on the 6th, gave him the opportunity to shoot down a Junkers 88 near Copenhagen and six days later Braham destroyed his twenty-ninth victim during a most exciting combat.

He was on an intruder mission over Denmark when he encountered an F.W. 190 and an Me. 109. He chased the 190 and did not see the Messerschmitt which managed to get on his tail and damaged the Mosquito's petrol tank. Braham continued his attack on the 190 and eventually sent it down to crash-land about ten miles south of Aalborg. As he turned to deal with the Messerschmitt, his Mosquito was hit by anti-aircraft fire and in spite of Braham's efforts at the controls, it slowly lost height. Luckily for Braham, the Messerschmitt had made off or the Mosquito would have been easy meat. Braham coaxed the Mosquito along as best he could, but soon realised that he would have to abandon it. He and Gregory baled out whilst still seventy miles from the English coast, but the Air/Sea Rescue boys had received his 'Mayday' call, and were quickly on the scene. Before long the two fliers were in the launch and on their way home.

Shortly after this incident, Bob Braham was awarded a second Bar to his D.S.O., and thus became the first R.A.F. pilot ever to win three D.S.O.'s and three D.F.C.'s.

After his escape on the 12th May, Braham was grounded for several weeks and did no more operational flying until D-Day when he took a Mosquito fighter bomber to raid a target in Normandy. A little over a fortnight later, Bob Braham made his last wartime sortie. On the 25th June, he took off with an Australian navigator, Flight Lieutenant Don Walsh, for another intruder mission to Denmark. He had no luck and was on his way out over the Danish coast when he was surprised by two F.W. 190's, which poured a stream of cannon shells into the Mosquito. With the port engine and wing set on fire and with absolutely no chance of getting away, Braham crash-landed the Mosquito on the beach. A few minutes later Braham and Walsh were surrounded by German soldiers. They spent the remaining ten months of the war in a prisoner of war camp.

In May, 1945, Bob Braham returned to England and accepted a permanent commission in the Royal Air Force. He resigned his commission in March, 1946, with the object of joining the Colonial Service, but he soon rejoined. However, in 1952 he changed his mind again, and this time left the R.A.F. for good. He emigrated to Canada with his wife and children and before very long had accepted a commission in the Royal Canadian Air Force.

5

'KILLER' FROM DOWN-UNDER

Group Captain C. R. Caldwell
D.S.O., D.F.C. and Bar
Polish Cross of Valour

THE top-scoring Australian fighter pilot of the Second World War, Clive Robertson Caldwell was born in Sydney, New South Wales, on the 28th July, 1910. He was educated first at Trinity Grammar School and later Sydney Grammar School. He joined the Royal Aero Club of New South Wales, and in 1938 had his first flying lesson. After only three and a half hours of dual instruction he made his first solo flight, and when the war broke out his log book showed just eleven hours' flying time.

Clive had made up his mind to become a fighter pilot if war came and so on the 4th September, 1939, sent in an application to join the Royal Australian Air Force. He was sent on an Officer Pilot Course in February, 1940, but on finding that all pilots on the course would become flying instructors, he obtained his release and rejoined in May, 1940, as an Aircraftman 2 Aircrew trainee under the Empire Air Training Scheme. After several months of intense training he finally completed the course and was commissioned as an Acting Pilot Officer in January, 1941. A fortnight later he embarked for the Middle East, where in May, 1941, he was posted to Number 250 Squadron which was in the process of formation in Aqir, Palestine. For a spell he flew bomber escort missions and ground strafing raids on aerodromes in Syria, and then was detached with two other pilots for the first fighter defence of Cyprus. He rejoined Number 250 Squadron at Alexandria and before long the squadron moved up to the front line in the Western Desert, where Caldwell scored his first victory on the 26th June.

The squadron was returning from an escort mission to Gazala when the Tomahawks and Blenheims were attacked by thirty Me. 109's between Capuzzo and Tobruk. In the general mix-up that followed Caldwell fired at several enemy fighters without observing much damage, before spotting an unsuspecting 109 just below his Tomahawk. He slid into position astern of the Messerschmitt and fired into its fuselage with short bursts of machinegun fire. Black smoke poured from the 109's engine and it went down in a gentle dive. Caldwell climbed back into the heavens to look for more opponents, but the Messerschmitts had been put to flight by the Tomahawks, so he rejoined the Blenheims and returned safely to base.

Four days later the Australian was piloting one of nine Tomahawks from Number 250 Squadron, who were guarding a convoy fifty miles east of Tobruk, when a force of twenty Junkers 87's escorted by thirty Messerschmitts attempted to attack the convoy. One flight of Tomahawks engaged the fighters, while Caldwell's flight headed for the Stukas. In a quarter of an hour it was all over and the enemy formation routed. The Tomahawks shot down six enemy planes without loss, Caldwell being credited with two Junkers 87's and sharing in the destruction of an Me. 110.

Caldwell, who by this time had earned himself the nickname of 'Killer', brought his personal score to four and a half when he shot down an Italian Fiat G.50 fighter while on an offensive sweep over the Bardia area on July 7th.

He was patrolling over ships of the Royal Navy on the Tobruk run on August 29th when he was surprised by two Me. 109's who dived on his Tomahawk from out of the sun. His plane was badly damaged during their first attack and Caldwell himself was wounded in the shoulder, back and leg. Most pilots would have called it a day at that, and headed for home, but not Killer who meant to have his revenge. He flung his Tomahawk about the sky with such skill that he cleverly out-manoeuvred the German planes, and when one overshot the Aussie, he promptly took advantage of the other pilot's mistake and shot it down into the sea. The other made off quickly, probably, Caldwell thought, because he had run out of ammunition, while the Aussie struggled back home with his damaged fighter. His wounds were soon attended to by the Medical Officer and he was operational again, although a bit sore, on the afternoon of September 1st, when he was lucky to avoid being hit again when attacked by an Me. 109.

Caldwell led his flight with great skill on escort missions, patrols and ground strafing attacks on enemy airfields and supply columns during the next few weeks, but he did not shoot down any more enemy aircraft until the 23rd November. On this day his flight met six Me. 109's west of Capuzzo. Caldwell selected the leading Hun as his target and after much chasing about finally shot it down in flames. Recalling his flight they continued their patrol and then returned to their aerodrome where Caldwell's ground crew refuelled and rearmed his Tomahawk and then added another little swastika to the row indicating his victories. There were now seven and a half swastikas beneath the cockpit of his Tomahawk, and they made a very impressive border. This border grew very rapidly a fortnight later on the 5th December when Killer Caldwell reported that he had shot down no less than five Junkers 87's in a single patrol.

It happened during the *Crusader* offensive, when Caldwell was leading a force of nineteen Tomahawks from Numbers 250 and 112 Squadrons in an offensive sweep. They encountered a formation of about sixty Junkers 87's heavily escorted by Me. 109's about ten miles west of El Gobi. What followed can only be described as a massacre, for within half-an-hour the Tomahawks had shot down twenty-seven of the Stukas and scored the most brilliant air success of the campaign in the Western Desert. Caldwell attacked three Stukas which were close together, and with his first burst of gunfire from slightly above on their starboard beam caused the second Stuka to explode and the third to catch fire and go down in flames. He then shot down another three 87's before the battle was over.

He destroyed a Messerschmitt 109 during an escort mission to Benghazi on the 20th December and on Boxing Day, 1941, received the simultaneous award of the Distinguished Flying Cross and Bar. By this time Caldwell had made quite a reputation for himself as a fighter ace and had become one of the top-scoring pilots in the Desert Air Force. Although he was at his best when he could go off on some 'lone-wolf' operation, he had proved that he was also a brilliant tactician and a fine leader and it came as no real surprise when he was given further promotion on the 6th January, 1942, to Squadron Leader and took command of Number 112 Squadron. This means that he had risen from the rank of Pilot Officer to that of Squadron Leader in less than twelve months, setting up the record for the Australian pilots.

At the end of January, 1942, the enemy began the offensive which pushed the Allied armies into Egypt and it was about this time that Number 112 Squadron carried out a record number of sorties, sixty-nine to be exact, for a single day. The squadron's pilots shot down many German and Italian planes, and Caldwell's row of swastikas grew steadily longer. In March, the Kittyhawks, with which the squadron had recently been re-equipped, were fitted with bomb racks, and dive-bombing the enemy supply lines and positions was added to the squadron's activities. After they had dropped their bombs the 'Sharks', this was the nickname given to the squadron, would resume their normal role as fighters and go off looking for Messerschmitts. Usually they did not have to look very far, for the Messerschmitts were prevalent on these dive-bombing occasions.

The Australian Government had asked for Caldwell's return to Australia for operations, but Sir Arthur (now Lord) Tedder had been able to refuse this as he had asked Caldwell, and had been assured by the Aussie that he was not 'combat fatigued'; Tedder had told Caldwell that he was giving him command of a Spitfire Wing then about to be formed in the Desert. This was to consist of two squadrons coming from Britain, and the third was to be made up of experienced desert pilots who would be chosen by Caldwell. Soon afterwards this programme had to be deferred for lack of Spitfires and so Caldwell was informed that in these circumstances Tedder could now no longer refuse his return to Australia. When saying goodbye, Tedder asked for Caldwell's log-book in which he wrote an 'assessment', a signal honour of which Caldwell is very proud.

At the end of this first tour of operations Caldwell had flown continuously on missions for over 550 hours during which he had destroyed twenty enemy aircraft and shared in the destruction of one more. He left Cairo on the 12th May, 1942, and shortly after arriving in London was posted to the Kenley Spitfire Wing. He remained at Kenley only for a few weeks before being recalled to London, where he became attached to the Royal Australian Air Force Headquarters. Caldwell was awarded the Polish Cross of Valour on the 4th August for his 'buoyant co-operation with Polish pilots when commanding Number 112 Squadron', this being the first award of its kind to be made by the Poles to a member of a Dominion Air Force. Soon afterwards Caldwell was on his way to Australia, via the United States.

Caldwell arrived in Australia in September, 1942, where he received a great welcome as his country's leading fighter pilot, after which he was posted to Number Two Operational Training Wing. Here he taught young trainees all he knew about air fighting, and also found time to carry out combat handling tests on a new Australian fighter plane, the Boomerang, and to participate in 'G' suit tests. In January, 1943, Caldwell became Wing Commander Flying of Number One Fighter Wing, which on moving to Darwin in Northern Australia, soon became the target of

Japanese raiders. Killer led the wing several times into action against these Japanese raiders and on the 2nd March scored his first success in Australia.

He led six Spitfires to engage a force of sixteen Japanese fighters and bombers raiding Coomallie in Northern Territory. In a short time the Spitfires had driven away the raiders and Caldwell himself had accounted for two of the Japanese planes. He destroyed two more Japanese aircraft exactly two months later when he led the Wing against a force of forty-eight enemy planes which were making a daylight raid on Darwin.

Caldwell's next success, his 25th confirmed victory, occurred on the 20th June, 1943, when over fifty Japanese aircraft attacked Darwin. He took off at the head of forty-nine Spitfires to meet the raiders, but through failure of his radio was obliged to hand over the lead of his wing. The Spitfires met the Japs on the way in to Wynellie harassed them over the town, westwards out to sea, and south of Melville Island. Caldwell tried to attack the bombers but was prevented from doing so by the Zero fighters. The Zeros were very manoeuvrable and he found it difficult to get into position to make an attack, but eventually he caught one unawares. Pressing the firing button he saw large pieces fly off the Zero as his cannon shells bored into the fuselage of the Jap fighter. The Zero made a quick turn to port to try to avoid his pursurer, but Caldwell stuck to it like a leech and after another short burst the Zero rolled over and crashed into the sea. The dogfight had carried Caldwell well away from the main battle so he set course and landed safely at his base a quarter of an hour later.

On the 28th June, Killer intercepted and destroyed a Japanese twin-engined bomber near Darwin, and two days later added another Zero to his bag. He scored his last kill, bringing his final total to twenty-eight and a half, on the 17th August, when he engaged and shot down a Japanese reconnaissance machine near Darwin.

Relinquishing command of his Spitfire wing a month later, Caldwell became Chief Flying Instructor at Number 2 Operational Training Unit. Soon after this he was awarded the Distinguished Service Order when the official citation stated that 'by his confidence, coolness, skill, and determination in the air, he set a most excellent example to all pilots in the wing. His skill and judgement as a leader are outstanding'.

Returning to operational service in May, 1944, as leader of Number Eighty Fighter Wing, Caldwell was promoted to Group

Captain in the following August, and in February, 1945, led the wing to the Morotai Isles. They never saw any Japanese aircraft after the night of their arrival, and so spent the time strafing enemy aerodromes, installations and barges as far afield as the Celebes. In April, 1945, Caldwell became attached to the headquarters staff of the First Tactical Air Force, Royal Australian Air Force, at Morotai, but a month later relinquished this post to take up a similar position in Melbourne.

Caldwell remained in the R.A.A.F. until February, 1946, when he went into a business firm in Sydney. Since then he has gained control of the business, which has become so successful that it now has subsidiary companies operating in all states in Australia, as well as overseas.

6

COCKNEY FIGHTER ACE

Group Captain F. R. Carey
C.B.E., D.F.C. and Two Bars,
A.F.C., D.F.M., Silver Star

Two Hurricanes were patrolling over a convoy of fishing vessels escorted by corvettes in the North Sea on the 30th January, 1940, when suddenly a German Heinkel 111 dived out of the clouds and headed towards the ships. The British fighters turned to intercept the raider, and then opened fire in a head-on attack. The Heinkel hurriedly jettisoned its bombs into the sea and headed at full throttle towards the clouds. One of the Hurricanes managed to get in a good burst of fire, which caused pieces to fall off the Hun, before it finally reached the cover of the clouds. The Hurricane pilot, Frank Carey, was credited with one Heinkel 111 damaged. It was his first meeting with the Luftwaffe and his first victory. He was an unknown Sergeant Pilot at this time, but before the end of the Second World War, he was to rise to the rank of Group Captain and to become one of the most successful fighter aces in the Royal Air Force.

Born in Brixton, London, on the 7th May, 1912, Frank

Reginald Carey had first become interested in flying while he was still a young boy at Belvedere School in Haywards Heath, Sussex, as he stood in the quadrangle and watched a fighter aircraft which fairly regularly gave the boys an aerobatic treat when the pilot flew over a particular house which was near the school. Frank made up his mind there and then that as soon as he was old enough he would become a pilot. Consequently a few days after his fifteenth birthday, having obtained his parents' consent, he enlisted in the Royal Air Force as an aircraft apprentice. After three years at Halton Aircraft Apprentice School he spent three years as a mechanic in the same flight ('A' Flight) of Number 43 Squadron in which he was later to be a pilot and then flight commander. He returned to Halton for a further year's engineering and then, after a few months at Worthy Down, went to Netheravon on a flying course. The course was long and arduous in those days, but Carey took to flying as a duck takes to water and at last in 1935 qualified as a pilot. A long leave followed and then in September, 1935, he was posted to Number 43 Squadron at Tangmere as a Sergeant Pilot. Carey remained with this famous squadron at Tangmere until the outbreak of war, when they were transferred to Acklington on the East Coast, to begin defensive patrols over convoys in the North Sea.

If the pilots of 43 Squadron had expected to emulate the exploits of the Royal Flying Corps pilots of the First World War, they were to be disappointed, for they never even saw a single enemy aircraft until the 30th January, 1940, when as already described Sergeant Carey damaged a Heinkel 111, to chalk up the squadron's first success. Thirteen days later, on the 12th February, the squadron got its first confirmed Hun and again Sergeant Carey was involved. He and Flight Lieutenant Caesar Hull were patrolling as usual over a convoy when a Heinkel 111 attempted to bomb the ships they were guarding. The two Hurricanes chased the enemy raider and after several attacks finally shot it down near the mouth of the River Tyne. For their skill and courage in this attack, both pilots were awarded decorations; Flight Lieutenant Hull received the Distinguished Flying Cross and Sergeant Carey the Distinguished Flying Medal.

A few weeks later Carey was commissioned as an Acting Pilot Officer and posted to Number 3 Squadron, which early in May, 1940, flew out to France to reinforce the overworked Royal Air Force already there. A few hours after landing in France, Pilot Officer Carey shot down Number 3 Squadron's first Hun. He took off with two other pilots and headed east from Merville.

After a few minutes he spotted a number of Heinkel 111's circling and bombing Courtrai. This was the first time he had seen more than one enemy aircraft in the sky and in his initial excitement he attacked first one and then another without much result. Eventually he decided to settle on one, which after a few short bursts crash-landed in a cloud of dust. Carey continued attacking the others until he had used up all his ammunition and then returned to Merville to refuel and rearm. Later in the day on another patrol, he destroyed a Dornier 17 and two Junkers 87's and probably destroyed two more of the Stukas.

Carey was continuously in action during the next few days, when the R.A.F. fighters in France were striving desperately to keep the Germans at bay. But as fast as the Hurricanes shot down the Huns, more and more came on to take their place. And, although the British pilots fought courageously and shot down many enemy aircraft, they also suffered losses. After five days of very little sleep and a great deal of operational flying, Frank Carey had added nine more Huns to his bag and then, on the 15th May, he was himself shot down by the rear-gunner of a Dornier 17. The bomber was in fact diving vertically to its destruction after Carey had attacked it, when the rear-gunner with a last desperate burst hit the Hurricane and also slightly wounded Carey who, however, managed to bale out and reach the ground safely. He spent the next few days in a Belgian hospital and then returned to England where he was awarded the Distinguished Flying Cross and Bar for his exploits in France.

By the end of June, he was fit again for action and was posted to his old squadron, Number 43, as a flight commander. This was one of the fighter squadrons which bore the brunt of the fighting during July and August over Southern England and which enhanced its reputation as one of Fighter Command's crack squadrons. Under the leadership of Squadron Leader Tommy Dalton-Morgan (later a Group Captain with D.S.O., D.F.C., and Bar, and seventeen confirmed victories), ably supported by his flight commanders, Carey and 'Iggie' Kilmartin (later Wing Commander, with D.F.C. and Bar, and fourteen kills), the pilots of Number 43 Squadron fought with such ferocity that they soon became one of the top-scoring squadrons who fought in the Battle of Britain. Carey, who at this time was the ace pilot of the squadron, personally shot down seven more enemy aircraft to bring his total bag to eighteen, before he was again shot down and wounded towards the end of August, 1940. He returned to Number 43 Squadron in September, 1940, at Usworth, where they were resting and re-forming after their losses in the Battle of Britain. Soon after this, the squadron turned to night fighting operations and at the same time Flight Lieutenant Carey was sent to Debden as an instructor in Number 52 Operational Training Unit. Later he was posted to Number 245 Squadron stationed in Northern Ireland. He remained with this squadron only for a few weeks before he was promoted to Squadron Leader and ordered to form a new Hurricane squadron. He formed Number 135 Squadron and took command of it when it became operational. Towards the end of 1941, he led his new squadron overseas to join the Royal Air Force contingent in Burma, which was having quite a tough time trying to throw back the hordes of Japanese fighters and bombers.

Very little is known of Carey's fighting career in the Burmese jungles during the next few months, for the R.A.F. kept no record of combats fought in this area at this time and Carey himself lost his log-book whilst out there. Carey does remember shooting down a Jap 97 fighter early in January, 1942, which was the first aircraft to be destroyed by Number 135 Squadron. After this he destroyed several more 97's over Rangoon, an Army 02 Oscar in the Arakan and another unidentified aircraft which fell into the Sittang River.

On another occasion Carey had just landed from an escort mission at Chittagong, when thirty Oscars made a raid on the aerodrome. As the enemy circled the field in line astern prior to bombing, Carey's Hurricane was refuelled and he prepared to take off as the Japs came in low, guns blazing. With bullets thudding into the Hurricane, Carey took off to intercept. Six Oscars immediately dived on his tail, as he flew only a few feet above the ground. The Japanese fighters were fitted with special telescopic sights which gave their pilots extremely accurate aim for their guns, but blinded them to anything not shown in their sights. In this instance, among the items not shown was a small hill, over which Carey gently lifted his Hurricane. One of the Japs did not climb and smacked right into the hill. The other Oscars, scared that the same thing might happen to them, made off in a hurry. Carey flew back to Chittagong and landed unhurt although his plane was riddled with bullet holes.

Another combat which Carey remembers took place in February, 1942, soon after his promotion to Wing Commander. It was the first occasion on which he led his Hurricane wing – a strafing attack on the Japanese aerodrome at Moulmein. As soon as they arrived over the Jap base they were met by a large number of

97's and dog-fights broke out all over the place. Carey shot down one 97 with a beautiful deflection shot and a few minutes later sent down a second in flames.

No one seems to know how many victories Carey scored in Burma, he himself says he cannot remember, but from various reports we can safely assume that he destroyed at least ten Japanese aircraft. When he returned to England the Air Ministry credited him with a total of twenty-eight confirmed victories, whilst one Sunday newspaper stated that he had shot down at least forty enemy planes and was easily the leading British fighter ace. Carey himself, in a letter, reckoned his score was 'about thirty, as far as I can remember'. In any case, regardless of how many aircraft he did shoot down, he was without a doubt a great fighter leader and helped in no small measure to win supremacy of the air for the Royal Air Force in Burma in 1942.

He returned to England in 1943, and after being awarded a second Bar to his D.F.C., was sent to a gunnery school. On completion of the course, Wing Commander Carey returned to India to form and command the first Air Fighter Training Unit in India, at Calcutta. He remained in charge of this unit until November, 1944, when he was promoted to Group Captain, and transferred to the Middle East, where he took command of Number 73 Operational Training Unit at Abu Suweir, near Ismalia.

When the war ended in 1945, Carey returned to England as Group Captain (Tactics) at the Central Fighter Establishment and later on spent a year at the Royal Air Force Staff College at Camberley. He learned to fly jets next and in 1949 was made Wing Commander (Flying) at the R.A.F. Station at Gutersloh, in Germany. He has now retired from the R.A.F. and is living in Australia.

7

FIGHTING FRENCHMAN

Wing Commander P. H. Clostermann
D.S.O., D.F.C. and Bar

PIERRE CLOSTERMANN was just twenty-one years old when he was posted to a Royal Air Force Fighter Squadron as a Sergeant Pilot in January, 1943, and he had flown exactly twenty-one missions with Number 341 (Alsace) Squadron as part of the renowned Biggin Hill Wing before he claimed his first successes against the Luftwaffe. On his 22nd mission on the 27th July, 1943, he shot down two Huns, both F.W. 190's, the best German fighter aircraft at this time. Clostermann himself describes this combat in detail in his autobiography *The Big Show*, but for the purposes of our story, a brief account is necessary.

The Biggin Hill Wing were escorting a force of American Marauder bombers on an afternoon raid on the airfield at Tricqueville. They were between Le Havre and Rouen when a dozen F.W. 190's of the notorious Richthofen Squadron dived on the Spitfires from out of the sun. Immediately Commandant René Mouchotte, the Biggin Hill Wing Leader, turned the Spitfires to meet the Huns head-on. In a few seconds the two opposing formations split up and individual dog-fights broke out all over the sky. Sergeant Clostermann fired at a pair of F.W. 190's who had converged on the tail of his section leader. His shells scored hits on the fuselage of one of the enemy fighters. Flames trailed out behind the plane and then suddenly it disintegrated. Clostermann was delighted, but not too delighted to forget that other Huns were about. He fired at several F.W. 190's that passed close in front of his aircraft, without any luck, and then suddenly found himself in an advantageous position behind and above a second F.W. 190. He closed quickly, lined up the 190 in his sights and fired two short bursts. That was all that was necessary. The cockpit flew off, the German pilot baled out and the 190 went down vertically trailing clouds of black smoke.

A month later, on the 27th August, the Commanding Officer

of the Alsace Squadron, Commandant Réné Mouchotte, failed to return from an escort mission to St. Omer. Sergeant Clostermann, who was flying wingman to Mouchotte, lost his leader after violent manoeuvres to evade an attack by thirty F.W. 190's which had surprised the French Fighter Squadron. Spitfires and Focke-Wulfs twisted, dived, climbed and turned in an effort to shoot each other out of the skies. Machine guns and cannons barked out an incessant chatter. The vanquished fell, and the victor rose to look for more victories. It was all over in a few minutes, the sky was clear, except for the trails of heavy black smoke and the parachutes which were swinging lazily towards the ground far below. Beneath one of the parachutes was the German pilot of an F.W. 190 shot down by Clostermann, thus avenging the death of his squadron leader.

On a lone dawn patrol to Beauvais on the 26th September, Sergeant Clostermann intercepted and shot down a Messerschmitt 109, but this was his last victory whilst flying with a French fighter squadron, since two days later Clostermann was commissioned as an Acting Pilot Officer and posted to Number 602 Squadron, one of the best known Spitfire Squadrons in Fighter Command, which had already shot down well over a hundred enemy aircraft and had included in its personnel in earlier fighting such famous fighters as Paddy Finucane, Al Deere, Archie McKellar and Finlay Boyd.

When Clostermann joined 602 Squadron, it was engaged in operations which gave little opportunity for him to add to his victories. Ground level strafing raids and dive bombing missions were both dangerous and exhilarating, but Clostermann was glad when the squadron changed over to more orthodox fighter defensive and offensive patrols after the invasion of Normandy. In less than three weeks of hectic fighting over the beachhead Clostermann destroyed five F.W. 190's. Two of these fell before his guns in one battle on the 2nd July, in which he also claimed one probable and two damaged.

Clostermann had now completed over two hundred operational missions, and a few days later, after being presented with the D.F.C. by Sir Archibald Sinclair, the Minister of Air, at an airfield in Normandy, the French ace was taken off operations and transferred to the Headquarters of the Free French Air Force in London.

In December, 1944, Clostermann was sent on a conversion course on Typhoons and Tempests, the latest, biggest, heaviest, fastest and best from the Hawker line of fighters. Then Clostermann began his second tour of operations with Number 274 Squadron who were stationed as part of Number One-two-two Tempest Wing at Volkel in Holland. It was to be an incredible tour of operations for in less than three months Clostermann flew over two hundred missions, shot down twenty-four German aircraft, won the D.S.O., and a Bar to his D.F.C., in addition to French, Belgian and American decorations, and received rapid promotion to command the wing to which he came in March, 1945, as a Flight Lieutenant.

Clostermann scored the first victory of his second tour on the 5th March when he attacked four Me. 109's over Hanover and finally shot one down in flames. There followed a period of ground strafing raids in which he destroyed several locomotives, tanks and motor vehicles and then another sweep to Hanover on the 14th March when he led eight Tempests into combat against forty Me. 109's In the ensuing fight the Frenchman destroyed one Me. 109, probably destroyed another and damaged one more.

More strafing raids followed, in spite of the heavy losses suffered by the Squadron at the hands of the German anti-aircraft defences. At least one aircraft was lost on every raid carried out by the Tempests and in less than a week the squadron lost a dozen of its pilots. Several times Clostermann's own aircraft, *Le Grand Charles*, was hit, but each time he was able to fly it safely back to base. But his luck could not last much longer. On his third mission on the 28th March, shortly after shooting down a Junkers 88 night fighter, his Tempest was hit by flak and Clostermann himself was wounded by shell splinters in the right leg. He managed to crash-land on his own airfield and was then rushed off to Eindhoven Hospital, where he remained for the next few days.

On the 2nd April he was proclaimed fit for combat again and on the same day took command of Number 3 Squadron in One-two-two Wing. Within a few hours of joining his new squadron he was leading a sweep over Lake Dummer. He personally destroyed one F.W. 190 in air combat, two Junkers 188's on the ground, and over thirty vehicles on Aldhorn aerodrome, before leading his Tempests safely back to base. The following day he led the squadron on three more strafing missions, the first to Hanover, the second to Lake Steinhuder and the third to Enshelde. Four pilots were lost, but the Germans lost many locomotives and vehicles. On the 5th April the Frenchman led two missions during which he shot down a Junkers 88, and two Me. 109's. He also damaged three Junkers 88's and two

F.W. 190's. On his second mission the Tempests attacked twelve F.W. 190's and four Me. 109's. Clostermann's own aircraft was hit by several 20 mm. and 37 mm. cannon shells and he had to make a crash landing at base, but he climbed out of his Tempest uninjured.

Clostermann made another crash landing on the 20th April. He had already shot down a large four-engined Junkers 290 over the Skaggerak on the morning patrol, and as the sun began to set he led three Tempests from Volkel for an offensive patrol along the Bremen-Hamburg autobahn.

The weather became worse as they headed west and before very long the rain was pouring down, the mist became thicker and Clostermann had considerable trouble in following the straight, white autobahn. Suddenly there was a bang in the bottom of the cockpit of Clostermann's Tempest and simultaneously he felt a sharp pain in his right leg. In the same instant Clostermann pulled back the control column and as he swung round in a steep climbing tight turn he saw about thirty F.W. 190's flying almost at tree-top level. At full throttle he roared down on the Huns, only to find another dozen 190's coming towards him from the side.

Bullets and cannon shells thudded into his Tempest and the next moment Clostermann felt something burning beneath his feet. He skidded violently to elude the enemy, and then found an F.W. 190 in his sights. He fired one long burst. The enemy plane fell away and ploughed through a row of trees before exploding. A quick look around and Clostermann noticed a lone aircraft heading towards Bremen. He gave chase, opened the throttle flat out, and slowly but surely drew nearer to the aircraft, which he soon identified as an F.W. 190. At two hundred yards' range the French ace fired two long bursts and instantly the 190 rolled right over and then landed with wheels still retracted in a marshy field, throwing up a shower of mud before coming to a sudden stop. Its pilot jumped out of the cockpit and took to his heels like a scared jack rabbit.

With sparks glowing in his cockpit Clostermann headed for base at top speed, at the same time climbing in case he had to bale out. Fifteen minutes later he crash-landed on his own aerodrome, bouncing and bumping across the tarmac and eventually rolling to a standstill between an ambulance and a fire tender, which for once were not needed, thanks to the flying skill of Clostermann plus a lot of luck.

At the beginning of May, 1945, Clostermann became the first

French fighter pilot to lead a British fighter wing when he was given command of Number One-two-two Wing. The extra responsibility seemed to serve as an extra incentive for him to add to his already impressive personal score, and on the 3rd May he completed a memorable day's fighting.

In the early morning he destroyed one F.W. 190 over Kiel and then damaged two more on the ground. During the afternoon he led a reconnaissance mission along the coast of Denmark and damaged a 500-ton U-boat in Auger Fiord. In the evening on his third sortie, he led twenty-four Tempests in a special raid on the great naval-air base at Grossenbrode, where over a hundred multi-motor transport aircraft lay at their moorings, protected by more than two hundred Me. 109's and F.W. 190's patrolling over the base. Ordering twenty of his pilots to engage the fighters, Clostermann led the other three Tempests down in a strafing attack on the grounded aircraft. He was the only one to survive the attack. His three comrades, Flight Lieutenant Bone, Flight Lieutenant Worley and Sergeant Crow, were all shot down by the murderous anti-aircraft fire. The Frenchman set fire to a Junkers 252, and then shot down two Dornier 24's which were about to land. He came round for another strafing attack and destroyed two Arado 232's and two Blohm and Voss 138's before climbing away to join in the enormous dogfight going on overhead. He shot down an F.W. 190 and Me. 109 and then led the remnants of his wing triumphantly back to base. They had shot down fourteen enemy aircraft for the loss of ten pilots. Clostermann's own personal share was four enemy aircraft destroyed in air combat and five more destroyed on the ground.

The next day Clostermann led his wing on their last operational mission, an attack on the naval-air base at Schleswig. He destroyed two Dornier 18's to bring his final score to thirty-three confirmed victories, thus making him the top-scoring French ace of the Second World War.

8

BILL COMPTON

Group Captain W. V. C. Compton
D.S.O. and Bar, D.F.C. and Bar, Silver Star,
Croix de Guerre, Legion d'Honneur

THE most highly decorated New Zealand fighter pilot of the Second World War, William Vernon Crawford Compton was born in Invercargill, New Zealand, on the 2nd March, 1916. He was educated at New Plymouth High School and on leaving school began work in a store in Waiuku. His heart was set on flying, however, and towards the end of 1938 he got a job on a transport vessel as a ship's carpenter, with the object of working his passage to England, so that he could join the Royal Air Force. It was a very slow journey and Compton visited many lands before the ship finally arrived in Liverpool three days after the outbreak of war. He volunteered for the R.A.F., was accepted to train as a fighter pilot and, in due course, went to various flying training schools before completing his training and qualifying as a pilot. He was posted to Number 603 (City of Edinburgh) Auxiliary Squadron at Hornchurch as a Sergeant Pilot and spent the next few weeks learning the tricks and tactics of aerial fighting.

Toward the end of May, 1941, Compton was commissioned as an Acting Pilot Officer and posted to Number 485 Squadron, a New Zealand Spitfire Squadron, which was in the process of formation and had not yet flown on operations. By August, 1941, the squadron was ready for action and moved south to Kenley to take part in fighter sweeps and escort missions. After several uneventful patrols, Pilot Officer Compton at last had a chance to show his skill when the squadron met a number of Me. 109's during a fighter sweep on the 21st September. He fired several bursts at one Messerschmitt which went down with black smoke pouring out behind it. Before he could see what finally happened to it, he was attacked by more 109's and had to be content with one probable. A fortnight later during another sweep, Bill again fired at a 109 and this time there were no complications. The

Messerschmitt caught fire and its pilot baled out, so Compton was able to claim his first confirmed Hun.

His second success occurred on the 12th February, 1942, by which time he was a Flying Officer and a section leader. The squadron, led by Squadron Leader E. P. 'Hawkeye' Wells, took part in the attack on the *Gneisenau* and *Scharnhorst* in the Channel. They flew across the Channel at 5,000 feet, above a cloud bank, and maintained their position until they were approaching the Belgian coast. Squadron Leader Wells led them down through a break in the clouds and saw four Me. 109's about a thousand feet below. He ordered Compton's section to attack.

In the mêlée that followed Bill blew the wing off one of the Messerschmitts but did not see what happened to it, for he was too busy pursuing the other 109's. They made off at top speed for the Dutch coast and the protection of the coastal defences. Compton recalled his section and as they re-formed over the sea sighted six more 109's. He led an attack but once more the 109's made off. The Spitfires re-formed again and were gaining height when Flight Sergeant Sweetman shouted:

'Look out, Bill – there's one on your tail!'

Compton dived and turned, and then saw two Spitfires send the Messerschmitt into the sea.

'Thanks, chaps,' he yelled and attacked another Messerschmitt. He fired three long bursts, which caused the 109 to crash on the beach five miles west of Ostend. The Spitfires reformed again and having exhausted all their ammunition returned to Kenley, where Bill was credited with one destroyed and one damaged. A few days later he was awarded the D.F.C.

On the 26th March, 1942, the New Zealanders were going as cover to Bostons on an operation against the shipping and docks at Le Havre when, some five miles short of the target, they met a strong formation of Messerschmitts and a running battle followed. Bill sent one Me. 109 crashing into the sea off Le Havre, and then dived onto the tail of another which was attacking a Spitfire. He fired several bursts and the 109 crashed near Fecamp.

Two days later the station commander, Group Captain Victor Beamish, D.S.O., D.F.C., A.F.C., led Number 45 Squadron on a sweep from Cap Gris Nez to Dunkirk. They were flying high at 20,000 feet when Beamish spotted some Spitfires far below in a fight with about forty F.W. 190's. He led the New Zealanders down to join in the fight and in a few minutes they had shot down five 190's, one of them falling to Compton, thus bringing his confirmed victories to five. Beamish himself was shot down and killed in this fight and Fighter Command lost one of its most brilliant leaders.

A late afternoon sweep on the 24th April provided Compton with his next success. The New Zealanders engaged four F.W. 190's flying below them in tight formation over Abbeville. They destroyed two and probably another, but the fourth got away. Bill got the first to be destroyed, a yellow-nosed 190 which spun down in flames.

A few weeks later after a hectic dog-fight over the Channel, during which his Spitfire was severely damaged, Compton crash-landed at Kenley and broke his wrist. He was sent off to hospital and did no more operational flying until the following August when he was posted to Number 611 Squadron as a flight commander. He flew with this squadron during the Commando raid on Dieppe on the 19th August, and on his first patrol in the early morning persuaded an F.W. 190 to crash-land after a brief engagement over the beaches. A few hours later, while escorting Fortresses back from an attack on Abbeville airfield, F.W. 190's attacked the Spitfires. Bill chased one, opened fire and kept on firing until he had to break away to avoid a collision He saw one enemy machine catch fire, and then four more 190's attacked him. He was now separated from his flight and tried to lose the enemy by doing steep climbing turns but the 190's had the advantage and kept up the attack Eventually, however, Bill worked his way to the coast, but was chased halfway across the Channel before the 190's finally left him.

On the 28th August, 611 Squadron were escorting Fortresses attacking Meaulte, near Amiens. Near the target Bill led his flight down to engage five F.W. 190's which were coming up from behind. After giving the leading Hun one short burst he saw the pilot bale out. Then together with another Spitfire, he attacked another 190, which went spinning down. They did not see what happened to it after this, so they claimed only one damaged.

Compton shot down his tenth confirmed Hun early in November, 1942, when the squadron was making a sweep over St. Omer with the Biggin Hill Wing, as a diversion to a large scale attack on Le Havre. Bill spotted eight F.W. 190's some 4,000 feet below the Spitfires and warned the wing leader, who led the Spitfires down in a diving attack. The Focke-Wulfs split up in all directions and each Spitfire pilot chose a target. Bill selected one which shot up almost vertically. Bill waited for it to straighten out and then opened up with his cannons. Pieces fell off the tail of the 190, which flicked over on to its back and then dived inverted towards the ground. The pilot baled out before it hit the ground with a terrific explosion.

Soon after this Compton was awarded a Bar to his D.F.C. He flew on several more operations with Number 611 Squadron but gained no more victories with them. He left the squadron on Christmas Day, 1942, to take command of Number 64 Squadron, who were engaged on patrolling over convoys in the North Sea and at this period rarely saw any enemy aircraft. Compton flew on many of these uneventful patrols and was getting rather bored with the whole business, when he was again posted south to the main battle zone, to become Wing Commander (Flying) of the Hornchurch Spitfire Wing in July, 1943. This was much more to his liking and during the next six months he flew on nearly 200 escort missions with American heavy bombers on daylight raids. The Yanks thought so highly of him as a fighter leader that they awarded him the Silver Star, and the R.A.F. also decorated him with the D.S.O., in September, 1943, for destroying thirteen enemy aircraft.

He got his eleventh soon after taking command of the Hornchurch Wing. He and his Number Two had become separated from the rest of the Wing, when they were jumped on by three F.W. 190's near Rouen. Compton's wingman was shot down immediately, but the New Zealander eluded the attacks of the enemy fighters and then sent one of them down in flames. Suddenly eight more 190's appeared and chased Bill all the way to the French coast, where his engine began to smoke. To his relief a Spitfire squadron came to the rescue and escorted him safely back to Hornchurch.

On another occasion Compton was leading his wing on an escort mission when they were attacked by thirty F.W. 190's. Two Spitfires and a Liberator bomber were shot down immediately, but the Spitfires had their revenge for in the running engagement that followed they shot down eight of the 190's. Compton himself destroyed two of them, but in doing so his Spitfire was hit in the wings and fuselage by German cannon shells. However, he landed safely back at Hornchurch and a few days later on another escort mission to Antwerp he shot down another F.W. 190.

On the 13th December, 1943, Compton relinquished command of the Hornchurch Wing and was sent to the United States with Wing Commander Ray Harries to give a series of lectures about R.A.F. tactics in air combat. He gave over a hundred lectures in

51

three months, and then returned to England in April, 1944, to become Wing Commander (Flying) Number One-four-five Wing, Second Tactical Air Force, in command of four Free French fighter squadrons and Number 74 Squadron.

It was not long before he was adding to his successes. On the 7th June he shot down his only bomber. He was patrolling over the beachhead in Normandy when he sighted five Junkers 88's coming towards him. He climbed above them and then roll-turned to come down in a screeching dive behind the last of the five. The Junkers rear-gunner put a bullet through each of the Spitfire's wings, before he was himself hit and his guns ceased firing. Bill gave the 88 another burst, flames shot out behind, and then it spiralled down to crash near Caen, sending up a column of black smoke. Compton climbed to attack the remainder of the bombers, but by now they had completely disappeared so he set course for base, feeling quite satisfied with his morning's work.

Soon after this, Bill formed a habit of shooting down two enemy aircraft on one patrol. On three successive occasions he performed this feat, thus bringing his final tally to twenty-one and a half enemy aircraft destroyed. His last two victims were shot down one morning when he was leading his Free French Spitfires on a sweep. He sighted a number of F.W. 190's and Me. 109's taking off from Evreux airfield, and led down two of his squadrons to attack. Bill destroyed one fighter with his first burst and a few minutes later sent down another Hun in flames, whilst his colleagues accounted for four more.

Just before leaving One-four-five Wing in January, 1945, Compton narrowly escaped death, this time on the ground. Two enemy fighters came in low for a strafing run across the airfield, as Bill was driving round the tarmac in his car. He flung himself out of the vehicle as the cannon shells smashed into the earth nearby. A few seconds later he jumped to his feet and breathed a sigh of relief as he eyed a couple of large petrol tanks a few yards away, which fortunately for Compton the Huns had failed to explode.

A few days later Compton ended his third tour of operations, having completed the grand total of 453 sorties involving over 800 hours' flying time – a record for a New Zealander – during which he had destroyed twenty-one and a half enemy aircraft. He was awarded a Bar to his D.S.O. and at the same time the Free French decorated him with the *Croix de Guerre* and the *Légion d'Honneur*, for his fine leadership of Free French squadrons in his wing.

He took over the post of Wing Commander in charge of plans at Number Eleven Group Headquarters, which position he still held when the war ended in May, 1945. Subsequently he took a six months' course at the Royal Air Force Staff College, at the end of which he was offered, and accepted, a permanent commission in the R.A.F. He was then posted to the Middle East where he was attached to the Headquarters Staff of the Mediterranean Air Command in Cairo, returning to the British Isles in 1948. Later on he became Air Attaché in Oslo.

9

'THE RED KNIGHT'

Wing Commander M. N. Crossley
D.S.O., O.B.E., D.F.C.

ONE of the finest fighter aces of the Royal Air Force during the dark days of 1940, when the gallant 'Few' had to fight against such tremendous odds, was the tall, handsome Michael Nicolson Crossley, who quickly earned himself the nickname of the 'Red Knight' when, after three months of continuous fighting with the Luftwaffe, he became Fighter Command's top scorer with twenty-two confirmed victories by the end of August, 1940.

Born in Halford, Warwickshire, on the 29th May, 1912, he was educated at Eton and later at the College of Aeronautical Engineering at Chelsea. He joined the Royal Air Force on a short-service commission in 1936 and qualified as a pilot a year later. Promoted to Flying Officer in 1938, he was made a flight commander with Number 32 Squadron just before the war started, but did not fly on operations until May, 1940, when his squadron was detailed to patrol over the French coast. For the first few days Crossley flew on several patrols, but although he could see the fierce fighting going on below his Hurricane, he could find no trace of the Luftwaffe in the sky. He had to wait until the 18th May before he sighted his first Huns over Dunkirk. He led his flight down to attack a number of Heinkel 111's, but to his great disappointment he had just lined up a Heinkel in his sights when he discovered that his guns could not fire owing to some mechanical fault.

The next day, during a patrol over the Dutch and Belgian coasts, Number 32 Squadron encountered a formation of Messerschmitt 109's. Mike was just turning to join in what he called the 'general rough and tumble', when he noticed four 109's flying away from the dog-fight. He banked sharply to give chase, but even as he did so another 109 flew right across in front of Mike's Hurricane. He pressed the gun button and this time his guns belched forth flame and smoke, and hot lead poured towards the Messerschmitt. Fragments flew from the 109's tail, and it fell away. Out of the corner of his eye, Mike saw another Messerschmitt trying to get on his tail, and immediately swept up and round, opening fire when the enemy fighter was only twenty feet away. Petrol shot out of the fuselage tank in a flaming jet, and the 109 went down bursting into flames before it hit the ground. The first 109 he had fired at was later confirmed by another pilot so that made a total of two destroyed by the Red Knight.

During the next week Crossley was in action almost every day, flying offensive patrols and escort missions over the coast of Northern France, and by the 25th May, when the squadron was taken off operations for a few days rest, he was the squadron's leading scorer with five confirmed victories to his credit.

On the 7th June, Number 32 Squadron returned to its base at Biggin Hill to resume its battles with the Luftwaffe; on the following day Crossley was leading them on a patrol over the English Channel when they sighted a large formation of Heinkel 111's flying 3,000 feet below them. It was an opportunity not to be thrown away, and Crossley gleefully led his Hurricanes down in a diving attack, each pilot selecting his own target. At 300 yards' range Mike opened fire and immediately the wheels of a jet-black Heinkel fell down. Another burst and the Heinkel fell out of formation with thick black smoke streaming from its starboard engine. It crash-landed in a field far below. Meanwhile Crossley had selected a second victim and after several short bursts this Heinkel crashed in flames no more than a mile from its unfortunate comrade. Crossley had little fuel left, so he landed at Rouen-Boos aerodrome to refuel and rearm. He was back at Biggin Hill for lunch and then was off on another patrol over the Dover area where he engaged and shot down a Messerschmitt 109.

A few days later Flight Lieutenant Crossley received the Distinguished Flying Cross from His Majesty the King at a special investiture held at Biggin Hill aerodrome.

Soon after this Number 32 Squadron was taken out of the line for a rest period, during which its aircraft were repaired and renewed, and its personnel changed. New pilots came in to take the place of pilots who had been killed or wounded in action and there were changes, too, in the command of the squadron. Mike Crossley was promoted to Squadron Leader, was given command of the squadron and, early in August, 1940, led it back to Biggin Hill to resume its unfinished business with the Luftwaffe.

On one of the first patrols on which he led Number 32 Squadron as its Commanding Officer, Crossley was about to land at Biggin Hill, when he noticed anti-aircraft shells bursting over the port of Dover. At once he turned and led his Hurricanes to investigate. They discovered a number of Junkers 87's and Messerschmitt 110's dive-bombing a convoy which, only a few minutes before, the Hurricanes had been guarding. Crossley sped after a 110 which had just released its bombs and was heading for the French coast almost at sea level. Slowly he crept up on the twin-engined fighter and at 800 yards' range gave it a short three-second burst of machine-gun fire. The Messerschmitt slowed down and began swerving from side to side. Mike kept his Hurricane steady and each time the 110 passed through his line of fire he pressed the gun-button. Smoke began to appear out of the starboard engine and then, suddenly, the Messerschmitt shot up into a steep climbing turn and hung for a moment outlined against the rising sun, before diving straight down into the depths of the Channel.

August 15th was the day of the heaviest fighting to date, when Goering sent over 1,800 aircraft in an all-out effort to smash the Royal Air Force. Fighter Command met the Huns and tore them to pieces. Mike thoroughly enjoyed himself, shooting down no less than three enemy aircraft, in addition to sharing in the destruction of another.

The morning was unusually quiet but after lunch the squadron was scrambled and soon after arriving over Portsmouth they saw ahead of them three hundred of the enemy stepped up in layers. Without hesitation Crossley led the squadron at the nearest formation of Junkers 88's, and managed to shoot down two of the Junkers before running out of ammunition. Ninety minutes later he was again at the head of his squadron patrolling over Maidstone, when the Fighter Controller informed him that an attack on Croydon was pending. Turning and heading at full throttle towards the City of London, the Hurricanes soon found scores of Me. 109's dive-bombing the airport. Leading his squadron straight past the Huns, Crossley turned and attacked out of the sun. With his first burst, Crossley hit a Dornier 17 and it quickly caught fire and went down in flames. He attacked another Do. 17 from astern and set its port engines on fire. He broke away and another Hurricane took up the attack. Yet another Hurricane had a go at it and then all three Hurricanes made a combined attack. The crew baled out and the Dornier crashed in flames in a wood near Sevenoaks.

Two days later Crossley led his Hurricanes in a head-on attack on over fifty Dornier 215's and Junkers 88's, escorted by an umbrella of Messerschmitt 110's A five second burst was enough to send a Ju. 88 crashing down near Ashford, and Mike also claimed an Me. 110 as a probable before breaking away from the fight. Early in the evening of the same day the tall, keen-eyed ex-Etonian claimed his twenty-first victim, an Me. 109 which crashed at Herne Bay, and then had to bale out of his own fighter after it had been set on fire by several more 109's.

Squadron Leader Crossley shot down his 22nd Hun in the last battle in which he led Number 32 Squadron, on the 25th August, for on the very same day Number 32 Squadron was taken off operations with the record of being the top-scoring squadron in Fighter Command with 102 enemy aircraft confirmed destroyed. A few days later Mike Crossley was awarded the Distinguished Service Order, and shortly after this was promoted to Wing Commander. Later on he was sent to the United States of America as a test pilot with the British Air Commission.

10

'CAT'S EYES'

Group Captain J. Cunningham
D.S.O. and Two Bars, O.B.E., D.F.C. and Bar,
Silver Star

JOHN CUNNINGHAM was born on the 27th July, 1917, at Addington, near Croydon, and was educated at Whitgift School. He was brought up more or less in the centre of the triangle of airfields formed by Croydon, Biggin Hill and Kenley, so it was not surprising that he was bitten by the aviation bug when he was only a little boy. At school he became keen on making model aircraft and helped to start the School Aeromodelling Club. When he left school in 1935 he decided to make his career in aviation, and joined the De Havilland Aeronautical Technical School at Hatfield. At about the same time he joined Number 604 Squadron of the Auxiliary Air Force, where he learned to fly on Avro 504k's. In 1938, after this joint technical training and flying background, he was asked by De Havillands to take a part in the test flying of light aircraft. So well did he perform this work that by the time he was twenty-one he had become a full-time assistant test pilot under Geoffrey de Havilland.

Cunningham continued as assistant test pilot until war came when he joined his squadron, Number 604, for active service. They were equipped with Blenheims at this time, and for the first nine months of the war they were engaged on convoy protection and escort patrols. They did not even see any enemy aircraft and the pilots became very discouraged. At last in June, 1940, the squadron moved to Middle Wallop to commence operations against night bombers. At this time night fighting was very ineffective. The pilots could not find the enemy aircraft and even if they had been able to, the Blenheims were too slow to overhaul them! At last, however, towards the end of October, 1940, the Blenheims began to be replaced by Beaufighters, equipped with all the latest night fighting devices. Less than a month later, John Cunningham destroyed a Junkers 88, the squadron's first night fighting success. Warrant Officer J. R. Phillipson, the radar operator of the Beaufighter, found the spot on the radar screen and led Cunningham towards it. He found a Junkers 88, chased it for ten minutes off the south coast, and climbed to nearly 20,000 feet. Cunningham then put a single burst of four seconds into the fuselage of the Junkers 88, which blew up. A few weeks later he sighted another enemy aircraft, after some more expert radar operating by Phillipson. Cunningham stealthily crept into position, identified it as a Heinkel 111, pressed the gun button and the Heinkel exploded immediately.

Cunningham, who had been given the nickname of 'Cat's Eyes' by the press in January, 1941, was awarded the first Distinguished Flying Cross to be given to a night fighter pilot. The citation reported:

> He has carried out twenty-five night sorties during the past three months and succeeded in making seven interceptions. He has at all times shown the utmost enthusiasm to seek and destroy night raiders, and has operated with confidence and success in extremely bad weather.

In February, Cunningham scored his third night fighting success, his victim this time exploding as it hit the ground. March was a poor month, but in April, Cunningham and his new radar operator, Sergeant 'Jimmy' Rawnsley, shot down no less than eight Heinkel 111's, three of them on the night of the 15th. This was the first time that a night fighter had destroyed three aircraft in one night and led to the award of a well-earned Distinguished Service Order to Cunningham.

He caught the first Heinkel on his first patrol that night with a very short burst of shells, which caused the enemy raider to fall in flames. On his second patrol, his radar operator picked up a raider near Marlborough and Cunningham followed it all the way to the south coast, before getting close enough to get in another deadly burst of cannon shells. The raider, another Heinkel 111, exploded as it crashed into the ruins of a bomb-damaged building in Southampton. Returning to Middle Wallop, Cunningham was put on to another Heinkel by the ground controller and, skilfully stalking the bomber with the aid of Rawnsley and his radar set, Cunningham closed in and sent down his third Heinkel to crash near Lymington.

Less than a month later, Cunningham shot down another Heinkel 111 whilst the King was on a visit to the station at Middle Wallop, and on the last day of May, 1941, he scored his thirteenth confirmed victory, when he set fire to another Heinkel 111.

In August, 1941, Cunningham was promoted to take command of Number 604 Squadron, which at the same time moved to Coltishall in Norfolk to continue night fighter operations. Although they were stationed at Coltishall for only about six weeks, Cunningham managed to add two confirmed victories and one damaged to his bag during this period. Two of these he accounted for during one patrol. The second one shot back and put out of action one of the Beaufighter's engines. Cunningham, however, flew sixty miles to Coltishall on one engine and landed safely.

A few days later the squadron returned to Middle Wallop in September, 1941, Cunningham was awarded a bar to his D.F.C. Its citation stated:

> Wing Commander Cunningham continues to uphold and improve his outstanding record as a night fighter pilot. With his observer/navigator Pilot Officer C. F. Rawnsley, D.F.C., D.F.M. and Bar, brilliant tactics and perfect teamwork have been displayed in the pursuit of enemy aircraft at night. Since April, 1941 they have added a further four enemy aircraft to previous victories. Throughout the operations Wing Commander Cunningham has been greatly assisted by Pilot Officer Rawnsley, whose skill has been outstanding.

Cunningham with fifteen victories to his credit was now the leading R.A.F. night fighter ace. He continued to fly on night operations with 604 squadron until June, 1942, when he relinquished command of the squadron and became Wing Commander Training at Eighty-one Group Headquarters responsible for the training syllabus used by new night fighter pilots in the Operational Training Units. At the same time he was awarded a Bar to his D.S.O. for his 'brilliant leadership' and 'matchless skill', and for destroying sixteen enemy aircraft, fifteen of them at night. The last of these victories had been achieved without firing a shot. He had got on the tail of a Heinkel 111 in very bad weather, on a cloudy day, and was about to press the gun button, after a lot of chasing about, when the Heinkel dived straight down and crashed not far from Cunningham's own airfield.

Wing Commander Cunningham began his second tour of operations in February, 1943, as Commanding Officer of Number 85 Squadron, then stationed at Hunsdon, but which moved to West Malling in the following May. This squadron was equipped with Mosquitos, probably the best night fighter aircraft in the world at this time. During the period he commanded this famous squadron Cunningham shot down four more Huns; an F.W. 190 over West Malling on the 13th June, 1943, another 190 near Dunkirk on the 23rd August, 1943, a third F.W. 190 on the 8th September, 1943, and his last victim, an Me. 410 which crashed in flames on the beach near Le Touquet, on the 2nd January, 1944. He completed his second tour of operations in February, 1944, with a final bag of twenty enemy aircraft destroyed, two probably destroyed and a further seven damaged.

He was promoted to Group Captain and posted as Group Captain Night Operations at the Headquarters of Number Eleven Group at Uxbridge. At the same time he received a second Bar to his D.S.O., the citation describing him as 'a magnificent leader, whose exceptional ability and wide knowledge of every aspect of night flying has contributed in a large measure to the high standard of operational efficiency of his squadron, which has destroyed a very large number of enemy aircraft'.

The citation ended: 'His iron determination and unswerving devotion to duty have set an example beyond praise.'

When the war ended in 1945, Cunningham returned to De Havillands and was appointed Chief Test Pilot to the Engine Company. He also rejoined the Auxiliary Air Force and re-formed Number 604 Squadron, which he commanded until he was forced to relinquish the post owing to the pressure of work with his test flying. Since then he has become famous the world over for his successful testing and demonstrating of the Comet, the first jet airliner in the world and still one of the best.

11

THE FIGHTING KIWI

Group Captain A. C. Deere
D.S.O., O.B.E., D.F.C. and Bar, A.F.C.,
American D.F.C., *Croix de Guerre*

ALAN CHRISTOPHER DEERE was born in Auckland, New Zealand, on the 12th December, 1917, and educated at St. Canice's School, Westport, and Wanganui Technical College. He worked first on a sheep farm but soon became tired of it and went into a solicitor's office. This also bored him, and on seeing a Royal Air Force recruiting advertisement, he threw up this job and joined the R.A.F. on a short service commission soon after his nineteenth birthday. He trained conscientiously, won his wings, and on the 1st January, 1939, was posted to a Gladiator Squadron as an Acting Pilot Officer.

When the Second World War broke out in September, 1939, Al Deere was serving with Number 54 Squadron and his name was already well-known in the services for he was the R.A.F. middle weight boxing champion and had represented the R.A.F. at rugby. He was also an excellent fighter pilot, although he did not get a chance to prove this until May, 1940, when 54 Squadron first met the Nazis in air combat. Alan scored his first successes on the 23rd during a special mission; he and Pilot Officer John Allen were detailed to escort a Miles Master trainer to Calais Marck aerodrome to pick up Squadron Leader F. L. White of 74 Squadron, who had been shot down there in the morning. Deere, Allen and Flight Lieutenant Leathart, was was piloting the Master, took off at 12.30 p.m., climbed to 5,000 feet and fifteen minutes later arrived over Calais Marck aerodrome. Leathart landed whilst Deere and Allen circled over the aerodrome on guard. As the Master taxied out, with Squadron Leader White in the rear cockpit, and took off, twelve Me. 109's were sighted at 6,000 feet heading towards it. Leathart circled to land again, as a 109 dived and fired a burst of cannon shells at it. Deere tore after the 109 and opened fire. The enemy fighter climbed, stalled, turned over on to its back and then dived into the sea near Calais. Another 109 screamed down towards Deere, who pulled up steeply, flicked over, and then saw five 109's chasing Allen. They were so intent on the Spitfire that they did not see Deere coming up behind. He closed to within 150 yards of the last Messerschmitt and fired a long burst. The 109 burst into flames and dived towards Calais where it crashed and exploded. Another 109 came in at Deere, but the New Zealander out-manoeuvred the Hun and came in on its tail. His guns roared and then suddenly ceased as he ran out of ammunition. As he broke away Deere saw the 109 flying low with smoke pouring from its engine. The Master took off again and the two Spitfires escorted it safely back to base.

A few hours later on another patrol over the Dunkirk beaches, Deere shot down his third 109. Already on his first day in action, the 'Fighting Kiwi' had proved his worth as an air fighter.

Two days later he was adding to his successes. Number 54 Squadron were patrolling at 20,000 feet over Dunkirk at about 10 o'clock in the morning when they encountered a formation of Junker's 88's escorted by twenty Me. 110's. They dived to attack the Huns, and Deere opened fire on a Messerschmitt. It immediately caught fire and went down to crash near Dunkirk. As Deere watched the 110 burning, he was attacked by another 110 which damaged his Spitfire, so he broke off the combat and headed for Hornchurch. He made a crash landing, the first of many and found a cannon shell had exploded in his port wing, making a hole about a foot square and puncturing his tyre. The following day, his Spitfire repaired, Deere was again patrolling over Dunkirk with 54 Squadron. He dived after a Junkers 88 at full speed and after several bursts of fire sent it down in flames.

On the 27th May, Deere was leading a section of 54 Squadron Spitfires on patrol over the Dunkirk beaches. At 0400 hours he sighted some Dornier 17's and began to close in on one of them. The Dornier's rear-gunner hit Deere's aircraft and damaged his gycol tank, but Al kept up his attack and finally shot down the Dornier. The New Zealander then made a crash-landing on the beach and was knocked unconscious. He soon recovered, jumped out of his *Kiwi One* – as he called his Spitfire, the first of a line of *Kiwis* – and walked five miles towards Dunkirk. He got a lift on a Belgian troop bus and finally arrived at Dunkirk in an old car which he had found at the roadside. He went to the beach, joined the queue of soldiers who were boarding a destroyer and arrived in England after a five-hour trip across the Channel. He returned to Hornchurch about twenty-four hours after being shot down to find that he had been awarded the Distinguished Flying Cross for shooting down five enemy aircraft and assisting in the destruction of others.

As soon as the evacuation of Dunkirk had been completed, 54 Squadron was taken off operations and sent to an aerodrome in the north of England to rest and replace the pilots lost in the fierce battles already fought. They returned to Hornchurch early in July to take part in the first phase of the Battle of Britain.

On the 9th July, Deere was leading his flight at 8,000 feet over the Goodwin Sands, when they saw a silvery seaplane approaching close to the water, with an escort of twelve Me. 109's flying at 1,000 feet, and another five 109's acting as top cover. Deere ordered one section to attack the seaplane and led the other to attack the five 109's who immediately formed a defensive circle. The New Zealander dived into them, put a burst into one Me. 109 and shot it down in flames. Another 109 came in behind him. Turning to meet the Hun head-on he opened fire at the same time as the Nazi. The Spitfire and Messerschmitt closed at a combined speed of around 700 m.p.h. and suddenly there was a loud thud as they collided. The 109 fell in pieces as its tail was sheared off and Deere felt as if he had been hit by a sledge-hammer. His faithful *Kiwi* shook and shuddered, but continued on its way, with Deere struggling to open the cockpit canopy which refused to budge. Black smoke poured from the engine, enveloping the cockpit and preventing Deere from seeing the ground which was now getting ever closer. As Deere struggled with the cockpit cover there was a terrific jerk and he was tossed all round the cockpit. Then silence. Quickly he broke open the hood, ran to a distance and then surveyed the scene. His Spitfire was blazing furiously and had left a trail of debris, including the complete tail unit, extending for almost a furlong. Deere himself was uninjured apart from singed eyebrows, and bruises on his knees.

Deere was back in action again the following day in a new Spitfire, but he did not score any more victories until the 24th July when he shot down his ninth victim. This time there were no further complications.

A few days later on the 8th August he destroyed his tenth and eleventh Huns. The Squadron intercepted twenty Dornier's escorted by 109's over the Thames. Another formation of 109's joined in the dog-fight that followed. Deere got one 109 over Margate and then spotted another Messerschmitt turning towards France. He chased it and gave it a burst which caused glycol to stream from it. Another burst and the 109 dived into the Channel.

On the 10th August, 54 Squadron, who were patrolling together with a Hurricane Squadron, encountered a huge formation of fifty Dorniers escorted by about one hundred Me. 109's. The Hurricanes attacked the bombers, whilst 54 Squadron took on the escorting fighters. The New Zealander found one Me. 109 on the tail of a Hurricane and opened fire. The 109 exploded instantly. A minute later, whilst closing on a second 109, Deere was similarly caught, and his Spitfire was hit repeatedly. He broke away, limped back to Hornchurch and made an excellent crash-landing: he was getting used to them by this time, for this was his fourth crash-landing within ten weeks.

The Squadron attacked a formation of two hundred bombers and fighters on their first patrol on the 15th August and Deere added another Me. 109 to his score. A few hours later during a second patrol the New Zealander chased two Me. 109's across the Channel. As he turned over the German aerodrome at Calais five more 109's dived on him.

Bullets seemed to be coming from everywhere and pieces were flying of my aircraft [he reported later*]. My instrument panel was shattered, my eye was bleeding from splinters, my watch had been shot clean off my wrist by an incendiary bullet which left a nice diagonal burn across my wrist, and it seemed only a matter of moments before the end. Never did it take so long to get across 30 miles of sea and never had my aircraft gone so slowly. My good Merlin carried me safely across, however, and I had just reached Folkestone when my pursuers broke off the engagement. None too soon. Two minutes later my engine – I was not at 800 feet – burst into flames. Desperately I tore off my straps, pulled back the hood and prepared to bale out. I was still doing about 300 m.p.h. so I pulled the stick back to get a bit more height. At about 1,500 feet I turned my Spitfire over on to its back and pushed the stick hard forward. I shot out a few feet and somehow became caught up by the bottom of my parachute. I twisted and turned but wasn't able to get either in or out. The nose had now dropped below the horizontal and was pointing at the ground which appeared to be rushing up at a terrific speed. Suddenly I was blown along the side of the fuselage, hitting my wrist a nasty smack on the tail. Then I was clear. I made a desperate grab at the rip-cord and with a jolt the parachute opened. None too soon. I hadn't time to breathe a sigh of relief before I landed with a mighty thud in a plantation of thick shrubs.

Within a week Deere had recovered from his injuries, claimed

*As told to David Masters in *So Few*, published by Corgi Books.

a new Spitfire from the maintenance section and rejoined the hunt for the Nazis. He found them again on the 28th August, at 34,000 feet over the hopfields of Kent. After the first onslaught by the Spitfires, the enemy 109's broke up all over the place. Deere fastened on to one of these and within a few seconds shot it down in flames. When the New Zealander looked around he found himself in the middle of about a dozen Me. 109's, who promptly sent a shower of lead in the direction of Deere and shot away his rudder controls. As his plane fell away into a spin and smoke began to pour from his engine, Deere decided to abandon his Spitfire; at 10,000 feet he took a header over the side. His parachute opened immediately this time and he floated down to land in the middle of a plum tree.

Deere had another near escape three days later. He had already flown on two sorties and was about to take off on a third, when a number of German bombers made a lightning raid on Hornchurch airfield. One bomb burst a few yards in front of Deere's Spitfire and the next instant his aircraft was lifted up and flung upside down along the runway. A few minutes later the door of the cockpit was pulled off and Deere was tugged out of the wrecked fighter. His head was bleeding profusely from a slight cut, and he was feeling very dazed, but otherwise unhurt.

Although grounded by the Medical Officer, Deere somehow wangled a sortie on the following day, and found a Dornier which he chased and shot down into the Thames. This was the New Zealander's seventeenth confirmed victory and was to be his last for some considerable time. A few days later 54 Squadron was rested from operations and at the same time Flight Lieutenant Deere was posted to an operations room as a controller. He was also awarded a Bar to his D.F.C., for his 'outstanding dash and determination as a leader'.

A spell of flying instruction followed during the winter months and then in May, 1941, Al Deere began his second operational tour as Squadron Leader of the famous City of Glasgow (602) Squadron. Soon after Deere's arrival, the Spitfires moved south for escort missions, fighter sweeps, and ranger patrols. Deere carried out well over a hundred sorties during his spell with the Glasgow Squadron, but Huns were hard to find at this period of the war and he succeeded in adding only two more victories to his bag.

In 1942 Deere was sent to the U.S.A. to give a series of lectures to American pilots and on his return attended a course at the R.A.F. Staff College. At the end of this course in 1943 he was promoted to Wing Commander of the Biggin Hill Wing. He led his Spitfire Wing, consisting of French, Canadian and New Zealand Squadrons so successfully that within a short period Biggin Hill chalked up its 1,000th confirmed victory. Deere added to his score by destroying two F.W. 190's and damaging several more. These were his last victories in air combat, and brought his final score to twenty-one and a half destroyed, nine probables, and nineteen damaged, a most impressive total. During this third tour of operations he was awarded the Distinguished Service Order, the American Silver Star and the French *Croix de Guerre* with Palms.

Deere was now appointed to command the fighter wing of the Central Gunnery School, which position he held until May, 1944, when he took command of an advanced airfield with the Allied Expeditionary Force. Later on he was appointed Wing Commander (Plans) of Number Eighty-four Group. Soon after the end of the Second World War he took command of the R.A.F. Station at Duxford; he remained there until 1947 when he was sent to the Mediterranean as a member of the Air Headquarters Staff at Malta. He returned to England in 1952 to take command of the R.A.F. Fighter Station at North Weald. Since then he has been awarded the Order of the British Empire and has written his autobiography, entitled *Nine Lives*. He was appointed an Aide-de-Camp to Her Majesty the Queen in April, 1961.

12

'MOSES MORLAIX'

Wing Commander Jean Demozay
D.S.O., D.F.C. and Bar, *Légion d' Honneur, Ordre Libération, Croix de Guerre*, D.F.C. (U.S.A.), *Croix de Guerre Belge,* Czech War Cross

WITH creaking undercarriage and groaning airframe, the battered patched-up Bristol Bombay troop-carrier lumbered laboriously across the airfield and with a valiant effort its two engines pulled the giant aircraft into the air. Its occupants, mainly soldiers, gave a shout of triumph as its wheels left the ground. They had worked like Trojans to make the plane airworthy again, after finding it abandoned and neglected twelve days earlier Now they were on their way to England. A couple of hours later the Bombay landed near London and its passengers went their separate ways to rejoin their respective Army units. Its pilot, a young Frenchman by the name of Jean Demozay, made his way to the Headquarters of the Free French Forces in London, where he filled up an application form to join the Royal Air Force.

Jean Demozay had been born in Nantes on the 21st March, 1916, and educated at the local school at Beaugency and later at Locquidy College in Nantes. In 1936 he joined L'Armée de l'Air, but a month later was invalided out on medical grounds; so he became a pilot with a civil airline. When the Second World War began, Jean offered his services to the Royal Air Force, becoming Liaison Officer at the British Headquarters at Rheims, and two months later was transferred to the operations room of Number Sixty-seven Wing at Dussylacoge. In January, 1940, he became the official interpreter with Number 1 Squadron and he served continuously with this squadron throughout the campaign in France until the squadron returned to England in June, 1940. On the 16th June, Jean received orders from French Headquarters to join them immediately, but he did not take this order as he knew what was likely to happen as far as France was concerned. Instead he went to Nantes airfield where he found the abandoned Bombay which, with the help of sixteen British soldiers, he repaired and flew to England.

Changing his name to 'Moses Morlaix' to avoid possible reprisals by the Germans against his family who were still in Nantes, Demozay was soon on his way to Number Five O.T.U. to brush up on his flying. It took about ten weeks for him to complete the course and then he was off to Wittering to rejoin Number 1 Squadron, this time as a fighter pilot. Of course he was still inexperienced as far as air fighting was concerned and he had to carry out all sorts of combat training. In fact he was on a training flight in a Hurricane on the 8th November, 1940, when he scored his first victory. He was flying east of Sutton Bridge, when he caught sight of a plane flying beneath him, so he dived down for a closer look at it. He saw the black crosses first, identified it as a Junkers 88, and then instinctively ducked as the German rear-gunner opened fire and he saw the enemy tracers curving towards his fighter. Demozay closed to two hundred yards' range and pressed the gun button on his control column. His own tracers buried themselves in the enemy plane and the next moment smoke trailed from the 88's starboard engine and its propeller stopped turning. It dived to the left into some clouds and that was the last Demozay saw of it. He landed prepared to claim one Junkers 88 damaged, but was overjoyed when he was told that the bomber had been seen to crash and that he could therefore be credited with his first destroyed Hun. A few days later on another training flight he intercepted and destroyed a Messerschmitt 109.

In February, 1941, the squadron was re-equipped with Hurricane II's, and began to make patrols over convoys of ships in the English Channel. During one of these convoy patrols on the 24th March, Demozay brought down his third victim, another Me. 109, which fell into the sea after a long twelve-second burst of cannon shells. He failed to see any Huns for several weeks after this, so he decided to try his hand at night fighting, since there always seemed to be plenty of German night raiders about. He found one, a Heinkel 111 illuminated by three searchlights over the East India Docks on the night of the 10th May. Demozay closed in to thirty yards, slightly below and directly astern of the raider, and fired one long burst at it. The Heinkel turned on to its port side with smoke pouring from its port engine and then dived to the ground where it exploded.

Demozay was essentially a lone wolf in the air, the majority of his victories being obtained whilst flying alone and, whenever he was given the chance, he preferred to go hunting for the Luftwaffe on his own. On one occasion on the 25th May, 1941, he took off with three other Hurricanes to patrol over Canterbury, but over Ramsgate lost his colleagues in some clouds, so he decided to head for the French coast to look for the enemy. Soon he noticed a rescue boat heading from France escorted by eight Me. 109's, and then he sighted three Me. 110's. He stalked them for some miles, slowly closing in until he was within 250 yards of the rearmost 110 which he deliberately and carefully lined up in his reflector sight. He fired and the 110 turned steeply to port, caught fire and dived into the sea.

On June 18th Demozay was posted to Number 242 Squadron at Stapleford Tawney, but his stay with this squadron was what might be described as 'short and sweet' – short, because he only remained with the squadron for ten days; sweet, because he destroyed another two Me. 109's during his short stay. On June 28th he flew to Hawkinge to become a flight commander with Number 91 Squadron, the celebrated 'Jim Crow' Squadron, who were often called the 'Eyes of Fighter Command' because of their achievements as a reconnaissance unit, particularly in the Battle of Britain, when they won fame under the nameplate of Number 421 Flight. It was a thoroughly international squadron, its pilots coming from as far afield as Australia, New Zealand, France, Belgium, Canada, Scotland, Ireland and England, and it had established a reputation for individual attacks rather than operating as a team, mainly because its duties were lone shipping reconnaissances along the French and Belgian coastlines. This, naturally, suited Demozay prefectly and victories came quickly as he frequently met enemy fighters during these one-man patrols.

He set fire to a Henschel 126 on the ground on the 12th July, probably destroyed an Me. 109 on the 16th, sank a minelayer the following day, and shot the elevator and rudder off a 109 on the 25th. During another weather and shipping reconnaissance between Ostend and Gris Nez on the last day of July he attacked four Me. 109's flying in two pairs line astern over Dunkirk. His first burst of fire from 200 yards astern of the rear aircraft caused it to explode into tiny pieces after the starboard wing had fallen off. He fired a second burst into the next one in the formation, which caught fire and crashed on the shore just west of Dunkirk. He then pursued the leading pair and as they crossed the coast fired a longish burst from 300 yards' range. One of the pair was hit and its cockpit hood came off before Demozay broke off the combat and returned to his base.

Between August 9th, 1941, and January 2nd, 1942, Demozay shot down another eight Messerschmitt 109's for certain, as well as two more which he did not actually see crash and so were counted as 'probables'; shortly afterwards he was taken off operations and posted to the Headquarters of Number Eleven Group.

Demozay began his second tour of operations on the 25th June, 1942, when he again returned to Number 91 Squadron, this time as its Commanding Officer. Victories eluded him for a time, although on the 2nd August he was surprised by two Me. 109's half-way across the Channel, who managed to shoot pieces out of his Spitfire before disappearing into the mist. Demozay was unhurt and had his revenge on the 23rd September. One of his young pilots, Pilot Officer Edwards, was missing from a reconnaissance mission to Ostend and Demozay took off from Hawkinge at 10.25 a.m. to search for him. He swept between Calais and Gris Nez for an hour without success, and was about ten miles northwest of Gris Nez when he saw an F.W. 190 flash past him. At the same time he spotted another 190 firing at him from astern. He turned steeply to port and continued turning as both of the 190's made repeated attacks. One of the enemy fighters then made a wide turn to starboard and came at Demozay from the side. The Frenchman throttled back and turned towards the 190 firing a two-second burst with all his guns from about a hundred yards, allowing slight deflection. The German pilot seemed to have misjudged his attack and, realising that if he went on he would fly right through Demozay's line of fire, he banked steeply. In doing so his fighter appeared to stall, then it rolled over and went straight into the sea on its back. The other 190 climbed away and escaped into the clouds.

Shortly after 5 p.m. on the 31st October, 1942, Demozay was scrambled to intercept a number of F.W. 190 fighter bombers which had just made a lightning raid on Canterbury. He flew straight to Dover where he sighted four 190's flying line astern in pairs. He came down and attacked the rear one of the port pair from astern and slightly below at a range of 150 yards. It went down vertically with smoke and flames appearing at the wing root and was seen to go into the sea by the coastguards at Dover. Demozay could not find the other three F.W. 190's so he returned to Hawkinge to refuel and rearm. Ten minutes later he took off again heading for the coast at Folkestone, where five minutes later he saw another four F.W. 190's flying at sea level. The enemy planes split up into pairs and climbed towards him. He fired at the leader of one pair and then turned towards the second pair, who immediately swung round towards Dover. Demozay chased these two firing in short bursts. Ten miles east of Dover one of the 190's went straight into the sea. The Frenchman was unable to catch up with the other aircraft, so he gave one final burst of shells and then returned to base where he landed at 5.45 p.m.

Demozay had been awarded the D.F.C. in November, 1941, to which had been added a Bar in July, 1942, and now in December, 1942, he received the D.S.O. Six days later he was promoted to Wing Commander and posted once again to the Headquarters of Number Eleven Group, where he remained until the following February when he was sent to North Africa to form a flying school for Free French fighter pilots. Demozay was recalled to London in April, 1944, and then sent on a special mission to the U.S.S.R. On August 9th he was given command of a bomber group and from then until the end of the war he flew on most of the missions carried out by this unit. In December, 1944, he was awarded the *Légion d'Honneur* and in the citation to the decoration was credited with twenty-one confirmed air victories, in addition to five more which he had destroyed on the ground. It was also stated that he had taken part in more than four hundred operational sorties.

A brilliant future in *L'Armée de l'Air* awaited this intrepid flier when the war was over and on the 24th October, 1945, Demozay was made deputy commander of all flying training schools in France. Less than two months later, however, his career was cut short. He was returning from a special mission to London on the 19th December, when the aircraft in which he was flying crashed at Le Duc. All the occupants were killed instantly.

13

SHARK LEADER

Wing Commander B. Drake
D.S.O., D.F.C. and Bar, D.F.C. (U.S.A.)

'THE SHARKS' was the nickname given to Number 112 Squadron in 1941, after its pilots had painted the noses of their Kittyhawks to resemble killer sharks with their teeth showing. This squadron had already established a reputation for aggressiveness when stationed in the Western Desert in the early months of the war, which had later been enhanced during the campaign in Greece. But it was in 1941 and 1942 that its gaily painted Kittyhawks really came to be feared by the Luftwaffe when, with veteran ace fighter Billy Drake as its Commanding Officer, the Sharks roamed far and wide clearing the skies of enemy aircraft, and then going down to dive-bomb and strafe them on their own airfields.

Billy Drake had been born in London on 20th December, 1917, and had joined the Royal Air Force on a short service commission in July, 1936. On being commissioned in 1937 he had been posted to Number 1 Squadron, and when the Second World War started in September, 1939, Drake, by this time a Flying

Officer, had gone to France with Number 1 Squadron as part of the Advanced Air Striking Force. At first the squadron rarely met any German aircraft as they patrolled day and day over the Maginot Line, and Drake had to wait until May, 1940, before bringing down his first Hun. He had become separated from the rest of the squadron after an engagement with the Luftwaffe, when he was surprised by two Messerschmitt 109's over Metz. He eluded their attack and, as both of them dived away towards the German lines, he pushed forward the nose of his Hurricane and gave chase. As the two 109's split up and went off in different directions, Drake followed one, which went down to tree-top height and headed at full speed for Germany. The German pilot swung and skidded his fighter from side to side in an effort to elude his persistent pursuer, and finally flew under some high-tension power cables. Billy Drake followed, more determined than ever that the 109 should not escape him, and a few minutes later he got within range. He pressed the gun button and eight streams of lead tore into the vitals of the enemy machine. It rolled over and crashed into a wood, which burst into raging flames as the Messerschmitt's petrol tanks exploded.

Within the next few days Billy Drake shot down two more Huns, and then he was himself brought down. He was patrolling with his flight on the 13th May, when something went wrong with his oxygen equipment and he had to turn back. On the way back to his airfield he ran into four Dorniers, which he immediately attacked. He destroyed one of them and probably destroyed another, before he was caught unawares by some Messerschmitt 110's. Wounded in the leg and back by bullets and cannon shell splinters, and with his Hurricane beginning to burn, Drake struggled out of the cockpit and parachuted down to the ground. A few hours later he was in a French hospital. After an operation for the removal of the bullets and splinters, he was flown back to an R.A.F. hospital in England where he remained for several months recovering from his wounds.

Towards the end of October, 1940, Drake returned to operations as a flight commander with Number 91 Squadron who were engaged on reconnaissance duties. Awarded the Distinguished Flying Cross in January, 1941, for 'carrying out a reconnaissance which proved of great value', and for 'displaying fine qualities of leadership and perseverance', Drake was promoted to Squadron Leader a month later and posted to Number 53 Operational Training Unit at Llandow as a flying instructor. He remained at Llandow until September, 1941, when he was sent overseas to command Number 128 Squadron based in West Africa. There was not much chance of action in this remote spot and Drake was very glad when he relinquished command of the squadron in April, 1942, and was ordered to report to Air Headquarters, Middle East. On arrival he was surprised and highly delighted to find that he had been given the very enviable post of Commander of the Shark Squadron. He joined the squadron on the 24th May, 1942, at Gambut, to find that they were mainly engaged in dive-bombing operations, although whenever the chance occurred they were always ready to 'mix-it' with the Luftwaffe. On such an occasion on the 6th June Billy Drake scored his first victory with 112 Squadron, when he probably destroyed an Me. 109 during a bombing raid on Bir Hakeim.

Soon after this Rommel's army began an offensive which caused the Eighth Army to make a gradual withdrawal, and the Sharks were moved from airfield to airfield without having time to settle down. In one period of ten days, from the 18th June, the squadron made four moves and found themselves on occasions dive-bombing the airfield which they had left only a few hours before. Eventually, at the end of June, 1942, the squadron settled in at Amriya, and for the next month concentrated on dive-bombing attacks and bomber escort missions, during which Billy Drake destroyed two Me. 109's, probably destroyed another, and set fire to a Junkers 88 which he left burning furiously on landing strip Number 21. He was awarded a Bar to his D.F.C. during July, 1942, and was described in the official citation as 'a skilful pilot and a fine leader, who has led his squadron on every sortie in the latest battle of Libya'.

The squadron was given a rest from operations during August, but returned to action on the 1st September, when they were scrambled in the afternoon to intercept a number of Me. 109's. After dispersing the enemy fighters, the Sharks sighted over fifty Stuka's escorted by thirty Me. 109's heading due west over the Quat-el-Abd area. Billy Drake led his Kittyhawks to the attack and in the ensuing dogfight personally shot down two Junkers 87's, whilst the rest of the Sharks got two more without loss.

Drake led the whole of the fighter wing to which 112 Squadron was attached on the 13th September in an effort to intercept a number of 109's which had made a dive-bombing attack on El Alamein. They encountered some 109's shortly afterwards and Drake very quickly sent one of them down in flames.

There was another big dogfight during the squadron's second sortie on the 1st October, when the Sharks were covering Number

73

250 Squadron. They found fourteen Junkers 87's and twenty Me. 109's at 6,000 feet over El Maghara, and in the resulting fight Drake and Flight Lieutenant Garton shared a Junkers 87, and then probably destroyed two more Stukas. Altogether in the fight the Sharks destroyed two, probably destroyed four and damaged a further two enemy aircraft.

The Eighth Army began its own offensive and the advance from El Alamein on the 23rd October, and for a few days Drake and his Sharks were continuously in action, shooting down many Huns. On the 26th October, Drake damaged a 109 which went down vertically with glycol pouring out and was later confirmed as destroyed. The following day his victim was a Macchi 202, and on the last day of October he added another Stuka to his bag. He led the Sharks to attack six Me. 109's at 12,000 feet west of Fuka during the morning of the 5th November, and personally destroyed one and damaged another.

During the next ten days the squadron was again continuously on the move, this time trying to catch up with the rapidly retreating Luftwaffe. Drake finally caught up with them on the 15th when he destroyed a Heinkel 111 west of Cirene. Four days later the Sharks flew in to a new base at Martuba and were in the midst of refuelling when they were ordered to scramble. They took off singly as they finished refuelling, Drake getting off first and returning thirty minutes later claiming one Me. 110 destroyed and one Me. 110 damaged.

A few days later Billy Drake learned that he had been awarded the Distinguished Service Order, when again mention was made of his 'utmost courage', and 'great determination'. He was now nearing the end of his third tour of operations and had been involved in scores of air battles, but none more exciting or eventful than the mission he led on the 11th December. The Sharks were escorting Number 66 U.S.A.A.F. Squadron on a bombing and strafing raid on enemy tents and motor vehicles. All went well until the target had been successfully attacked and the squadrons were on their way home. Suddenly they were attacked by half-a-dozen Messerschmitt 109's and several Macchi 202's. Drake turned into the Huns and fired at a 109 which fell behind the enemy lines. He then chased a Macchi for several miles along the coastline, before 'the Macchi spun into the sea voluntarily' as Drake reported later. The hunter then became the hunted, for almost before the Italian aircraft had disappeared into the briny, Drake was set upon by seven Me. 109's. He used every trick in the book in an effort to keep out of range of the enemy cannonshells, but the odds were too much even for such an experienced duellist as Billy Drake and after several minutes his Kittyhawk was so badly shot up that he had to make a hurried wheels-up crash-landing amongst the 11th Hussars. He returned to the squadron's new base at Belandah the same afternoon in a borrowed Hurricane, none the worse for his experience.

Two days later Drake scored his last confirmed victory with the Sharks, when he shared in the destruction of a 109 with Sergeant Shaw. A few weeks later he relinquished command of 112 Squadron and left for Cairo, where he was promoted to Wing Commander and assigned to a Training Unit as a flying instructor.

He resumed operational flying when he was given command of a Spitfire wing in Malta in June, 1943, and during the next four months he brought his score to twenty-four confirmed victories. Returning to Britain in November, 1943, he spent the next six months with Number Twenty Wing as wing leader and then was sent off to the U.S.A. on special duties. On his return in 1945 he became deputy commander of Biggin Hill fighter base and later served in the operations room at S.H.A.E.F. Headquarters.

Billy Drake remained in the Royal Air Force after the war ended and after a spell in the Far East was granted a permanent commission in 1948.

14

TEST PILOT

Squadron Leader N. F. Duke
D.S.O., O.B.E., D.F.C. and Two Bars, A.F.C.

Born at Tonbridge, Kent, on the 11th January, 1922, Neville Frederick Duke was educated at the Convent of St Mary and at Judd's School, Tonbridge. He first became interested in flying through watching aircraft flying over Tonbridge from the nearby R.A.F. fighter stations at Biggin Hill and Kenley. He began to collect photographs of aeroplanes and by the time he was seven had quite a large collection of model aircraft. He went up for his first flight when he was ten and thereafter decided on a career in flying. He left Judd's School in the summer of 1939 and for six months, whilst waiting until he was old enough to join the R.A.F., he worked in an auctioneer's office. In June, 1940, he passed all the medical and academic examinations and a few weeks later was on his way to Number Four Initial Training Wing. Several months of intensive training followed, before he was finally commissioned as an Acting Pilot Officer and posted to Number 92 (East India) Squadron at Biggin Hill.

Duke flew on several missions with Don Kingaby, Brian Kingcombe and Jamie Rankin, and learned a lot about the technique of air fighting from such splendid tutors, but he did not shoot down any enemy aircraft until June 25th. He was returning alone from an escort mission to St Omer, having been separated from his squadron, when he saw a Messerschmitt 109 attacking a Spitfire near Dunkirk. He dived on the unsuspecting enemy fighter and from 150 yards opened fire. White smoke streamed out behind the damaged fighter, and it went straight down to crash a few miles inland. Quite naturally Duke felt very pleased with himself.

On his very next mission, whilst diving to avoid an enemy attack, Duke cracked his ear drums and it was another three weeks before he flew again. He returned to operations as wingman to 'Sailor' Malan, the Biggin Hill Wing Leader, and during the next few weeks learned a great deal about combat flying from the celebrated South African ace.

Duke only scored one more victory over Northern France. This was on August 9th when he destroyed an Me. 109 over Boulogne. Then he was transferred to a fighter squadron in the Western Desert.

He joined Number 112 Squadron at Sidi Hannish on November 12th, 1941, and the following day took off in a Tomahawk, an American fighter with which the squadron was equipped. He tried to land it in the same way as a Spitfire and ended up in a heap. Undismayed, the following morning he took up a Tomahawk again, flew around for an hour and landed correctly. After this Duke soon mastered the intricacies of the aircraft and within a few days had shot down another Me. 109, and shared in the destruction of a Fiat C.R.42, an Italian biplane fighter.

It was not long before Duke himself was shot down. It happened on November 30th, soon after the squadron had attacked about thirty enemy aircraft near El Gobi. Duke pursued a Fiat G.50, which finally plunged into the desert. Several more G.50's and Me. 109's then attacked Duke and he had to make a crash landing after a cannon shell had exploded in his port wing. A few moments later Duke crouched behind some scrub nearby and watched the enemy fighters completely destroy his Tomahawk. He began walking, but a short while later was picked up by an Army lorry and returned to his unit safe and sound.

Duke added a Macchi 200 to his tally on December 4th and the following day had to make another crash landing after a mix-up with some 109's, during which his Tomahawk was badly damaged and he himself was slightly wounded in the leg. He was out of action for a fortnight, but on his first flight on rejoining his squadron, he destroyed a Messerschmitt 109 and probably destroyed two Junkers.

After celebrating Christmas at Msus, 112 Squadron went to Suez to re-equip with Kittyhawks, a much improved version of the Tomahawk. They moved back to Msus, with a new Commanding Officer, Squadron Leader 'Killer' Caldwell, D.F.C. and Bar, the famous Australian ace, but did no operational flying for some weeks because of the bad weather. Towards the end of January, 1942, began the retreat to El Alamein; the Kittyhawks were fitted with bomb racks and ordered to dive-bomb the advancing panzer columns. Duke missed some of these missions when he was sent to Cairo and by the time he returned the squadron had moved to Gambut. One of his first sorties on his return was very costly to the Huns. It was on February 14th when the Kittyhawks found a number of Macchis and Bredas strafing British troops near Acroma. The wing shot down sixteen Italian aircraft without loss, Duke accounting for one Macchi on his own, and then helping a fellow pilot to destroy another.

Early in March, 1942 Duke was awarded the Distinguished Flying Cross and a few days later completed his first operational tour. He had 161 sorties, 220 operational flying hours and eight enemy aircraft to his credit. Posted to the Fighter School at El Ballah as an instructor, he remained at school teaching trainee pilots to fly and fight with Tomahawks and Kittyhawks until his rest period ended in the following November, when he was detailed to join his old squadron, Number 92, which had recently arrived in the Middle East, and was now stationed at Sidi Barrani. The trend of the battle in North Africa had now changed and Rommel was on the run again, chased by the Eighth Army and the Desert Air Force. Within a few days 92 Squadron moved up to Msus and, together with 601 and 145 Squadrons, began sweeps over El Agheila and Agedabia. The advance continued and the wing moved on first to Antelat, then to El Hassiat and again to Norgra. They spent Christmas in El Merdunne but were on the move again before the New Year was in, this time to El Chel. Duke had little chance to add to his score during all this moving, but finally the squadron settled in at Tamet, where they caught up with the Luftwaffe again. On the 8th January Duke shot down a Macchi 202 and three days later, on his 21st birthday, he celebrated by shooting down two more Macchi 202's, the pilots of which were a Wing Commander and a Squadron Leader. An unusual birthday present! Another double victory, this time the victims were Junkers 87's, came Duke's way on the 21st January and this was followed by promotion to Flight Lieutenant and the award of a Bar to his D.F.C.

The squadron moved to Castel Benito airfield and life became rather quiet for a period when there was very little flying. By March, however, the wing was at Medanine and the war was on again. The Commanding Officer of 92 Squadron was away for a period and Duke was appointed Acting Squadron Commander. He had an eventful week during which he shot down seven enemy aircraft. On the 1st March he destroyed two Macchi 202's during one sortie, both the pilots baling out. Two days later he sent a 109 down in flames, and the following day got another two Me. 109's. He destroyed another 109 near Medanine on his first mission on the 7th March, and later in the day added yet another 109 to his rapidly increasing list of kills.

A few days later 92 Squadron moved on again, this time to Bu Ghara, and whilst returning to this base on March 23rd Duke pursued a lone Junkers 88. He scored hits on the bomber and claimed it as damaged, but his own Spitfire was hit in the wings, airscrew and undercarriage and he had to break off the combat. Four days later, the Air Officer in Command of the Desert Air Force, Air Marshal Broadhurst, rang up to inform Duke that he had been awarded an immediate D.S.O. mainly because of his fine leadership of the squadron during the first week in March.

Duke celebrated two days later, on the 29th, by shooting down his 20th confirmed Hun during a patrol north of Gabes. He shot down two Italian three-engined bombers on a sweep on the 16th April and soon after this was taken off operations and posted to an Operational Training Unit near Ismalia as a Chief Flying Instructor.

The months passed slowly at Ismalia and Duke became restless to return to operations, but at last in February, 1944, he began his third tour as Squadron Commander of 145 Squadron stationed near Caserta in Italy. Things were so quiet in this area at this time that although he flew on many patrols over Anzio and Cassino, he did not meet the Luftwaffe in the air until the squadron moved to Venafro in May. He shot down two Me. 109's and two F.W. 190's during three missions and was awarded a second Bar to his D.F.C. Then he was shot down himself; he was leading a strafing attack in the Rietti area on June 7th when his Spitfire was hit by flak and he had to bale out. He landed in Lake Bracciano, but swam ashore, where he was sheltered by some friendly peasant farmers, until he was picked up a few hours later by a patrol of American G.I.'s.

The wing moved on to Fabrica, near Lake Vico, and took on a new role. The Spitfires were fitted with racks to carry a 500-pound bomb, and for several weeks Duke and his squadron were engaged in dive-bombing attacks against a number of varied targets.

During the final battle for the Gothic Line the Spitfires moved to Loreto, and it was from this airfield that Duke flew to shoot down his last two victims. With Flying Officer Hamer as his wingman, Duke took off on the 3rd September to patrol the battle area between Pesaro and Rimini. They found three Me. 109's and immediately gave chase. Duke caught one with a burst at long range, which caused the 109 to slow down and enabled Duke to close up for a point-blank shot. The cockpit cover flew off and the enemy pilot baled out. Duke turned his attention to the other 109's, closed to 200 yards and opened fire. One 109 caught fire and again the pilot baled out. The third 109 disappeared into some nearby clouds.

Duke managed to get in a number of dive-bombing attacks and also a few more combat patrols before his third tour of operations ended on September 20th. He had now completed 496 operational sorties and was top-scoring fighter pilot of the Middle East Command with a score of twenty-eight enemy aircraft destroyed, six probably destroyed, and ten damaged.

Returning to the United Kingdom, Duke was sent to the Hawker Aircraft Company as a test pilot. He liked the job so much that in June, 1948, he resigned his commission in the R.A.F. and became a permanent test pilot with Hawkers. In 1951 he was appointed Chief Test Pilot and as such was responsible for seeing the Hawker Hunter jet fighter through all its teething troubles. In 1953, Hawkers decided to make an attempt on the world's air speed record. On the 31st August, Duke broke the record, flying a Hunter at 722 m.p.h. over a three-kilometre course near Littlehampton in Sussex. On September

7th, Duke flew faster still and set up a new record speed of 727 m.p.h.

A few weeks later appeared two books written by Duke: *Test Pilot*, an autobiography, and *The Sound Barrier*, a technical book, both of which further enhanced the reputation of this modest, fearless fighter ace and test pilot.

15

'PADDY'

Wing Commander B. E. Finucane
D.S.O., D.F.C. and Two Bars

THE eldest of five brothers and sisters, Brendan Finucane was born in Dublin on the 16th October, 1920. His parents were very humble and, from the time he left O'Connell's Irish Christian Brothers' School in Dublin, he had to work hard as an office boy in an accountant's office and gave his salary towards the upkeep of a large family. His heart was set on flying, however, and in May, 1938, by which time some of his brothers were working, he gave up his office job and joined the Royal Air Force. Paddy qualified as a fighter pilot and on being commissioned was posted to 65 (East India) Spitfire Squadron at Hornchurch.

He flew his first operational sorties during the Battle of Britain, over fifty in fact in just over a fortnight, and on the 12th August shot down his first enemy aircraft. By the end of August, 65 Squadron had deserved a rest and consequently were moved to Turnhouse in Scotland to reorganise and rest. They were called upon to help out the hard-worked Spitfires and Hurricanes of Number Eleven Group from time to time during the next few months, but did not actually return to operations until November, 1940, when they were moved to Tangmere. The main part of the German attempt to establish air supremacy over Southern England was now over and the only Huns that ventured across the Channel were mainly fighter-bomber Messerschmitts escorted by 109's. Paddy got into a few fights with these elusive Huns, and by the end of the year his log-book recorded victories over four Me. 109's and one Me. 110.

A few days after his fifth victory Finucane had his first narrow escape. He was patrolling with his Number Two on a roving mission over the Channel when they found a lone Junkers 88 flying almost at sea level. Immediately the two Spitfires dived to attack. The enemy rear-gunner opened up with several accurate bursts of fire and Paddy's Spitfire was riddled with bullets. He continued to attack, however, and eventually the 88 crashed into the sea. Turning for home, Paddy nursed his damaged engine and breathed a sigh of relief as he brought it in at Tangmere twenty minutes later for a wheels-up landing.

In the spring of 1941 Finucane was awarded the D.F.C. and in April was promoted to Flight Lieutenant, and given command of 'A' Flight in Number 452 (R.A.A.F.) Squadron, a new squadron which was in the process of formation at Kirton-in-Lindsay in Lincolnshire. A few days later, with the arrival of new Spitfires a concentrated course in formation flying and fighter attacks was begun, which ended early in July, 1941, when the Australian Squadron made its debut on operations. It turned out to be an uneventful sweep and Paddy and the Australians returned to base very disappointed.

On the 11th July on another sweep across the Channel, the Aussies met the Huns in the air for the first time. Eight Me. 109's came down out of the sun in a diving attack. Paddy saw them first and pulled his Spitfire round to meet the attack. The leading Hun broke away and instantly Paddy was on his tail with his section trying to follow him. A short three-second burst from a hundred and fifty yards' range and pieces flew off the wings of the 109. Another burst and the German pilot baled out. Paddy swept round, his section trailing him, to find the sky was clear. The Luftwaffe had vanished. There was no chance of further victories that day, but Paddy was satisfied. He had chalked up the squadron's first kill.

On the 3rd August Paddy got two Me. 109's on one sortie. Five 109's had attacked his section and Finucane fired at one of the 109's as it swept past. He turned in behind it, followed it straight down through a cloud and on emerging saw it two hundred yards ahead. He fired and the 109 exploded into a thousand pieces. Climbing back to rejoin the rest of the squadron Paddy found a group of 109's going round in a big circle. He picked off one straggler, hit it in the fuselage and, as flames and smoke appeared, set off to rejoin the Aussies before the other Messerschmitts had a chance to attack him.

In less than a month Paddy destroyed nine Me. 109's and probably destroyed two more; this led to his being awarded a Bar to his D.F.C. The citation to the award said that he had 'led his flight with great dash, determination and courage in the face of the enemy and had been largely responsible for the fine fighting spirit of 452 Squadron'.

Paddy was making a name for himself. On the 16th August he scored three victories, all over Messerschmitt 109's. He shot the first one down into the Channel on the early morning sweep. In the afternoon on his second sortie, 452 Squadron was part of a wing of Spitfires escorting Blenheims in a raid on St Omer. They were on their way home nearing the coast when the 109's attacked them. Paddy caught one at seventy-five yards and had just sent it down in flames when his gun sight failed. As he struggled to fix his spare sight another section of Messerschmitts came in on his tail. Skidding round in the tightest of turns, Paddy eluded the attack and as the 109's flashed past, poured in a burst of cannon shells at point-blank range. One Messerschmitt blew up, the bits and pieces showering over Finucane's Spitfire as he pulled away to set course for Kenley.

Two more 109's fell before the guns of Finucane's Spitfire on his next mission, when the skies over Northern France seemed to be crowded with the iron crosses of the Luftwaffe. He followed the first 109 from 18,000 feet right down to 2,000 feet at well over 400 miles an hour before the 109 finally exploded. He was on his way out of France at low level when another 109 came at him from the port bow. Paddy turned head-on into the German's line of fire and as they rushed at each other at a frightening speed each pilot kept his thumb pressed on the firing button. The Hun broke first and caught the full fury of the Spitfire's cannon shells in its belly. It winged over and fell away towards the sea, streaming smoke and flames. Paddy's score was nineteen victories when he was awarded a second Bar to his D.F.C. on the 26th September and he destroyed his twentieth victim, another Me. 109 which crashed into the Channel, on the 2nd October. The following morning the newspaper headlines proclaimed 'Finucane wants one more!' They were referring, of course, to Finucane's score and relating it to his twenty-first birthday. Just three days before his birthday his squadron met some 109's while on a sweep. In the ensuing fight Finucane destroyed two Messerschmitts and damaged a third before running out of ammunition and breaking away. The following day, October 14th, Paddy added two more 109's to his tally. By his twenty-first birthday on the 16th October his score was twenty-four confirmed kills. He was awarded the D.S.O. the very same day for his 'brilliant leadership and example'.

A few days later Finucane fractured his ankle whilst jumping over a low wall in the blackout and spent the next two months hobbling around on crutches.

In January, 1942, 452 Squadron moved to Kenley and at the same time Finucane was promoted to Squadron Leader and given command of the renowned 602 (City of Glasgow) Auxiliary Squadron, also stationed at Kenley. One of his first missions as Commanding Officer of his new squadron was very nearly his last. It was on February 20th, 1942, when flying with Pilot Officer R. Lewis, an Australian. They dived down to attack an enemy transport vessel near Dunkirk. As they broke away two Focke-Wulf 190's made a head-on attack on the Spitfires. Finucane was hit in the leg and thigh and broke away.

'Return to base,' he ordered his wingman.

But Lewis, seeing Paddy's plight, mounted guard near his leader. The 190's made several determined attacks to finish off the damaged Spitfire, but Lewis fought them off. Eventually after Lewis and Finucane had managed to shoot down one of the 190's, the English coast appeared and the other 190 left them. Finucane made a perfect landing at Kenley, and taxied up to the dispersal point, but he did not get out of the cockpit. He had lost consciousness through loss of blood!

The injury was not as serious as had been first supposed, however, and within three weeks Paddy was in action again. On the 13th March, on his first sortie after coming out of hospital he shot down two F.W. 190's over Hazebruck. Two more fell to his guns during a sweep from Le Havre to Dunkirk on the 28th March, and on the 26th April he shot down another F.W. 190. Three weeks later on the 17th May he destroyed his thirty-second victim, to become joint top-scorer of Fighter Command, equalling the record set up by 'Sailor' Malan.

On the 27th June, Finucane was appointed Wing Commander Flying of the Hornchurch wing. A large-scale fighter sweep had been planned for July 15th and Squadron Leader D. Carlson was due to lead one of the squadrons. On the day of the operation Carlson was ill, so Finucane took his place. The Spitfires attacked a number of enemy ships near Ostend and set fire to three before going on to shoot up a German airfield in the hope of making the Huns come up to fight. The Germans, however, chose to remain on the ground, in the safety of their air-raid shelters. Paddy re-formed his wing and swung round to head for Hornchurch at low level. As the Spitfires passed over the beaches of Pointe du Touquet at less than fifty feet an enemy machine-gunner blazed away and a single bullet hit the radiator of Paddy's Spitfire. The engine temperature rose swiftly, and the Spitfire began to slow down.

Paddy called over the radio-telephone: 'I shall have to get out of this. I have had it. Am turning out.'

Pilot Officer Aikman, a Canadian and Paddy's wingman, saw the Irishman open the cockpit hood and take off his helmet, after which he bent down in the cockpit presumably to prepare his parachute. But he was too low to bale out and had not enough revolutions to climb. The engine temperature soared past the danger point and the next minute the engine stopped altogether. Then came Finucane's last words. He was perfectly calm.

'This is it, chaps,' he said.

The next instant his Spitfire plunged into the Channel and sank immediately, taking its gallant young pilot with it.

Paddy's death was a blow to Fighter Command and people all over the world sent money towards a fund to build the wing of a hospital as a permanent memorial to the fearless young Irishman, who gladly gave his life to uphold his faith in the free world.

16

A GALLANT CZECH

Sergeant J. Frantisek
D.F.M., Czechoslovakian War Cross,
Virtuti Militari, *Croix de Guerre*

A REGULAR member of the Czech Air Force, Josef Frantisek had to leave his native land when the Nazis invaded it. He flew to Poland and in March, 1939, enlisted in the Polish Air Force. Hardly had he become accustomed to flying the Polish fighter planes when the Germans invaded Poland, and Frantisek again took to the air to fight the Huns. Before the collapse of Poland he had shot down his first enemy machines and proved himself to be a pilot of considerable skill, for he was fighting in an obsolete fighter against German aircraft which were much faster, more powerful and carried more and bigger guns and cannons. When Poland was defeated after three weeks of violent fighting, Frantisek flew to Rumania where he was interned. Within a week he escaped from the internment camp, and making his way through the Balkans, finally arrived in Syria, where with the help of the French authorities he boarded a ship bound for France. He arrived in France in May, 1940, and immediately was posted to a fighter squadron of *L'Armée de l'Air*. For the next three weeks he flew and fought over Belgium and Champagne bringing his total of confirmed victories to eleven and winning the French *Croix de Guerre*.

When France collapsed in June, 1940, Josef Frantisek was on the run again. This time he came to England where he enlisted in the Royal Air Force. A quick conversion course on Spitfires and Hurricanes followed and then at the end of August he was posted as a Sergeant Pilot to Number 303 Hurricane Squadron. This was the 'Kosciusko' Squadron, the first of the Polish units to be formed in the Royal Air Force. Frantisek was the only Czech in the squadron, but this suited him perfectly for he was a lone wolf in the air. He liked to hunt on his own and several times left the squadron after take-off in order to chase the Huns alone. Finally the Squadron Commander gave him a roving commission and permission to fly after the Hun whenever and wherever he wanted – which was very often, for Frantisek had a fierce hatred of the Luftwaffe.

Frantisek opened his account in England with the destruction of an Me. 109 on the 2nd September. He was flying over Dover when he sighted two Me. 109's at the same height. He attacked one head on, firing from a hundred yards' range. The 109 broke away, but the Czech followed and hit the 109 in the fuselage. Josef closed in to point-blank range and fired again. This time a great cloud of black smoke issued from the engine and the 109 went down to crash about two miles from Dover.

The following day Frantisek dived on a Heinkel 113 and only used a short two-second burst, which must have killed the pilot, since the enemy fighter dived slowly away into the sea and disappeared.

The Polish Squadron intercepted fifty Me. 109's and Junkers 88's over the Thames Estuary during the afternoon of the 5th September and Frantisek was soon in the thick of the fighting. He followed his section leader Flight Lieutenant Forbes in an attack on a bunch of Junkers 88's but a 109 dived and attacked Frantisek from above. The 109 failed to use deflection and overshot; quickly the Czech was on his tail opening fire at a hundred and fifty yards. One short two-second burst sent the 109 down vertically in flames, so Frantisek rejoined his Flight Commander in an attack on the bombers. He fired from below and astern of one 88 and saw his bullets hitting the starboard engine and cockpit. Suddenly the engine burst into flames and the 88 sideslipped into the sea. Frantisek who by this time was short of ammunition returned to Northolt to rearm.

The next day Frantisek attacked two Me. 109's over Sevenoaks, and after sending one down in flames was himself hit by a cannon shell and had to make a hurried retreat.

On the 9th September, Frantisek flew with the squadron in a combined attack on a large formation of Heinkel 111's escorted by swarms of Messerschmitts, and his own Hurricane was so badly damaged that he had to make a crash landing near Brighton. When the battle began, Frantisek attacked an Me. 109 from the starboard beam and after several short bursts of gunfire, the Messerschmitt began to burn. The German pilot tried to escape by climbing; then he opened the cockpit hood apparently with the intention of baling out. Before he could do so the engine blew up and the machine fell in flames. Frantisek turned his attention to the bombers, but was immediately attacked by two Me. 109's. He dived into some thick cumulus cloud, avoided his pursuers, and came out of the cloud to find himself dead astern of a Heinkel 111. He nearly collided with it, swung away and then pulled in behind it again, aiming at the cockpit of the bomber. The front of the Heinkel fell to pieces, with the cockpit and both engines in flames. As he broke away the two Messerschmitts again attacked him, one from above and the other from underneath. Frantisek's Hurricane was hit by cannon shells in the wing, the petrol tank and the radiator. Completely at the mercy of the Huns, Frantisek waited for the end. Then, suddenly, two Spitfires arrived on the scene and quickly disposed of the 109's. With his engine temperature mounting dangerously, the Czech pilot looked for a suitable landing place. On a hill near Brighton he found a field of cabbages and a few minutes later glided in to make an excellent crash landing. An hour later he was on a train heading for his base.

When the Poles intercepted over eighty enemy aircraft at midday over London on the 15th September, Frantisek attacked two Me. 110's, and shot down one of them in flames before having to break away, Three days later he left the squadron to go hunting across the Channel where he found an Me. 109 heading south with its engines smoking slightly. He dived and caught it near the French coast. He fired two short bursts which caused the 109 to go into the sea in flames and then flew back to Northolt joining up with Flying Officer Feric on the way.

Sergeant Frantisek destroyed two Heinkel 111's which he chased from Portsmouth to the French coast on the 26th September, and the following day in the early morning he shot down a Heinkel 111 and a Messerschmitt 110. After his first burst the starboard engine of the Heinkel burst into flames, but to make sure Frantisek fired again and set the other engine on fire. He then flew south and noticed six Me. 110's circling, one of which broke out of the circle as the Hurricane approached. The Czech closed to a hundred yards and with his first burst hit and stopped the starboard engine of the 110. The enemy fighter then glided down towards a landing field and Frantisek, thinking it was going to land, held his fire. At the last moment when the Messerschmitt was only a few feet from the ground, the German pilot opened his throttle and began to climb. Instantly Frantisek pressed his gun button and the 110 crashed into the airfield and burst into flames.

On the last day of September, 1940, Sergeant Frantisek got his twenty-eighth confirmed kill. The squadron had been scrambled to meet an incoming raid in the afternoon, but Frantisek had some trouble in starting his engine and consequently took off on his own hoping to join up with the squadron later. Flying above the clouds in a south-easterly direction he suddenly encountered six Me. 109's. The enemy fighters quickly formed a defensive circle, but one of them came out of line slightly and in an instant the Czech had taken advantage of the other's error and got in a burst which caused the 109 to spin down. Frantisek followed and again fired and immediately the 109 burst into flames. Frantisek then found another 109 and got in a good burst of fire which caused the 109 to smoke, before he lost it in some clouds. He was unable to find it again, so he returned to Northolt.

A few days later, on the 8th October, Josef Frantisek flew for the last time. He was returning from an early morning patrol with the Poles; one by one they were coming in to land at Northolt to refuel and rearm. When it was Frantisek's turn, his Hurricane glided in as usual, touched down at eighty miles an hour. Then came disaster. The wing tip of the Hurricane touched a slight bump in the ground, the fighter somersaulted over, and the next instant was blazing furiously. The gallant Czech died before his comrades could get him out of the wreckage.

Frantisek was posthumously awarded the highest Polish award for valour, the *Virtuti Militari*, and at the same time received his one and only Czechoslovakian decoration, the War Cross. Perhaps the Czech authorities had not realised before his death that Josef Frantisek, the little Czech Sergeant, had shot down twenty-eight enemy aircraft. He was the leading Czech fighter ace of the war and also, at the time of his death, the highest-scoring pilot of Fighter Command.

17

NEW ZEALAND ACE

Wing Commander C. F. Gray
D.S.O., D.F.C. and Two Bars

THE boys left the school hall chattering excitedly. They had just been listening to a talk about the Royal Air Force given by a Wing Commander, and most of them had immediately decided to make a career of flying. As the months passed, however, many of them found new interests, so that by the time they left school, only a very few remembered the talk. Two of them remembered it so well that as soon as they were old enough they sent in applications to join the R.A.F.

The two boys were twin brothers, Colin and Kenneth Gray, who had been born in Papanui, Christchurch, New Zealand, on the 9th November, 1914. When they finished their education at Christ's College, Christchurch, they had both gone into offices as junior clerks, in order to kill time until they were old enough to become flyers.

Now they waited anxiously for the postman to call with the replies to their letters of application. At long last he arrived. They tore open the envelopes and read with dismay that, because the demand for pilots was so low in days of peace, their applications had been turned down.

The brothers, more determined than ever to become pilots,

stuck to their clerking duties, but all the time kept their eyes open for an opportunity to join the R.A.F. The opportunity came in 1938 when the R.A.F. began its long-overdue expansion scheme. Both brothers immediately sent in applications and a few days later were instructed to report for a medical inspection at Wellington.

Colin had an attack of influenza on the day of the examination but nothing would stop him from going with his brother. The result was inevitable, Colin was turned down. Kenneth passed the tests with ease and soon afterwards came to England to train as a pilot. He became a bomber pilot and won the D.F.C. before being killed on a raid over Germany.

Meanwhile, Colin, in order to build up his strength, took a job as a farm labourer. Eight months later he was on his way to England, having passed the medical tests and been accepted as a trainee for a short-service commission in the R.A.F. He was still at a flying training school when the war broke out, but soon passed out as a fully fledged Pilot Officer and subsequently was posted to Hornchurch fighter station to join Number 54 Squadron, where he met another young New Zealander by the name of Alan Deere. They became great friends and also great rivals in their chosen business of shooting down the Luftwaffe.

For several months Colin and Alan were able to practise combat flying with each other, and other pilots of the squadron, in complete peace in the pleasant skies over Southern England, whilst just over an hour's flying time away the R.A.F. Hurricanes and Luftwaffe Messerschmitts slugged it out over the Maginot and Seigfried Lines.

The squadron's first taste of action came in May, 1940, when they were ordered to patrol over the beaches of Dunkirk whilst the Allied Armies were being evacuated from France. Colin and another pilot attacked a Messerschmitt 109 high above the British Tommies, who were being constantly dive-bombed by Stukas and Junkers 88's. Very soon the Messerschmitt was on fire and its pilot baled out. Colin watched fascinated as the German pilot fell head over heels, but was instantly activated by a violent bang, which caused his Spitfire to fall away into an uncontrollable spin. He fought to regain control of his fighter but his ailerons had been shot away, so as the ground rushed towards him at an alarming rate, he pushed back the perspex hood of his cockpit and prepared to bale out.

Just as he had given up all hope, his stricken Spitfire suddenly levelled out above the blue waters of the English Channel. With sweat dripping from his forehead, Colin carefully surveyed the damage to his Spitfire. He tried out the various controls and found that he could just manage to keep his aircraft flying – provided he did not meet any more Huns. Luck was on his side and thirty minutes later he crash-landed on the first British airfield he saw. As he climbed out of his rather sad-looking Spitfire, he remembered one of the unwritten laws of air-fighting – 'Always keep a sharp look out – it's the one you don't see that gets you.'

A brief respite followed the Dunkirk operations, and Colin Gray did not meet the enemy again until July 13th, and this time he shot down a Messerschmitt 109 without any more complications. After this the Battle of Britain was on in real earnest and the long tiring days that followed were full of excitement, danger, emotion, success and failure for the short, wiry, curly-haired New Zealander.

Gray learned quickly and on the 24th July he shot down his second Me. 109 in a dogfight over Margate. The following day his flight of five Spitfires took on a vast armada of forty Junkers 87's and fifty Me. 109's near Dover. He fired at several Messerschmitts in a sky that was full of black crosses and swastikas, but was unable to claim any victims, owing to his having to break off combat every few seconds or so because of the danger of colliding with the enemy.

The New Zealander shot down two Me. 109's on the 12th August, gave a repeat performance three days later and on August 18th he set fire to a Messerschmitt 110 over the Thames Estuary. On a second sortie on the same day he scored hits on a Dornier 17, whilst in the afternoon on his third patrol, he hit a Messerschmitt 109 which crashed into the centre of Clacton. He destroyed an Me. 110 which he pursued almost to the French coast on the 24th August, and two days later blew up a Messerschmitt 109 with a burst of gunfire which must have hit the enemy fighter in the petrol tank.

Gray's last four days of fighting in the Battle of Britain, from the 31st August to the 3rd September inclusive, brought him six more confirmed victories, one probable, and also two lucky escapes. His first lucky escape occurred on September 1st, when he attacked three Heinkel 111's flying high over Maidstone. He shot down the leading Hun all right, but when he came in to attack the other two his own Spitfire was hit by a cannon shell and fell away into a spin. Colin regained control, but in doing so found that his elevators would not work. He glided away, landed at Hornchurch, and found that the cannon shell had completely severed the elevator control wire. An hour later, his Spitfire having been repaired by his hard-working ground crew, Colin was again in combat. This time Number 54 Squadron tore into a pack of Me. 109's over Biggin Hill airfield and after a few minutes Colin forced one of the 109's to crash-land on the aerodrome.

The next day Colin had his second lucky escape. He had just sent a Messerschmitt 109 down in flames, when a cannon shell exploded about two feet behind his cockpit. Although there was a gaping hole in the Spitfire, the shell splinters missed its pilot completely and Colin was able to land safely at Hornchurch. Colin flew four more sorties in another Spitfire before the day ended and on one of these sorties accounted for an Me. 110 which exploded over Hornchurch. The following day he destroyed an Me. 109, and probably destroyed an Me. 110, and then went off with the remains of Number 54 Squadron to an airfield in the north of England for a rest from operations.

It was not until the following February that the squadron returned to operations again, with Colin Gray, newly promoted Flight Lieutenant, in command of 'A' Flight. Soon after this he was awarded a Bar to the D.F.C. he had won in August, 1940. Further promotion to Squadron Leader came in the summer of 1941 and on one of his first sweeps over Northern France as a squadron commander he shot down his seventeenth victim, an Me. 109 which crashed on its own airfield near Le Havre. After this Squadron Leader Gray was given command of the first squadron in Britain to be equipped with Spitfire IX's and he led them from Hornchurch, the same airfield from which he had taken off on countless occasions during the Battle of Britain.

A brief spell in Malta in 1942 enabled Gray to chalk up three more victims and then, after a rest period, the New Zealander moved on to Tunisia in January, 1943, to begin his third tour of operations. At first he took command of Number 81 Squadron, but later he was promoted Wing Commander in charge of five Spitfire squadrons, leading them during the Tunisian and Sicilian campaigns. He shot down five enemy aircraft over Tunisia and two more in Sicily.

On one occasion he had just taken off when he noticed bombs bursting on the airfield he had just left. Peering into the heavens he could just make out eight F.W. 190's who were now heading towards their base at Bizerta. Colin gave chase for a few minutes, but when he realised it was impossible to catch up he turned towards home followed by his wingman. Soon afterwards he sighted two low-flying Me. 109's and immediately roared down to make an astern attack on one of them. For several minutes the Spitfire and the Messerschmitt fought out a battle, barely a few feet away from the blistering sand of the desert. Eventually the New Zealander got in a deadly burst of cannon-shell fire which caused the 109 to go into a steep climb with white glycol streaming behind it. At 1,500 feet it rolled over and its pilot baled out.

Colin remembers well the day his squadron destroyed twenty-eight enemy aircraft for the loss of one Spitfire. It happened on April 18th, 1943, near Milazzo in the Straits of Messina. The Spitfires were flying at very low-level when they saw a number of Me. 109's and Macchi fighters patrolling at 7,000 feet. Almost at the same instant Gray observed scores of large, overloaded Junkers 52 transport aircraft straight ahead. They were bringing up supplies and reinforcements to the Germans on the beaches in the area. The Spitfires tore into the slow, cumbersome transports and before the escorting fighters realised what was happening the Ju. 52's were being slaughtered. When the 109's and Macchis did finally come to their aid the Spitfires had shot down over a score of the Junkers. Wing Commander Gray's share was two, both of which crashed blazing furiously into the sea.

A few weeks after this action Gray returned to England where he was posted for instructional duties. He had been awarded the D.S.O. and a second Bar to his D.F.C. whilst in the Middle East, and in November, 1943, went to Buckingham Palace to receive his decorations from the King. In 1944 Gray served another tour of operations in North West Europe, but his duties prevented him from doing much operational flying or adding to his long list of victories. By the end of the war these added up to twenty-seven and a half confirmed destroyed, all scored in a total operational flying time of 670 hours. As New Zealand's ace fighter pilot he was granted a permanent commission in the Royal Air Force in 1945 and served at the Air Ministry. In 1947–8 he was attached to the Directorate of Allied and Foreign Liaison and later on went to the United States of America under an exchange of pilots scheme.

18

WELSH WIZARD

Wing Commander R. H. Harries
D.S.O. and Bar, D.F.C. and Two Bars,
Croix de Guerre, Croix de Guerre Belge

THE son of a bank manager, Raymond Hiley Harries was born
in South Wales in 1916 and, on leaving school, decided on a
career in the medical profession, becoming a student at Guys
Hospital. His studies were interrupted, however, by the outbreak of the war, and Harries left the hospital and volunteered
for the Royal Air Force. He was trained as a fighter pilot and on
completing the course was commissioned and posted to Number
43 Squadron, a fighter unit stationed at Drem in Scotland and
engaged on convoy and interception patrols over Scotland and
the North Sea area. In the summer of 1941 the squadron carried
out a number of night interception patrols, and during one of
these on the 6th May Harries saw his first Hun. He attacked a
Heinkel 111 over the Firth of Forth, but was very short of fuel
and had to break off the engagement before doing any damage to
it. Two months later Harries was posted to Number 52 Operational Training Unit at Debden for duty as a Flying Instructor.

Early in February, 1942, he joined Number 131 Squadron at
Llanbedr in North Wales as a flight commander and within a
month had shot down his first victim, a Junkers 88 which fell
into the sea with both its engines on fire about thirty-five miles
west of his base. The squadron, which had only recently been
formed, was still officially non-operational during this period
and most of the time was spent in local flying, air-to-sea firing,
air tests and dogfighting practices. In fact, things were so quiet
that the Operations Book records that on the 27th April 'Flight
Lieutenant Harries gave an interesting lecture to pilots on the
Merlin engine'.

Less than three weeks later, however, the squadron was on its
way to Merston to become part of the Tangmere Spitfire Wing,
which took a leading role in the R.A.F.'s offensive fighter operations in the summer of 1942. During one of the squadron's first

fighter sweeps on the 5th June, they were surprised by fifteen F.W. 190's five miles north of Le Havre, but the Spitfires put up a stubborn resistance and, by the time the battle was over, Harries had probably destroyed one F.W. 190 and damaged a second.

Harries was protecting ships on the morning of the 19th August, 1942, during the Commando raid on Dieppe, when he sighted an F.W. 190 chasing a Spitfire. He made a head-on attack on the enemy fighter which did a flick half roll and then fell upside down until it hit the water about two miles off the coast. During another similar mission in the afternoon, Harries persuaded a Dornier 217 to dive into the sea. Six days afterwards Flight Lieutenant Harries was awarded the D.F.C., the first decoration to be won by 131 Squadron.

'A very interesting patrol' was how the Commanding Officer described a flight made by Harries and himself on the 3rd December, 1942, but the Welshman had other views on it. They took off at 8.30 a.m. and were ordered to investigate Raid Number 68. They were given three directions and finally made a perfect interception eight miles south-west of the Isle of Wight. The aircraft turned out to be a Halifax in difficulties with two of its engines stopped. The two Spitfires escorted it safely back to Tangmere, but during this trip Harries had a very shaky experience. He found himself in cloud with his instruments iced up. He realised something was wrong when he found himself hanging on his harness. The next moment he came out of the cloud at 1,500 feet diving vertically towards the sea. He hauled back on the control column and pulled out of the dive less than fifty feet above the waves.

Three days later Harries had a much more enjoyable flight to Calais where he shot down an F.W. 190. This was his last flight with Number 131 Squadron, since the following day he was promoted to Squadron Leader and left to take command of Number 91 Squadron, which was stationed at Hawkinge.

Harries was testing a new type of microphone on the 20th January, 1943, and had just landed at West Malling, when the tannoy announced a raid by German fighter-bombers against London. He took off without the microphone, but by plugging in to Biggin Hill Control and listening to their instructions to other pilots, he soon realised that the raiders were returning over Beachy Head. He flew there at full speed, just in time to see four Me. 109's crossing the coastline. He dived on the rear pair of Messerschmitts and opened fire at the port aircraft from a range of a hundred and fifty yards. The 109 whipped straight into the sea. Harries turned slightly to starboard and saw his shells scoring strikes on the second 109, when he glanced behind him and saw four F.W. 190's approaching. He whipped round in the tightest of turns and attacked the last of the four, which gave out a pall of smoke, before Harries had to break off the engagement owing to the appearance of about fifteen more enemy aircraft.

Harries destroyed two F.W. 190's in two flights over the Channel in March, 1943, and then the squadron was moved to Honiley and began to re-equip with Spitfire XII's. They did not return to operations until the 21st May and, whilst they were still training on their new aircraft, Harries was informed that he had been awarded a Bar to his D.F.C. for being 'a highly efficient squadron commander whose great keenness and energetic leadership have set a worthy example'.

Four days after returning to Hawkinge, Harries shot down two F.W. 190's in ten minutes. He and his wingman intercepted twelve 'tip-and-run' raiders, F.W. 190's, over Folkestone. Harries fired a three-second deflection burst of shells from a range of two hundred and fifty yards at one of the 190's which hit the sea tail first, split in two and then sank. He spotted another 190 to starboard, pulled up to a thousand feet and then dived right on its tail. After a four-second burst the enemy fighter gradually lost height with smoke and flames coming from it, skimmed for some distance along the surface of the water, came to a sudden stop and then sank. Seeing no more enemy aircraft in the vicinity, Harries flew around and took some cine-gun snaps of the oil patch and wreckage.

Towards the end of June, 1943, Squadron Leader Harries led his squadron to Westhampnett to join Number 41 Squadron to form a Spitfire Twelve Wing, whose main task was the escorting of bombers, although they also found time to carry out many fighter sweeps. During one of these sweeps on the 16th July Harries destroyed another F.W. 190 as it was taking off from Poix aerodrome. Two days later he attacked three Me. 109's near Abbeville and saw strikes on one which he claimed as damaged. He shot the tail off the second, and chased the third as it half-rolled and dived. Closing rapidly he opened fire at two hundred yards and saw his shells entering the fuselage of the 190. White smoke streamed out and it finally burst into flames. This was the Welshman's twelfth confirmed victory and led to the award of a second Bar to his D.F.C. in August, 1943, and also to his taking command of the wing during the same month.

The Westhampnett Wing became the top-scoring wing in

Fighter Command for the month of September when they destroyed a total of twenty-seven enemy aircraft, Harries himself accounting for three of these. Both of these facts were mentioned in the official citation to the D.S.O. awarded to Harries, which also spoke of his 'inspiring leadership and great tactical ability' and described Harries as 'an exceptionally skilful, courageous and determined fighter'.

On the 20th October his wing claimed another nine enemy fighters destroyed during a sweep over the Beaumont-Bernay region, Harries shooting down two of them between Rouen and Evreux. These were his last victories on this particular tour of operations, since the following month he relinquished command of the wing, and was sent to the U.S.A. to give a series of lectures to American fighter pilots.

He returned to England in the spring of 1944 and soon after D-Day became Wing Commander Flying of Number One-three-five Wing, with which he flew from bases in France and Germany for the next six months. He quickly found his shooting form, destroying an F.W. 190 whilst escorting Lancasters to St Cyr, near Versailles, on the 25th July. Subsequently he shot down two more enemy fighters, before he scored his last victory on Boxing Day, 1944, when he attacked and damaged one of Germany's newest and fastest planes, an Me. 262 jet fighter.

Harries was sent for a conversion course on Tempests at Predannock in January, 1945, and on his return was given command of Number One-three-five Wing, but he was only in charge of this wing for about a fortnight before he was posted to Number Eighty-four Group as Wing Commander (Training). He was still occupying this post when the war ended.

He had been awarded the French *Croix de Guerre* in August, 1944, to which was added the Belgian *Croix de Guerre* in June, 1945. A month later he was awarded his last decoration, a Bar to his D.S.O., when it was officially announced that he had destroyed at least twenty enemy aircraft. Harries remained in the R.A.F. after the war ended and saw service in many lands before he was killed in a most unfortunate air accident on the 14th May, 1950.

19

MALTA SPITFIRE ACE

Squadron Leader R. B. Hesselyn
M.B.E., D.F.C., D.F.M. and Bar

RAY HESSELYN, the man who was destined to become the leading Royal New Zealand Air Force fighter ace of the Second World War, and who became the only R.N.Z.A.F. pilot to win the D.F.M. and Bar, was born in Dunedin, New Zealand on the 13th March, 1921. He was educated at Waitaki Boy's High School, and Southland B.H.S., and then served with the New Zealand Territorial Army. On the outbreak of World War II he served with the Army before transferring to the Air Force in 1940. Pilots were needed badly at this time and after four months training, Hesselyn, now a sergeant pilot and whose name had been shortened to 'Hess' by his fellow trainees, was on his way to England, where in September, 1941, he was sent for further training to Number 61 Operational Training Unit at Heston. In November he was posted to his first squadron, Number 234 based at Ibsley, and for the next three months was engaged on interceptions, convoy patrols and sweeps.

In February, 1942, he was selected to go overseas and sailed with fifteen other pilots, plus ground crews and sixteen crated Spitfires, to Gibraltar. There the aircraft were assembled on H.M.S. *Eagle* and the pilots were given their orders. They were to fly the first Spitfires to Malta and to remain there to form a squadron. On the 7th March, 1942, they took off from the *Eagle*, flew nearly 800 miles to the besieged island and, on landing at Taikali aerodrome, took the nameplate of Number 249 Squadron. Within a week Hess had flown his first operational mission over Malta, and within a month had scored his first successes.

Hess and three other pilots were on patrol on the 1st April when they sighted a Dornier 24 escorted by Me. 109's approaching the island low down. Immediately the four Spitfires dived to intercept, the New Zealander making a stern attack on one of the fighters. The speed of his dive carried him past his target, but a few seconds later he found another 109 dead ahead. At fifty yards' range Hess opened fire – a short burst was sufficient to send the Messerschmitt into the sea. He then chased two more 109's out to sea, but he was unable to catch up with them and decided to return to Takali. Ninety minutes later Hess took off for his third sortie of the day and within minutes was involved in another large dog-fight against twenty more 109's. Forced down to less than a thousand feet before finally getting away from the Messerschmitts, Hess sighted a Junkers 87, crept up behind it and fired a two-second burst. The Stuka burst into flames and dived into the sea.

Although the handful of Spitfires and Hurricanes stationed on Malta were up to their necks in the furious fighting that took place as the Luftwaffe made an all-out onslaught to conquer the island, Sergeant Hesselyn did not claim his next victim until the 20th April when he chased a Messerschmitt 109 right across the island before sending it down into St Paul's Bay. On his way back to Takali he hit a Junkers 88 but did not see it crash, so he only claimed a probable.

The next day he shot down a Messerschmitt 109 and a Junkers 87 and also damaged another 109. He destroyed the first 109 with a beautiful deflection shot which caused the Messerschmitt to disintegrate, but was then attacked by another Me. which was shot off his tail by Flying Officer Johnny Plagis. Over Gozo, Hess then spotted several Stukas. He dived on the last one, which after a four-second burst went straight down in flames. The New Zealander was attacked by a bunch of 109's shortly afterwards, but he evaded them and found another 109 shooting up his base. Hess gave chase and scored hits on the enemy fighter before having to give up the chase because of the shortage of fuel.

An illustration of the great odds faced by the defenders of the George Cross Island occurred during Hess's next combat on the 26th April. He had taken off from Takali with two companions, one of whom was obliged to return with radio-telephone trouble. The remaining pair of Spitfires were climbing gracefully into the sun when they sighted a swarm of over twenty Me. 109's well above them. Four of the enemy peeled off and dived on Hess and his companion, who turned towards the Huns and met them head-on. The New Zealander saw his cannon shells hit the wing of one of the Messerschmitts and then had to quickly dive away as another six 109's came at him with guns blazing. Bullets tore holes in the wing and fuselage of his Spitfire before he finally eluded his pursuers and headed alone towards Takali where he found a crowd of Junkers 87's dive-bombing the field. He caught one just as it began to dive and fired two brief bursts. Vivid flames shot from the Stuka, the pilot and navigator baled out, and the dive-bomber hit the ground with a terrific explosion. But Hess had no time to watch the effect of his gunnery skill because even before the Stuka had hit the ground four more Messerschmitts came in behind, two from either side. Turning into each pair in turn and firing whenever the opportunity occurred, Hess eventually scored hits on one of the Messerschmitts and immediately all four of the enemy fighters headed for Sicily at top speed. A few minutes later the New Zealander landed safely between the bomb-craters on Takali to prepare for his next sortie.

A large naval vessel sailed into Malta's Valetta Harbour on the 10th May with supplies and reinforcements of men and machines and this was the prelude to an even fiercer onslaught by the Luftwaffe in an effort to sink the ship. Hess flew an average of three patrols each day from the 10th to the 14th May and, during this intensive period of operations, he destroyed five, probably destroyed one and damaged several more, hostile aircraft.

His second combat on the 10th May was perhaps the most exciting, and provided Hess with a narrow escape. He was patrolling at 25,000 feet with three other pilots when they intercepted about twenty German raiders. Hess managed to get on to the tail of a Junkers 88 and was about to open fire when there was a terrific explosion in the cockpit and his flying helmet was jerked forwards. An explosive bullet had come through the canopy of the Spitfire, torn a piece out of the New Zealander's helmet and then exploded against the instrument panel a few inches from his face. At the same time a cannon-shell burst near his feet, but Hess was not even scratched and, pulling his Spitfire round in the tightest of turns, he saw his attacker, an Me. 109, twenty yards away directly in his line of fire. Pressing his gun button, Hess saw his own shells strike the 109 over its fuselage and wings. It was almost as if he had shot away all the nuts and bolts in the 109 for it collapsed in bits and pieces of various sizes. In the meantime Hess had blacked out as the tremendous gravitational pull exerted by his turn had drained the blood from his head, but a few seconds later his eyes cleared and he was amazed to see the sky empty. He pulled his Spitfire out of its dive and landed at Takali without further mishap. It was suggested as he walked back to the Mess that he went out for a drink to relieve the tension. This he did, with the result that apart from a hangover, he was quite fit next morning to resume his unfinished business with the Luftwaffe.

It was the 12th May, however, before Hess was in combat again, when in less than half an hour he shot down an Me. 109 and probably destroyed another. The following day he accounted for another 109 and on the 14th he shot a Junkers 88 to pieces. After this the Luftwaffe remained at home to lick its wounds and Hess was able to enjoy a spell of relative quietness.

Whilst the Spitfires were awaiting the next Luftwaffe blitz, the decorations and promotions began to arrive, Hess being awarded the Distinguished Flying Medal on the 8th May for his 'outstanding determination in pressing home his attacks undeterred by the odds'. Ten days later the award of a Bar to this decoration was announced, when reference was made to the New Zealander's 'outstanding courage and devotion to duty'. Promotion quickly followed, and on the 28th May Hess was summoned to the Commanding Officer's office and informed that he had been commissioned as a Pilot Officer.

It was several weeks before Hess again met the Hun in combat and somehow he seemed to have lost his shooting form, for although he took part in two aerial battles on the 6th July he was unable to claim a single victory. Two days later, however, he despatched an Me. 109 into the sea and then set fire to a Junkers 88. A week later Hess flew his last operational mission from the island, but failed to add to his score. The following day he was on his way back to England.

A six months' rest from operations at Number 61 O.T.U. followed and then Hess joined Number 501 Squadron who were training in Northern Ireland. This squadron shortly afterwards moved to Westhampnett near Tangmere, where in April, 1943, flying as a wing with Numbers 601 and 485 Squadrons they began offensive sweeps and escort missions to Northern France. The Luftwaffe fighters were not very keen to 'mix it' with Fighter Command at this time and Hess, after his hectic experiences in Malta, was not used to flying so many missions without ever seeing an enemy fighter. However, when the Luftwaffe did appear, Hess took full advantage and on the 15th May shot down his first F.W. 190.

In July, 1943, Hess was posted to Number 222 (Natal) Spitfire Squadron where he was later appointed Flight Commander. A few weeks later, during an escort mission to Antwerp, he added two Me. 109's to his bag. The Spitfires soon after leaving the bombers had dived after a dozen 109's flying several thousand feet lower. The Messerschmitts split up, and Hess attacked one

of them from the starboard quarter. He saw strikes on the fuselage of the 109, which then rolled on to its back and went
down to crash near Neuzen. Hess then spotted another 109
about 600 yards ahead, closed in and opened fire from dead
astern. The pilot baled out and the tail broke off the enemy
fighter before it dived into a river.

By the end of September, 1943, Hess had become the leading
ace of the Royal New Zealand Air Force with eighteen and a half
confirmed victories and had been awarded the D.F.C. for 'his
great skill, courage and keenness'. Three days later after destroying three Huns on one mission he was himself shot down in
flames.

On the afternoon of October 3rd, the wing was briefed as high-
cover escort for Marauder bombers carrying out a raid on the
German airfield at Beauvais-Tille. The mission was uneventful
until the Spitfires arrived over Beauvais, although there were a lot
of enemy fighters about and more were being reported. As they
turned high above the bombers, Hess sighted some F.W. 190's
diving to attack the rear box of bombers. He reported to the
wing leader and then led his fighters into the Huns. He shot down
one of the 190's as it broke away, and then sighted more enemy
fighters, 109's this time, coming down on the bombers. His flight
was too late to catch them before they hit the bombers, but followed them down as they broke away. At about 4,000 feet Hess
managed to close on one and from dead astern fired a short burst
which caused the 109 to explode. Hess's wingman was still following, so they continued to chase the 109's, although by this time
they had lost contact with the rest of the wing. Hess caught
another 109 with a burst into the cockpit and saw it crash soon
afterwards. Then, realising the danger of staying so low down,
Hess and his Number Two climbed swiftly to rejoin the wing.
At about 18,000 feet, Hess saw an F.W. 190 moving in towards
him from the starboard beam, called to his wingman to watch out
for it, and then turned towards the 190. The German opened
fire at an almost impossible angle and suddenly there was a loud
explosion from the bottom of Hess's cockpit and it burst into
flames. At the same time several cannon shells exploded behind
the armour plating of Hess's seat and in the cockpit.

The Spitfire spun down, as Hess struggled to release the cockpit
hood which refused to budge. He managed to get the plane out
of the spin, only to have it go into an inverted spin. By this time
the heat was intense. At last he forced open the hood and managed to get out of the cockpit, which was like an inferno. His

parachute opened and as he swung beneath it he beat out the flames on his burning clothing. He landed near Bauvais where he was immediately surrounded by German troops, who took him to the local military hospital. Here he was treated for first, second and third degree burns, and for shrapnel wounds in the leg.

A month later he was packed off to a prisoner of war camp and there he remained for the rest of the war. He was not a model prisoner by any means and before long was organising escapes and counter intelligence. He did in fact manage to escape from the camp on one occasion himself, but was soon recaptured, so he went back to make more escape attempts. In 1946, after his return to England, Hesselyn was awarded the M.B.E. for 'distinguished services when a prisoner of war in Germany'.

Hess accepted a permanent commission in the Royal Air Force in 1947 and today he is still serving in the R.A.F. as a Squadron Leader at Fighter Command Headquarters.

20

'DUTCH' HUGO

Group Captain P. H. Hugo
D.S.O., D.F.C. and Two Bars,
Croix de Guerre, D.F.C. (U.S.A.)

THE shooting down of twenty-two aircraft, a share in the sinking of some twenty sea-going vessels, the destruction of at least fifty-five vehicles, a total operational flying time of over 1,100 hours – these are only a few of the wartime achievements of 'Dutch' Hugo and partly explain why he was a Group Captain at the age of twenty-four and why he was wearing ribbons of the Distinguished Service Order, the Distinguished Flying Cross (with Two Bars), the French *Croix de Guerre*, and the American Distinguished Flying Cross before the end of 1944.

The son of a French Huguenot sheep farmer, Petrus Hendrik Hugo was born on the 20th December, 1917, at Pampoenpoort, Cape Province, South Africa. He was educated at Victoria West

High School and later studied at the Witwatersrand College of Aeronautical Engineering. He came to England in 1938, attended a course run by the Royal Air Force at the Civil Flying School at Sywell in the early months of 1939, and was accepted for a short service commission in the Royal Air Force on the 1st April, 1939. He was sent to Number 13 Flying Training School for the next six months and at the end of the course was classified as an exceptional pilot, an excellent marksman and suitable for posting to a fighter squadron. He was duly posted to the Fighter School at St Athan, and then to Number 2 Ferry Pool, at Filton, and finally in December, 1940, was ordered to France to join Number 615 Squadron who were stationed at Vitry. This squadron was equipped with Gladiators at the time and Hugo had to make his first operational patrols flying these out of date biplane fighters. Fortunately for Hugo and his fellow pilots, the squadron began to re-equip with Hawker Hurricanes. The pilots just had time for a few familiarisation flights in their new fighters before they were thrown into action to meet the oncoming hordes of Messerschmitts, Junkers, Heinkels and Dorniers of the Luftwaffe, which seemed to fill the skies of France and the Low Countries as Hitler launched his all-out offensive, which ultimately caused the collapse of France and the evacuation of the Allied Armies from Dunkirk.

Before he returned with what was left of Number 615 Squadron to Kenley for a well-earned rest at the end of May, 1940, the young South African had managed to bring down his first Hun, a Heinkel 111 which he destroyed during a patrol between Arras and Douai on the afternoon of the 20th May.

In July, 1940, the squadron resumed its operations against the Luftwaffe, and on the 14th of the same month Pilot Officer Hugo was adding to his victories. His section had sighted three Stukas which they attacked. Hugo engaged the leading one of the trio and after a short burst from fairly close range noticed that the enemy rear-gunner had stopped firing back at him. Breaking away because he was overshooting the dive bomber, Hugo then fired a burst into the second of the Junkers 87's which had already been attacked by Flying Officer Collard and was eventually credited to him. Turning quickly so that he could engage the first Stuka again, Hugo closed in rapidly and fired two short sharp bursts. The Junkers caught fire in the starboard wing and then fell into the sea, where it left a patch of burning oil. The third Stuka had been shot down by his flight commander.

Three days later Hugo damaged a Dornier over Haywards

Heath and then on the 20th he shot down two Me. 109's during a single patrol. His section, comprising Flight Lieutenant Gaunce, Flying Officer Grey and Hugo, had been attacked by a large number of Messerschmitts near Dover. Firing haphazardly at a number of aircraft in his initial excitement, Hugo was gradually getting nowhere, when he suddenly found himself on the tail of a 109. A long burst from a range of a hundred and fifty yards found its target and the Messerschmitt spun down, leaving a trail of grey smoke behind it. A few seconds later Hugo spotted another 109 below him. He fired into the cockpit of the Messerschmitt, which gave out a cloud of black smoke, turned on to its back and then spun away. The South African then used up the rest of his ammunition on two more 109's before breaking off the engagement.

'Dutch' – this was the nickname given to him by the pilots of the squadron because of his rather pronounced Afrikaans accent – claimed another Me. 109 five days later and on the 27th helped his commanding officer, Squadron Leader Kayll, to shoot down a rather colourful Heinkel 59 ten miles north-east of Dover. This was one of the air-sea-rescue planes which the Luftwaffe were using to spy on our convoys and special orders had been issued by the War Cabinet that all such aircraft were to be shot down.

In an engagement on the 12th August, Hugo shot down another Me. 109. He wrote in his combat report:

Dense smoke and liquid poured from the German pilot's machine. Although my engine stopped I dived after him. Fortunately my engine restarted. The Me. pilot pulled out of his dive at about 6,000 feet and then started to dive again. I was hot on his tail and at about 3,000 feet opened fire. The German pilot continued to dive and landed in the water. Within a minute the aircraft had sunk, and I saw the pilot swimming about in the middle of a big patch of air bubbles which had been caused by the sinking of his machine. I sent back a message on my R/T asking for a launch to be sent out to the German airman's rescue and gave his position. I then flew to base.

Hugo himself was shot down four days later. He was concentrating on a Heinkel 111 over Newhaven which he later claimed as probably destroyed, when his own Hurricane was hit by cannon shells from a Messerschmitt 110, and Dutch was hit by splinters in both legs. He was only slightly wounded and two days later on the 18th August he was back in action again. Kenley had been bombed by the Luftwaffe and Hugo had taken off with other Hurricanes in an attempt to intercept the raiders, when he was ambushed by a number of 109's. Hugo was wounded in the left leg, left eye, and right jaw, and his Hurricane was so badly damaged that he had to make a hurried crash-landing. He was rushed away to Orpington Hospital and he was still in hospital at the end of the month when the news came through that he had been awarded the Distinguished Flying Cross.

When he reported fit again toward the end of September he rejoined 615 Squadron, who had in the meantime moved to Prestwick in Scotland. He saw very little action here and, in fact, it was to be almost a year before he met up with the Luftwaffe again, although during the spring and summer of 1941 the squadron did move south for convoy patrolling, first to Northolt and later to Kenley. In the late summer of 1941 the squadron's Hurricanes were fitted with four cannon guns, and from the middle of September to the end of November were engaged on raids on enemy shipping, and coastal installations in Northern France. Dutch Hugo, by this time a flight commander, led many of these strafing attacks and, between September 18th and November 27th, helped to sink over twenty enemy ships, ranging in size from a 500-ton cargo vessel to the tiny E-boats and R-boats of the German Navy. During the same period he also helped to damage a further ten ships and to set on fire at least three oil tanks, four distilleries, and a locomotive. On a raid against the Ostend seaplane base on the 14th October, Hugo shared with his Commanding Officer, Squadron Leader Denys Gillam, in the destruction of a Heinkel 59 seaplane and, on the 27th of the same month on a similar mission to the same target, he helped Flying Officer Strickland and Flying Officer Slade to destroy another Heinkel 59. For his part in these many and diverse activities of the squadron during this period Flight Lieutenant Hugo was awarded a Bar to his D.F.C. on the 5th November. The official citation to the award paid tribute to his 'great skill and determination', his 'high qualities of leadership and courage', and ended with the thought that 'his enthusiasm remains unabated'.

Promotion quickly followed, when he was given command of Number 41 Spitfire Squadron towards the end of November, 1941. His first victories with this squadron were scored on the 12th February, 1942, over the German battleships *Scharnhorst* and *Gneisenau* as they made their escape from Brest Harbour. The squadron sighted and attacked twenty Me. 109's in the early afternoon and in the ensuing battle Squadron Leader Hugo shot down one Messerschmitt and then knocked pieces out of a second. During March Dutch added two more 109's to his bag, one of which he shot down on the 14th over a German convoy near Fécamp. The other he destroyed on the 26th whilst the squadron was escorting twenty-four Bostons in a raid on Le Havre.

On the 12th April, Hugo took over command of the Tangmere Fighter Wing when Wing-Commander Michael Robinson, D.S.O., D.F.C., was shot down and killed, but he only had time to lead them on a few missions before he was again shot down and wounded. It happened on the 27th April during a running engagement between Dunkirk and Cap Gris Nez. In a fierce battle Hugo had already probably destroyed an F.W. 190 and damaged a second, when his own aircraft was hit and he himself wounded in the left shoulder. He baled out and landed in the Channel, but he was not in the water very long before he was picked up by a rescue launch.

Posted to the Headquarters of Number Eleven Group in order to rest and recuperate, the only thing of any importance that happened to Hugo during the next few months was the award of the Distinguished Service Order, which was announced in the *London Gazette* on the 29th May, 1942. The citation stated that Hugo had 'completed over 500 hours operational flying', had 'performed outstanding work in attacks on enemy shipping', credited him with the destruction of thirteen hostile aircraft (some of these being shared with other pilots) and ended with the following tribute to Hugo – 'Both as Squadron Commander and Wing Leader this officer had displayed exceptional skill, sound judgement and fighting qualities which have won the entire confidence of all pilots in his command.'

When Paddy Finucane was shot down in July, 1942, Dutch Hugo succeeded him as wing leader of the Hornchurch Spitfire Wing, but Hugo only remained with the wing for about six weeks before he was sent to North Africa where he joined Number Three-two-two Spitfire Wing. Here in a period of hectic scrapping over and around the North African coastline, Hugo added nine confirmed destroyed, two probables and five damaged to his list of kills in just over a month.

The first of these victories took place on the 12th November, when Hugo and Flight Lieutenant Eckford shot down a Dornier 217 near Djidjelli. The following day Hugo probably destroyed a Junkers 88 and damaged another near Bougie Harbour, and on the 15th was credited with a Heinkel 111 probable and a Junkers 88 damaged over Bone Harbour. The next day he was in two fights, during which he destroyed a Junkers 88 and damaged two Me. 109's. Another 88 fell before his guns on the 18th, followed by three Me. 109's which he shot down on the 21st, 26th and 28th November. On the 2nd December Hugo shot down two Italian Breda 88's near La Galite, one of them with the help of several Spitfires from Number 81 Squadron. His last victim of this exciting interlude was another Italian bomber, a Savoia 79 which he shot down on the 14th December, while patrolling over the cruiser *Ajax*.

Hugo took over command of Number Three-two-two Wing on the 29th November, 1942, when Group Captain Charles Appleton, D.S.O., D.F.C., was seriously wounded, losing his leg during a dusk bombing attack on Bone airfield, and Hugo continued to lead this wing until March, 1943, when he was posted to the Headquarters of the North West African Coastal Air Force. At the same time he was awarded a second Bar to his D.F.C.

In June, 1943, Hugo again took command of Number Three-two-two Wing and during the next eighteen months took it to Malta, Sicily, Italy, Syria, Corsica, Southern France and then back to Italy where it was disbanded in November, 1944. He shot down an Me. 109 on the 29th June, 1943, near Comiso, in Sicily, an F.W. 190 which crashed east of Mount Etna on the 2nd September, and obtained his last confirmed kill on the 18th November, 1943, whilst patrolling along the coast of Yugoslavia; he sighted, attacked and shot down in flames an Arado 196 floatplane.

In the summer of 1944 he led his Spitfires on a series of strafing raids against enemy transport and supply columns, during which over a thousand vehicles were put out of action. Hugo's personal share of this almost fantastic total was at least fifty-five vehicles destroyed and a further twenty-nine damaged, all of which he accounted for in less than six weeks between the 6th May and the 20th June, 1944.

On the 10th July, Hugo damaged a Messerschmitt 109 in an airfight over Alessandria in Northern Italy. This turned out to be his last victory in aerial combat and brought his final tally to twenty-two enemy aircraft destroyed, four probably destroyed, and thirteen damaged. Dutch continued to fly on operations, however, until November, 1944, when he was posted to the air staff of the Headquarters of the Mediterranean Allied Air Force, and seconded to Marshal Tolbukin's Second Ukrainian Army then moving from Rumania to Austria. Subsequently he returned to England to be sent to the Central Fighter Establishment, where he remained until the war ended. He retired from the

Royal Air Force in February, 1950, and settled down in East Africa with his wife and children.

21

ACE OF ACES

Air Commodore J. E. Johnson
C.B.E., D.S.O. and Two Bars, D.F.C. and Bar, D.F.C. (U.S.A.),
Legion of Merit, Air Medal, Order of Leopold, *Croix de Guerre Belge*

JAMES EDGAR JOHNSON was just another typical Royal Air Force fighter pilot, modest and unassuming on the ground, and cool and calculating in the air, until the summer of 1943 when, after a hectic six months of aerial combats over Northern France, he emerged as one of Fighter Command's top-scoring pilots. His name first hit the headlines when it was learned that this young, dark-haired Leicestershire lad had shot out of the sky nineteen of Germany's latest fighter planes in less than six months, and this at a time when the Luftwaffe thought twice before coming out to fight. To prove this was not just a flash in the pan, Johnson continued 'Knocking 'em down' and eventually became the top-scoring fighter pilot of the Royal Air Force. His final tally was thirty-eight enemy aircraft destroyed, all of them fighters, the hardest prey of all.

Johnson, who was born in Loughborough, Leicestershire, in 1915, was educated at Loughborough School and later went to the University College at Nottingham. He became a member of the Royal Air Force Volunteer Reserve, and consequently when war was declared on September 3rd, 1939, he was called up to train as a pilot. He was as keen as mustard from the very first moment he entered an aeroplane and he did his utmost to become a good pilot. He must have been pretty good, too, for in August, 1940, he was commissioned as an Acting Pilot Officer and posted to Number 616 Spitfire Squadron. He flew his first operational sorties as one of the famous 'Few' who won the Battle of Britain, but due to an old rugger injury, he had to undergo an operation which kept him out of action for several months.

He rejoined 616 Squadron in 1941 and one day in May, 1941, was flying with the Spitfire Wing commanded by the 'Legless Wonder', Wing Commander D. R. S. Bader, D.S.O., D.F.C., when the Spitfires were attacked by a large number of Me. 109's. 'Johnny' found himself in a perfect position behind one Messerschmitt and opened fire with his eight machine guns. The effect was instantaneous for the 109 exploded and fell near Gravelines in pieces.

Bader had such a high opinion of Johnson as a fighter pilot that very soon he made Johnny his Number Two, the pilot entrusted with the job of guarding the tail of the wing commander's Spitfire during missions. Conseqently he had very few opportunities of adding to his own score, but this was offset by the fact that his job as Bader's Number Two gave him an excellent opportunity of studying the legless pilot's tactics in combat and he learned a great deal about air fighting from his famous Commanding Officer. On the 9th August, 1941, however, Bader was shot down when his Spitfires were ambushed by a large number of 109's during a sweep. Johnny was quick to avenge his leader, for even before Bader had landed by parachute, the Leicestershire pilot had shot down one Messerschmitt, and a few minutes later was helping to put the finishing touches to another 109.

Johnson shot down another 109 a few weeks later and early in September, 1941, was awarded the Distinguished Flying Cross for 'completing successfully over fifty sweeps over enemy occupied territory'. About the same time he was promoted to flight commander, continuing to fly on sweeps with Number 616 Squadron. He remained with this squadron until July, 1942, when he took command of 610 Squadron. He led this squadron during the Dieppe raid on the 19th August, 1942, when in addition to shooting down a Focke-Wulf 190 he also shared in the destruction of two more. This brought his score to six confirmed victories and led to the award of a Bar to his D.F.C. in September, 1942.

Johnson remained with 610 Squadron until March, 1943, when he was promoted to Wing Leader of the Kenley Wing of Spitfires, which afterwards became known as One-two-seven Wing, whose main task during the spring and summer of 1943 was the escorting of American bombers on daylight raids on targets in France and the Low Countries. The wing in general, and Johnson in particular, met with tremendous success. The Canadians shot down more German aircraft than any other wing in Fighter Command and Johnson increased his personal score from six to twenty-five.

On the 3rd April, Johnson led his wing for the first time on a fighter sweep over the St Omer region. They met a score or so of F.W. 190's which were flying in fours, line abreast and at slightly staggered heights. The Canadians tore into the pack of German fighters, Johnny selecting an F.W. 190 which was lagging behind the main German bunch. He closed in at over four hundred miles an hour and opened fire at a hundred and fifty yards' range. One burst was sufficient to make the enemy pilot bale out, as his plane went down to crash near St Omer.

Two days later the Canadians were escorting a formation of American Fortresses during a raid on Antwerp when they saw thirty F.W. 190's circling above them and preparing to make an attack out of the sun. Immediately Johnson led one of the squadrons to engage the enemy and in the ensuing dog-fight, hit and damaged three of the German fighters.

It became relatively quiet for some time after this and Johnny and his wing escorted many bombers on raids without meeting any opposition. About the middle of May, however, the Huns again came out of their lairs and did their best to shoot down the American bombers which were blasting German targets to smithereens. This was the chance that Johnny had been waiting for and within four days he had added three more victories to his bag. On the 11th May he destroyed a 190 near Gravelines. Two days later Johnny and two Canadians, Flying Officer R. D. Bowen and Pilot Officer H. J. Dowding, intercepted two F.W.'s whilst returning from an escort mission to Meaulte and within a few minutes the three Spitfires had sent one of the 190's crashing down into the Channel. The next day, during a running engagement from Dunkirk to Coutrai, Johnson shot down another 190, when forty F.W.'s and Me.'s attacked the Canadians.

Johnny's next success was on June 1st when he led his Spitfires on an escort mission to the Doullens–St Pol area. They were returning to base after the attack when they were engaged by a number of 109's; Johnny attacked one of them and saw his cannon shells striking the tailpiece and fuselage of the Hun as it tried to shake off the Spitfire by means of sharp turns at high speed. Suddenly the 109 straightened out and put down its flaps; Johnny found himself overshooting the Hun and had to break away quickly. As he did so Flying Officer Bowen attacked the Hun and with one short burst sent it down to dive vertically into the north bank of the River Somme.

Johnson was leading two Canadian squadrons on a sweep a fortnight later, on the 15th, when they spotted fifteen F.W. 190's in line abreast at 24,000 feet over Rouen. The Canadians were well above the Huns and in an ideal position to attack so, ordering one squadron to act as top cover, Johnny led the other squadron in a diving attack on the unsuspecting Germans. Selecting his target Johnny opened fire as he closed in and hit one of the 190's at ten o'clock high, that is above him and to his left. Shouting to both of his squadrons to attack the higher bunch, he opened his throttle and headed straight into the 190's. All was confusion as the Huns scattered all over the place and before they had time to recover, Johnny had picked out a victim and poured a burst of cannon shells into it. As the Hun exploded and fell to earth in pieces, the rest of the German formation broke away.

Two days later, on the 17th June, Johnny chalked up his fourteenth victory. As usual he was out with his R.C.A.F. wing when they sighted about thirty aircraft west of Ypres. Johnny led his Spitfires in a wide arc to come up behind the enemy formation and then, leaving two squadrons to act as cover, led the third squadron down to attack four 190's who were flying in line abreast a few hundred yards to the rear of the main formation. He selected one of the F.W.'s and opened fire as he closed in, hitting the Hun in the cockpit and wing root. He found he was overshooting, so giving the 190 a final burst, he pulled up to 16,000 feet, levelled off and looked to see what had happened to the Hun. His bullets must have found a vital spot for the 190 was burning furiously and spiralling down to the ground.

Exactly one week later during an afternoon raid on a power-station at Yainville, between Rouen and Le Havre, about forty 109's came up to engage the Canadians and then shoved off. Johnson led his squadrons up sun to attack two F.W.'s and with Squadron Leader 'Buck' McNair dived on them. The Huns never saw them. Johnny saw cannon strikes on one and a large piece fell away from its tail. It spun away and crashed near Valmont. McNair got the other a few seconds later.

On the 27th Johnny got his sixteenth when during a morning sweep he destroyed one of six F.W.'s that he overtook as they turned away over the Channel. An afternoon sortie on the 15th July provided him with his next kill. He sighted eight 109's south of Abbeville, but all but two of them disappeared as the Canadians got up sun. He took down a section to attack these two and destroyed one of them, while Pilot Officer MacDonald disposed of the other.

The Canadians were detailed to escort a force of Bostons during a late evening attack on the German aerodrome at Schipol on the 19th July. Over the target they were met by a number of enemy fighters, who seemed quite determined to prevent the Bostons from bombing their objective. The Canadians were equally determined, however, and waded into the attack with guns blazing. A furious dog-fight followed before the Huns finally gave up the fight and scampered away. Johnson attacked a group of three 109's which had Italian markings on their fuselage and after much chasing about sent one of them down in flames.

Six days later during a similar mission to Schipol, Johnny added another 109 to his score. On the morning of the 30th the Canadians were again escorting American bombers to Schipol. On completing the attack Johnny noticed two Huns about 6,000 feet below, and about seven miles behind, his wing. Believing there might be others around, he took one of his squadrons down and found at least another six. He and Flight Sergeant G. M. Shouldice attacked one of the original pair of 109's causing it to go into a dive. Johnson followed, fired another burst of cannon shells, and as the 109 pulled out of its dive, saw its undercarriage fall down. The Canadian Sergeant continued to attack and finally the German pilot baled out.

A raid on Rotterdam on the 12th August produced a running engagement near Ghent, during the course of which Johnson and Warrant Officer Conrad shared in the destruction of one Me. 109 and the damaging of another. Five days later, during an escort mission to Schweinfurt, Johnson, Flight Lieutenant D. H. Drover, Pilot Officer J. Preston, and Flight Sergeant L. F. Foster shared in the destruction of an Me. 110. On the 23rd, during a sweep over the Béthune area, the Canadians engaged twelve 109's and in the ensuing fight Johnson destroyed one of them to put his score up to twenty-three. Three days later he got his twenty-fourth, an F.W. 190 which crashed near Caen, after the Canadians were engaged by fifteen 190's and 109's during an evening sweep to Tricqueville, Rouen and Caen. He led the 'Wolf' and 'Red Indian' squadrons as escort to Marauders in a large-scale attack on the railway yards at Lille on the 4th September. Over the target area, he led one of the squadrons to intercept nine F.W. 190's. He quickly destroyed one of them for his twenty-fifth victory. Five days later he completed the last sortie of his first tour of operations. Since March, 1943, when he first took over the Canadian wing he had shot down nineteen Huns whilst his wing had accounted for about sixty more. He had now completed well over two hundred sorties, during which his Spitfire had never been hit by either enemy fighters or anti-aircraft fire, a record of which any pilot would be proud.

After a six months' rest period at Fighter Command Headquarters Johnny began his second and final tour of operations in March, 1944, when he was given command of Number One-four-four (R.C.A.F.) Wing. He had such a feeling of respect and admiration for these Canadians that, as a token of his appreciation at being given the honour of leading them, he wore a flash on his shoulder with the word *Canada* written on it. A few days later, on the 28th March, Johnny celebrated his return to action by helping Flying Officer P. A. McLachlan to destroy a Junkers 88 on the ground at an airfield at Dreux in Northern France.

Two Canadian squadrons led by Johnson took off at 0730 hours on the 25th April on a diversionary sweep for Liberators and Fortresses on their way to France and Germany. As the wing swept along near Laon six F.W. 190's were sighted flying north-east at the same level. Johnny led his squadrons in pursuit, climbing and working into position for a surprise attack. After a chase of about twenty miles the Spitfires caught the enemy fighters. Johnny shot down two, his twenty-sixth and seventh, while the rest of the wing disposed of the other four 190's.

On the 5th May, Johnny's Canadians made an early morning sweep to Lille to clear the sky for the bombers following. He saw an F.W. 190 a mile below and sent it crashing into a field near Douai. This was Johnson's twenty-eighth Hun and made him the top-scoring ace still serving on operations with Fighter Command, one ahead of Wing Commander Johnny Braham, the night-fighter intruder ace who had shot down his twenty-seventh a few weeks before. Johnson's ambition now was to beat the thirty-two victories of the record holders, 'Sailor' Malan and Paddy Finucane, who had reigned supreme for over two years.

On the 15th June, Johnson's wing moved to an airstrip on Normandy and on the following day during an air battle over this airstrip Johnny shot down an F.W. 190. Six days later Johnson was leading seven Spitfires of the 'Caribou' Squadron when they became involved with a mixed formation of 109's and 190's low down just west of Argentan. The Canadians shot down four of the Huns, Johnny accounting for one of them, an F.W. 190, to bring his total a little nearer to the record. In the next fight, on the 28th, Johnson led one squadron to intercept seven Me. 109 fighter-bombers near Villers-Bocage. They chased the Huns eastwards, destroying four, probably destroying another, and damaging the other two. Johnny personally destroyed two of the 109's to put his score up to thirty-two and thus equal to the record of Malan and Finucane. Two days later Johnny led his Canadians into a fight with twelve 109's, and shot down one of the three 109's destroyed in this fight. Thus he became Fighter Command's Ace of Aces.

Johnny, however, had quite a bit of flying to do yet before his final tour of operations was ended and he was determined to set up an all-time record for Fighter Command. Consequently he went on fighting relentlessly, and added to his victories whenever the chance arose.

He led an evening sweep on July 5th, and when a dozen 109's were sighted near Alençon, took one squadron down to intercept. In a few minutes the Canadians had destroyed seven and damaged four more. Johnny got the first as it was putting a burst into the wing of a Spitfire and then shot down a second to raise his score to thirty-five.

Since taking command of Number One-four-four Wing in March 1944, Johnson had shot down ten Huns, whilst his wing as a whole had claimed seventy-three destroyed. Now, however, in the middle of July the wing was reorganised and Johnny became Wing Commander (Flying) of the old Kenley Wing. He seemed to put new life into this wing, for on the 23rd August they scored the outstanding air victory of the month.

Early in the afternoon, Johnny led two squadrons of his new wing on a sweep round Fontainbleau and Beauvais and flew into a large formation of F.W. 190's, with Me. 109's as top cover, near Senlis. Although considerably outnumbered the wing got twelve destroyed and three damaged for the loss of three pilots. Johnny fought superbly and destroyed two 109's.

The war in the air had been practically won by this time and very rarely did the Luftwaffe come out to challenge the R.A.F.'s supremacy. When they did Johnny and his Canadians were waiting for them.

In his last air battle on the 27th September, Johnny led the 'Hornet' Squadron on a midday patrol over the Nijmegen-Venlo area. Twenty miles east of Nijmegen they sighted and attacked nine 109's. They got three destroyed and two probables for the loss of Squadron Leader Wally McLeod, D.S.O., D.F.C. and Bar, leading R.C.A.F. pilot with twenty-one victories. Johnson shot down one of the 109's and then was himself hit and had to break away. This, incidentally, was the only time that Johnny's Spitfire was ever hit during the whole of the 515 sorties that he flew on operations. The victory that he scored in this fight, his thirty-eighth, was also Johnson's last, for although he continued to fly on operations until the 5th May, 1945, he never had another chance of adding to his score. He was promoted to Group Captain on the 6th April, 1945, and took command of a fighter wing.

When the war ended in May, 1945, Johnny decided to stay in the R.A.F. and during the post-war years served with many fighter units in various places. Honours were still bestowed on this ace of aces even as late as 1947 when the Belgian Government awarded him the Order of Leopold and the *Croix de Guerre Belge*, for his gallant efforts during the war years.

In 1950 Johnson was serving with the United States Air Force in Virginia, U.S.A., when he was sent to Korea to study and report on the lessons of air fighting. The Americans had such a high opinion of his qualities as a leader that they awarded him the American Air Medal in December, 1950, and the Legion of Merit in October, 1951. On his return from Korea Johnny became Wing Commander (Flying) of Number 135 (Vampire) Wing, B.A.F.O. under Group Captain Donaldson, D.S.O., D.F.C., and then later on was again promoted to Group Captain. Today he is an Air Commodore and Senior Air Staff Officer at the Headquarters of Number Three Group, Bomber Command.

22

THE 109 SPECIALIST

Group Captain D. E. Kingaby
D.S.O., A.F.C., D.F.M. and Two Bars, D.F.C. (U.S.A.),
Croix de Guerre Belge

THE son of a Church of England vicar, Donald Ernest Kingaby was born in Holloway, London, and educated at King's School, Ely. On leaving school he started work as a clerk in an insurance office, but soon took an interest in flying; in April, 1939, he joined the Royal Air Force Volunteer Reserve. He wanted to be a fighter pilot and by the summer of 1940 he had qualified as a pilot and was posted to Number 266 Squadron, which at the time was non-operational. Sergeant Kingaby shortly afterwards was transferred to Number 92 Squadron and first went into action when the Battle of Britain was at its height and fighter pilots were flying three, four and five sorties each day.

On the 12th October, 1940, Don Kingaby shot down his first Hun, in a battle in which the squadron tackled over fifty Me. 109's high above Rochester. During the rest of the month, in the hectic fighting over the south coast, he shot down two Me. 109's, an Me. 110, and a Dornier 17. Then, as if to prove this was no fluke, on the 15th November he went out and destroyed four Me. 109's in one day, three of them during one battle in the late afternoon.

Then came Don's first narrow escape. He had just landed at Manston aerodrome after a patrol and was walking towards the dispersal hut to make out his report when a formation of Messerschmitts made a lightning swoop on the airfield. Don threw himself flat on the ground as the leading Messerschmitt came in low with guns blazing. He saw the flashes of the fighter's guns and felt the thud of the bullets as they hammered into the earth all around him. A bullet shattered one of his fingers, but he had no time to consider the wound as a second Messerschmitt opened up. He rolled over, away from the stream of deadly lead, and went on rolling until the 109's had used up all their ammunition. He reckoned he was lucky to get away with only one smashed finger after that experience. As a matter of fact this was the only wound that he ever received throughout the war, although he was to have many more narrow escapes.

In November, 1940, Sergeant Kingaby was awarded the D.F.M. for 'displaying great courage and tenacity in his attacks against the enemy', and shortly afterwards the newspapers christened him 'The 109 Specialist' because most of his confirmed victories so far had been against this particular type of enemy aircraft. He shot down his eighth 109 during the afternoon of the 1st December.

When the R.A.F. went over to the offensive in 1941, Number 92 Squadron was detailed to fly on escort missions and sweeps to Northern France, but rarely met any German planes until the summer, although Kingaby added another 109 to his bag on the 14th February, when he chased it all the way across the Channel before sending it down to crash near Cap Gris Nez. On the 16th May he destroyed another 109 and damaged a second; his next victim on the 23rd June was also a 109, which spun into the ground during an escort mission to Béthune. Two further escort missions on the 2nd and 3rd July provided him with the opportunity to add three more Me. 109's to his score, although one of them he only claimed as a probable. These successes led to the award of a Bar to his D.F.M. The citation to the award said that 'he had continued to prove himself a very able section leader who fought with coolness and courage'.

'A blessing in disguise' was how Don described the combat on the 2nd July, when he destroyed two 109's. The squadron was returning from a sweep to Lille in the early afternoon when two aircraft which Kingaby thought were Hurricanes dived down in front of his section. Then he realised they were 109's, but by that time it was too late to do anything about it.

'The next moment two more 109's came diving down,' Kingaby said later, 'and obviously the first two had been bait for us while the second pair were supposed to shoot us up.'

Kingaby whipped behind this pair and fired a long burst into each before breaking off because he suspected there might be more 109's on the way down. As he climbed he saw two more Messerschmitts diving and then a more pleasant sight, first a parachute and then two large splashes in the water made by the 109's he had attacked so successfully.

Kingaby played a cat and mouse game with the Messerschmitts on the 9th August when the squadron attacked a bunch of 109's during a fighter sweep to the Boulogne area. He saw four 109's turning in behind him, so he climbed into the sun, lost his pursuers and then came down behind another pair of 109's near Le Touquet. He stalked this pair until he was in a position to attack the lefthand aircraft. He fired a two second burst from a hundred and fifty yards behind the Messerschmitt, which wobbled violently, turned over and went down with glycol and black smoke pouring out. Kingaby then climbed and beneath the clouds found the other Messerschmitt going round in steep turns evidently searching for the Spitfire which had shot down its companion. Kingaby nipped into the clouds for a few seconds and then came out behind the 109. For half a minute or so Kingaby chased the 109 round in circles until he eventually got in a burst of cannon fire which sent the 109 down to crash about five miles south of Le Touquet.

During September the Luftwaffe was not anxious to 'mix it' with the Spitfires, but on the 1st October Kingaby shot the tail off a 109 over Cap Gris Nez; two days later he destroyed his eighteenth victim, but in the same fight had a narrow escape. He was over Ostend at the time on an escort mission when his radiotelephone and reflector sight became unserviceable due to an electrical failure. A few minutes later he saw twenty Me. 109's behind the squadron and about to attack. He could not warn the rest of his squadron because his radio was out of action, so he decided to turn into them. He fought with about six of the Messerschmitts before his cockpit was suddenly flooded with glycol and he thought he had been hit. He decided to make for the English coast before his engine failed and went into a dive with seven 109's following him. Eventually he managed to elude all the Messerschmitts except one, which gradually crept up on him. Kingaby realised that he would have to turn and fight. After two complete turns, Kingaby had got on the tail of the 109 and chased it down to five hundred feet with a short burst of both cannon and machine gun fire, aimed through a bead sight which Kingaby always had fitted to his aircraft. The burst caused smoke to issue from the 109, which next moment dived straight into the Channel. Kingaby flew back to England, landed at Manston, and discovered to his surprise that his Spitfire had not a single bullet hole in it. Thy glycol in the cockpit had come from the windscreen anti-freeze device, which had gone wrong due to the electrical failure.

Kingaby became the first R.A.F. pilot ever to win three D.F.M.'s when he was awarded a second Bar on the 2nd November. The official citation paid tribute to 'his great skill and courage' and 'his determination and sound judgement, combined with a high standard of operational efficiency'. On the same day he ended his first tour of operations and was posted to an Operational Training Unit at Grangemouth, where he was commissioned and then became a flying instructor.

He returned to operations in the summer of 1942 as a flight commander with Number 122 Spitfire Squadron at Hornchurch and before long had another near escape. He was on a sweep when his flight was ambushed by a number of Messerschmitts. Don broke away with several 109's on his tail, but by means of some excellent evasive action managed to work his way into some friendly clouds nearby.

During the Allied raid on Dieppe on the 19th August, 1942, Number 122 Squadron was ordered to provide air cover for the troops on the beaches, and in the violent air battles that took place over and around Dieppe throughout the day, reminding Kingaby of the fierce fighting in the Battle of Britain, he shot down his nineteenth Hun. This time, however, it was a Dornier 217 dive-bomber and his last victory for some considerable time, for although he was promoted to Squadron Leader and continued to lead the Bombay Squadron on fighter sweeps and escort missions, he did not obtain his next success until January, 1943, when in two days he destroyed an Me. 109F and an F.W. 190 and also damaged another F.W. 190.

'Squadron Leader Kingaby has taken part in more than 300 operational sorties and has personally destroyed twenty-one enemy aircraft,' said the citation a short time afterwards when Kingaby was awarded the D.S.O. Almost before he had time to put up the ribbon of his D.S.O. Kingaby had shot down another F.W. 190. He was leading Number 122 Squadron as bomber escort when a bunch of F.W. 190's and Me. 109's attacked him. He dived down at full throttle and at over 500 m.p.h. zoomed up like a rocket to come up beneath the belly of a 190 which had just made a pass at the bombers. Kingaby fired a two-second burst which caused an elevator to fly off the Focke-Wulf, and the plane to go down in a vicious spin. Kingaby watched the pilot bale out and then caught up with the bombers and accompanied them home.

In the spring of 1943 he became wing leader of the Hornchurch Spitfire Wing which he led until the end of his second operational tour in the autumn of 1943, when he was posted to Fighter Command Headquarters for a staff position. During the invasion of France in June, 1944, he managed to obtain permission to fly on several sorties and during one of these he shared in the destruction of an F.W. 190 over the Normandy beachhead. This was his last confirmed victory, and gave him a final score of twenty-two and a half enemy aircraft destroyed, eight probably destroyed and sixteen damaged, obtained in just over 450 operational sorties.

He was sent to the Advanced Gunnery School at Catfoss in July, 1944, and was awarded the American D.F.C. and the *Croix de Guerre Belge* in the following October. When the war ended Kingaby was given a permanent commission in the R.A.F. and became Commanding Officer of Number 72 Squadron. In June 1952, he was awarded the Air Force Cross and shortly afterwards took up a post at the Air Ministry in Whitehall.

23

OLD KUT

Flight Lieutenant K. Kuttelwascher
D.F.C. and Bar, Czech War Cross

ONE of the pioneers of night fighter intruder operations in the Royal Air Force was a Czech pilot called Karel Kuttelwascher, though he was better known by his nickname of 'Old Kut'. Born in Nemrecky, Czechoslovakia, in 1916, Kuttelwascher had been interested in flying from an early age and although he became a clerk when he left school, his heart was set on an aeronautical career. As soon as he was old enough he enlisted in the Czech Air Force.

Kuttelwascher took part in the resistance when the Nazis invaded Czechoslovakia and when his country capitulated he escaped to join the French Foreign Legion. Subsequently he transferred to the French Air Force, and for a short time after the outbreak of war he served with a French fighter squadron. However, he saw little action in France before he was on the run again, this time to England, where he was accepted as a Sergeant Pilot in the Royal Air Force in July, 1940. He was sent to an Operational Training Unit for a course on Hurricanes and Spitfires and then posted to Number 1 Squadron, which was resting and reorganising at Wittering. For several months he had to be content with practising formation flying, dogfighting with his colleagues in the squadron, firing at targets on the ground and in the air, and many other forms of air combat training.

He made his début on operations early in 1941 flying convoy patrols over and around the East Coast and he had carried out more than a score of such missions before he claimed his first air victory on the 8th April, 1941. He took off from Croydon at 8.30 a.m. with three other Hurricanes to patrol over Dungeness, but they had not been in the air very long before they sighted three Messerschmitt 109's flying near Cap Gris Nez. A dogfight followed and Kuttelwascher soon found himself chasing an all-black 109 which in turn was chasing another of the Hurricanes. The final outcome was that Sergeant Kuttelwascher got in a burst of cannon shells from thirty yards' range which sent the Messerschmitt crashing into a small wood some fifteen miles south of Gris Nez.

During the summer of 1941, Kuttelwascher flew on many escort missions and fighter sweeps to Northern France and shot down another two Me. 109's, before Number 1 Squadron was moved to Tangmere on the 2nd July to begin a period of intensive training for night flying operations. They were equipped with a new version of the Hurricane fitted with four cannon guns, in which they practised interception flights, co-operating first with ground searchlights and later with searchlights carried by the American 'Turbinlite' Havoc night fighter aircraft. By 1st November, 1941, they were fully operational as a night fighter squadron, but it was to be some considerable time before they scored their first night victories. In fact, many of the squadron's pilots, bored by the inactivity in the night sky, took their Hurricanes out in daylight to make attacks on enemy shipping in the English Channel. During one of these attacks on the 28th December, Kuttelwascher strafed and damaged two ships in Ostend Harbour. He also claimed hits on a destroyer on the 12th February, 1942, when the whole of the squadron was scrambled to attack the German warships *Scharnhorst*, *Gneisenau* and *Prinz Eugen*, who were making their way throught the Channel.

Soon after this Number 1 Squadron pilots became the R.A.F.'s first intruders, searching out enemy aircraft at night over their own aerodromes, a particularly dangerous and lonely operation since they flew only single-engined Hurricanes. If that engine failed, the best the pilot could hope for was a prisoner-of-war camp. Kuttelwascher seemed particularly suited to this type of mission and on the 1st April, 1942, he scored the squadron's first intruder victories.

He took off from Tangmere at 10.20 p.m., crossed the French coast west of Le Havre and then headed towards Evreux airfield. He circled the German aerodrome for several minutes, but could find no trace of any enemy planes, so he flew to Melun aerodrome which was illuminated. Soon after his arrival over the runway a red rocket was fired and he saw a Junkers 88 take off. He watched it climb to 1,500 feet and then closed in and gave it two short bursts of cannon shells from astern. He saw his tracers hitting the starboard engine of the 88 which then went into a dive and crashed. Meanwhile Kuttelwascher had flown back over the runway where he noticed another aircraft taking off. Again he closed, identified it as another Junkers 88, and then fired five or six bursts into it. By this time, however, the Huns had realised there was a British night fighter about and searchlights and anti-aircraft fire began to light up the sky. Kuttelwascher thought it was about time he departed so he set course for Tangmere and landed there safely at 1.25 a.m., to make out a claim for one Junkers 88 destroyed and one damaged.

Kuttelwascher flew an intruder patrol to another German airfield at St. André on the 16th April where he found two Dornier 217's with their navigation lights on. One of them switched off almost immediately and Kuttelwascher lost sight of it. He followed the other, however, fired four short bursts and saw the Dornier smack into the ground with a bright orange flash.

Victories came regularly after this, but not without some unnerving moments. On one occasion on the 27th April, for instance, after destroying a Dornier 17 at Rouen-Boos airfield, Kuttelwascher was himself surprised and hit by cannon shells from a Junkers 88. Although his engine was damaged, he shot down the enemy plane before returning safely to Tangmere.

Three nights later Kuttelwascher shot down two Huns during a single mission. He went to Rennes airfield first where he caught a Dornier 217 just as it was taking off. He fired twice at a range of a hundred and fifty yards, but this had no apparent effect so he went in closer and fired a longer burst. The nose of the Dornier dropped and it dived down to explode on the ground. Kuttelwascher flew around the airfield for another five minutes, but saw no further activity, so he flew north to Dinard. Here he found a Heinkel 111 taking off with all its lights on. He followed it until it had reached a thousand feet and then he closed in and shot it down into the sea close to the aerodrome.

He was unable to find any German planes on the 3rd May, so he attacked a goods train at St. Lo and then scored hits on a small motor boat at Caen. The following night he found plenty of aircraft and set up a record for intruder pilots when he shot down three Heinkel 111's in four minutes. He found six of these bombers orbiting the airfield at St. André just after midnight, each of them showing a white tail light. He came in behind one of them firing a two-second burst from astern and slightly below. The Heinkel's starboard engine caught fire and it dived to the ground north-east of the aerodrome. Kuttelwascher repeated the same tactics with a second Heinkel which dived in flames into a wood east of the airfield. He fired at a third and saw it go down steeply from a height of less than 1,500 feet before he lost sight of it. Thirty seconds later, however, he was able to fly over and take a camera-gun photograph of all three Heinkels burning simultaneously round the airfield.

He found a convoy of twelve ships near Fécamp on the 1st June, at which he fired a few rounds of ammunition, and continuing his patrol disabled two goods trains between Bolbec and Le Havre, after which he successfully attacked an E-boat. Two nights later the enemy sent over a large number of bombers and Number 1 Squadron was scrambled to intercept them. Kuttelwascher flew to Deal to cut off the raiders and quickly sighted a damaged Dornier, which he sent plunging down into the sea five miles off the Belgian coast. The following night he went back to his intruding, paying a visit to St. André, where he destroyed a Heinkel 111 and a Dornier 217, and damaged another Heinkel 111.

On the 29th June he had to visit five airfields before finding a customer which he identified as a Dornier 217. It took less than a minute for the Czech to dispose of it and then, unable to find any more Huns, he turned towards England. He had only just left the French coast behind him when he saw flak coming up from E-boats, so he dived down and attacked one which began to smoke and took a heavy list to starboard. He strafed another and saw his cannon shells scoring strikes before he had to break away because he had used up all his ammunition.

Kuttelwascher flew his last intruder mission with Number 1 Squadron on the 2nd July when he destroyed two Dornier 217's and damaged a third. This brought his total to twenty-two victories, of which eighteen were confirmed as definitely destroyed and four were granted as probably destroyed. Fifteen of those confirmed destroyed enemy aircraft had been shot down during only nine intruder missions between the 1st April and the 2nd July, 1942, and earned for Kuttelwascher the award of the D.F.C. in April, 1942, and a Bar to it five weeks later.

On the 9th July, 1942, Kuttelwascher, now a Flight Lieutenant, was posted to Number 23 Squadron, another night-fighter squadron which was equipped with Mosquitos. Although he flew several missions with this unit, he seemed to strike an unlucky patch, never once being able to even sight a German aircraft. In fact on at least three occasions he had to return soon after taking off because of electrical failures in his Mosquito. When the squadron was posted overseas Kuttelwascher was taken off operations and given a staff appointment.

Later in the war he was sent on a lecture tour of the U.S.A.

Kuttelwascher left the R.A.F. in 1945 and returned to his own country, but life had changed in Czechoslovakia, and after eighteen months he returned to England to become a pilot with British European Airways. He died in 1960.

24

'GINGER' LACEY

Squadron Leader J. H. Lacey
D.F.M. and Bar

ON THE morning of the 13th September, 1940, Buckingham Palace was bombed by a Heinkel 111k which, after the attack, turned south to head back to its base in Northern France. A lone Hurricane on patrol over Maidstone was ordered to look out for it. Its pilot, a red-haired Sergeant pilot, shortly afterwards spotted a twin-engined bomber which he soon identified as a Heinkel 111. Closing in for the kill, the Sergeant lined up the raider in his sights and pressed the gun-button at the same time as the German rear-gunner opened fire. The Heinkel went down in flames to crash near the coast, but the German gunner's burst had also found a vital spot in the Hurricane and the young Sergeant had to abandon his aircraft. It was not the first time he had baled out, and it certainly was not to be the last, for altogether during his first tour of operations the Sergeant – his name was James Harry Lacey, though he was known to everybody as 'Ginger' – had to crash-land or bale out of badly damaged Hurricanes on at least nine occasions. This time he landed safely and uninjured and within a few hours was back at his base, where he was told he had destroyed the actual Heinkel which had bombed the Palace. A few months later Ginger received the personal congratulations of Queen Mary.

Born in Wetherby, Yorkshire, in February, 1917, Ginger was educated at King James' Grammar School, Knaresborough, where he was more interested in sport than in the study of academic subjects. He was also keenly interested in the internal combustion engine and, although he became a chemist's apprentice when he left school, he began a serious study of scientific subjects at Leeds Technical College. He soon became so fascinated by engines and aircraft that he decided to join the Royal Air Force and in 1937 was accepted in the Volunteer Reserve. When the war broke out Ginger was posted as a Sergeant Pilot to Number 501 (County of Gloucester) Squadron. Although he was operational from the day war started, he failed to make contact with the Luftwaffe until the following summer.

The squadron was stationed at Tangmere when it received its orders to fly to France on the 10th May, 1940. A few hours later the squadron landed at Betheniville and before the day had ended Sergeant Lacey was making his first patrol over the Maginot Line. He was flying a Hurricane in a section of three led by Flight Sergeant D. A. S. Mackay, which took off from the French aerodrome at 2015 hours for a local patrol. In his eagerness to shoot down his first Hun, Ginger became separated from his section. He flew around until he had nearly exhausted his petrol supply, but could find no signs of German aircraft, nor of his own section, so reluctantly he turned to head for Betheniville. Unfortunately Ginger lost his way and had to make a forced-landing after dark in a field when his fuel gave out. He landed safely and spent the next couple of hours in a nearby French Army Mess before returning to his squadron.

Three days later Ginger shot down three German aircraft. In a big dogfight over Sédan he set fire to a Heinkel 111 and then destroyed a Messerschmitt 109; a few hours later on another patrol he sent down a Messerschmitt 110 to crash at La Chesne, northeast of Vouziers. After this brilliant start, Ginger never looked back. Although he was almost unknown outside flying circles, he soon became one of the outstanding pilots of Fighter Command.

During their short stay in France, Number 501 Squadron had a particularly busy time, shooting down more than sixty enemy aircraft. Their best day was the 27th May, when they shot down twelve German aircraft for certain and possibly three more. Soon after taking off from Boos, near Rouen, they intercepted twenty-four Heinkel 111's escorted by two dozen Me. 110's. As soon as the Hurricanes dived into the German formation the escort of Messerschmitts disappeared and left the Heinkels to their fate. In a quarter of an hour it was all over, twelve of the Huns lying in blazing heaps on the ground, two of them accounted for by Ginger Lacey.

On the 18th June, the squadron returned to England and shortly afterwards Sergeant Lacey was awarded the Distinguished

Flying Medal for his 'great determination and coolness in combat'.

The squadron never went north of the Thames during the Battle of Britain, being based at Croydon and Gravesend, and was continually in action for several months, fighting desperately to turn back the Luftwaffe when Goering launched his all-out offensive against Britain. Almost every day, except when the weather was too bad to fly, and this was very rare, Ginger took off several times between dawn and dusk, and time after time landed to report the successful conclusion of a combat. Between the 12th August and the 30th October he destroyed no less than sixteen enemy aircraft, probably destroyed four more, and damaged a further seven. However, he was not to get off scot free, for he was himself shot down on several occasions, sometimes managing to save his damaged Hurricane by making a crash-landing, but at other times his Hurricane was so badly shot up that he had to abandon it and save himself by using his parachute.

One of Lacey's first operations against the mass attacks of the Luftwaffe in August was on the 12th, when the squadron engaged between thirty and forty Junkers 87's over the Thames Estuary. Ginger shot down one of the Stuka's for certain and probably destroyed another in the ensuing combat. He destroyed a Junkers 88 on the 24th August, and on another patrol later the same day he severely damaged a Dornier 215. Five days after this Ginger sent a 109 into the sea near Gravesend after the squadron had been bounced by nine 109's over Hawkinge. On the 30th Ginger was himself forced down with a damaged radiator, but in two more sorties on the same day, he got a Heinkel 111 confirmed and an Me. 110 probable. The next day his victim was an Me. 109.

On the 2nd September Ginger helped himself to two 109's destroyed and a Dornier 215 which he claimed as damaged, although it almost certainly never reached its base. He shot down the first Messerschmitt on the dawn patrol, and before 8 o'clock was off with the squadron for a second patrol. They soon sighted fifty Dornier 215's, escorted by about fifty 109's, high over Ashford. The squadron went for the fighters first, Ginger selecting a trio of Messerschmitts which were flying slightly above the rest. He got on the tail of a red-cowled 109 and gave it a burst of about five seconds. The enemy fighter turned sharply, closely followed by Ginger, who was about to open fire again, when the pilot of the 109 baled out. Seeing that most of the other Messerschmitts were busy scrapping with the rest of the Hurricanes, Lacey dived down to engage the Dorniers. Almost as soon as he opened fire one of

126

the Dorniers broke out of the formation with smoke pouring from one of its engines. Ginger followed, firing in short bursts until he had used up all his ammunition. The Dornier was down to 5,000 feet, flying on one engine, but still losing height slowly, when Ginger left it over the Channel.

Three days later during the afternoon Ginger got mixed up with some 109's at 15,000 feet over Maidstone and, before breaking off the engagement, shot down two of them – kills which were confirmed by other pilots in the squadron. His next decisive combat was the fight already described when he shot down the Heinkel that bombed Buckingham Palace. The 15th September is often described as the R.A.F.'s greatest day during the Battle of Britain, but it can also be called a red-letter day for Lacey, since he claimed four victories during the course of two sorties. His first fight took place over Maidstone just after 11 o'clock, when he shot down a 109 and then damaged a second. After lunch the Luftwaffe decided to make a bombing attack on the squadron's airfield at Kenley and 501 Squadron were scrambled to intercept them. They met a large force of Dornier 17's and Heinkel 111's escorted by swarms of Messerschmitts. Ginger managed to shoot down one of the Heinkels before the 109's came diving down. He turned into the fighters and had caused pieces to fly off one of the 109's before he ran out of ammunition and had to break away.

It was Lacey's turn to be shot down on the 17th September. The squadron was surprised by twenty Me. 109's whilst patrolling over Ashford in the afternoon and Ginger's Hurricane was soon going down in flames. He was uninjured, however, and once more his parachute saved his life.

On the 27th September, Ginger shot down another 109 to bring his tally to nineteen enemy aircraft destroyed and a few days later was awarded a Bar to his D.F.M. The citation referred to his 'consistent efficiency and great courage' and 'his splendid qualities as a fighter pilot'.

During the month of October, 1940, Ginger shot down three more Me. 109's had to make another crash-landing on the 4th, reported he had been shot at by another Hurricane on the 15th and shot down a drifting balloon into the sea on the 29th. But after this there was little to enthuse about, apart from being commissioned in January, until the summer of 1941. By the summer Lacey had become a flight commander in his old squadron and began to make sweeps and offensive patrols over Northern France.

In a period of a fortnight in July, Ginger shot down three Me. 109's (two of them in one dog-fight on the 24th) and an He. 59 seaplane and then was taken off operations. He was posted to Number 57 Operational Training Unit as a Gunnery Instructor and here he remained until the spring of 1942, when he began his second tour of operations as a Flight Commander with another celebrated Auxiliary Squadron, Number 602 (The City of Glasgow) Squadron. He managed to claim three F.W. 190's damaged during his few week's stay with this squadron and was then transferred to the Headquarters of Number Eighty-one Group. In 1943 he became the Gunnery Leader of an Air Fighting School in India and did no more operational flying until the end of 1944, when he was given command of Number 17 Squadron in Burma.

He shot down his last victim, an Oscar II, on the 19th February, 1945, to bring his final bag to twenty-eight aircraft destroyed four probably destroyed, and another eleven damaged. Ginger remained on operations with his Squadron in Burma until the war ended and so can claim to be one of the relatively few R.A.F. pilots who was operational both on the day war broke out and on the day it ended.

25

'SAWN-OFF LOCKIE'

Flight Lieutenant E. S. Lock
D.S.O., D.F.C. and Bar

ERIC STANLEY LOCKE was born in Bayston Hill, Shrewsbury, Shropshire, in 1920 and as soon as he was old enough was sent to Prestfelde School. It was while he was still at school that he had his first taste of flying, when he went on a five-shilling trip with Sir Alan Cobham's air circus. Unlike most boys, he was not impressed by this first flight, and by the time he left school, he had forgotten all about it. He went into his father's farming and quarrying business and thought no more about flying until early in 1939, when he had already concluded that there was going to be a war and had decided that, if there was to be a war, he would be a fighter pilot. Consequently he joined the Royal Air Force Volunteer Reserve and within three months had been called up and sent to a flying training school. By the end of May, 1940, he had completed his training, qualified as a fighter pilot, and been posted to Number 41 Spitfire Squadron at Catterick as an Acting Pilot Officer.

'Lockie' took a couple of weeks' leave in July, 1940, to get married to Peggy Meyers, a former 'Miss Shrewsbury', and then returned to his squadron to take part in defensive patrols over the North of England. At first these patrols were rather boring to Lockie since the enemy only sent over lone raiders and Lockie never seemed able to catch one of them. At last, however, on the 15th August, Lockie met his first Hun in combat. He reported:

> I was flying in formation with 41 Squadron when we were ordered to patrol north of base [Catterick] at 20,000 feet. After flying for a while we saw a formation of Junkers 88 and Messerschmitt 110. The squadron then went into line astern and we made an attack. During our second attack, I fired two short bursts into the starboard engine of a Messerschmitt 110. I followed it down to 10,000 feet, firing at the fuselage. The machine-gunner stopped firing. Continuing my dive I fired at the port engine, which caught fire. I left it at 5,000 feet still in a vertical dive, with both engines on fire.

Lockie was only going to claim a probable, but another pilot of 41 Squadron had seen the Messerschmitt dive into Seaham Harbour and so was able to confirm Lockie's first victory.

On the 3rd September, Number 41 Squadron moved south to Hornchurch and at last, with the Battle of Britain in full swing, saw plenty of action over Southern England. Two days after arriving in the main battle zone, Eric Lock scored his first victories in the Battle of Britain. He was flying Number Two in Red Section of 41 Squadron when they intercepted a formation of enemy aircraft over the Isle of Sheppey. The Commanding Officer of 41 Squadron ordered his pilots to attack the bombers first, and down they went in a screaming dive, guns blazing, right into the middle of the bombers.

Lockie and his Flight Commander broke away to port, where they found a Messerschmitt 109, which the Flight Commander attacked and caused to blow up. A dog-fight developed and Lockie engaged a Heinkel 111, which attempted to get away by diving. Lockie followed, closed in, opened fire and the Heinkel crashed into a river. Lockie then climbed back to 8,000 feet and saw another Heinkel 111 which had left the main formation. He closed in from the starboard quarter, pressed the firing button, and immediately set the enemy's starboard engine on fire. He closed in to about seventy-five yards and fired two more long bursts. Smoke poured out behind the Heinkel, its undercarriage dropped down and it began a shallow glide. Lockie stopped firing and followed it down.

It was a bad mistake, for immediately a Messerschmitt 109 dived on the tail of Lockie's Spitfire and opened fire, wounding Lockie in the leg. Lockie pulled the stick back hard into his stomach and zoomed up in a climbing turn. The Hun tried to follow, but stalled and fell away. Now it was Lockie's turn. He closed in, waited for the 109 to come out of its dive, and then gave it several short bursts. It exploded in mid-air, with a blinding flash. Lockie looked round for the bomber he had been following, and saw it land on the sea, about ten miles from the first one in the mouth of the river. Eric circled round and round a boat which he spotted nearby and led it back to the enemy bomber. The last thing he saw before turning towards base was the German bomber crew being taken prisoner by the occupants of the British boat. On his way back, Lockie saw his first Heinkel still floating in the mouth of the river with a small rubber dinghy near it. There was no doubt at all about all his three victories on this day being confirmed.

Pilot Officer Lock's injuries could not have been very serious, for he was in action again early the following morning shooting down a Junkers 88 into the Channel at 0900 hours. Three days later he destroyed two Messerschmitt 109's over Kent and on the 11th shot down a Junkers 88 and a Messerschmitt 110. This brought his total bag to nine Huns, eight of which he had destroyed within a period of a week, and led to the award of the Distinguished Flying Cross. The official citation to the award concluded: 'He has displayed great vigour and determination in pressing home his attacks'.

On the 14th September, Lockie added two more Messerschmitt 109's to his score, and on the following day, the R.A.F.'s greatest day in the Battle of Britain, he shot down a Messerschmitt 109 and a Dornier 217, both of which crashed south-east of Clacton. Two days' rest followed and then, on the 18th September, he got one Messerschmitt 109 probably destroyed on his first patrol and later in the day on a second sortie destroyed one Messerschmitt 109 over Gravesend and probably destroyed a second.

The next day was blank, but on the 20th he was patrolling over the Dover area when he encountered three Heinkel 113's. These were the Luftwaffe's newest fighters, but they held no terror for Lockie. In a few minutes he had shot one of them into the sea near Dover and sent the other two scampering away towards France at full speed. Continuing his patrol he found a Henschel 126, which he chased as far as the French coast before sending it down to crash near Boulogne. When he finally returned to Hornchurch, his Commanding Officer greeted him with the news that he had been awarded a Bar to his D.F.C. for destroying fifteen Huns within a period of sixteen days. During the same period he had been slightly wounded once and forced to bale out on three occasions. The official citation referred to Lockie's 'great courage in the face of heavy odds' and his 'skill and coolness in combat'.

A few days later, Number 41 Squadron was withdrawn from the line for a brief rest to re-form and bring the pilots and aircraft to full strength after their inevitable losses in the last few weeks. They returned to Hornchurch early in October and immediately Lockie continued his run of successes. On the 5th he got one Messerschmitt 109 confirmed and two more probables over Kent; on the 9th he destroyed another 109 ten miles from Dover, and seconds later probably destroyed another. He shot down another Messerschmitt 109 into the sea off Dungeness on the 11th and destroyed yet another 109 over Biggin Hill aerodrome on the 20th October, to bring his total bag to twenty confirmed victories.

A quiet spell followed and, apart from probably destroying a Messerschmitt 109 south-east of Dover on the 25th October, Lockie had no further successes until 17th November. On this day he was patrolling with Number 41 Squadron over the Thames Estuary, at 20,000 feet, when he saw about seventy Messerschmitt 109's about 2,000 feet below. He warned his Commanding Officer who immediately took 41 Squadron down to attack. Pilot Officer Lock picked out a 109, which went down in flames after his first burst of fire. He selected another 109 and, attacking it from behind, set it on fire. As he watched the Messerschmitt go down to crash in the sea, Lockie was jumped on by another 109 and bullets and cannonshells smashed into his cockpit. He was badly wounded in his right arm, and both legs. His throttle lever was forced fully open by a bullet and then knocked off, but this undoubtedly saved Lockie's life for his Spitfire leapt forward at full bore and tore out of the dog-fight at well over 400 m.p.h., leaving the Messerschmitt far behind and out of range.

Lockie's troubles were only just beginning, however. There he was at 20,000 feet, at full speed, his left arm the only limb in action, and with his throttle lever shot off, and had no means of slowing down his engine. He daren't bale out because of his wounded legs, so he had to go on roaring down at 400 m.p.h. At 2,000 feet, he managed to switch off his engine and then pulled back on the control column to level out his Spitfire. Putting down his wheels, Lockie flew on until he came to a large piece of ground, where he made a crash landing on what turned out to be Martlesham Heath.

For two hours he sat in his cockpit unable to move and bleeding from his wounds before help finally arrived in the form of a couple of soldiers. Lockie told them how to make a stretcher out of two rifles and an overcoat and they carried him for two miles, dropping him three times on the way, once into a dyke of water, before he lost consciousness. He woke up in hospital, to find that he had been awarded the Distinguished Service Order for 'his magnificent fighting spirit and personal example which have been in the highest traditions of the service'.

During the next three months this intrepid airman underwent fifteen operations for the removal of shell splinters and remained in hospital until the end of May, 1941, apart from a day in April when he went to Buckingham Palace to receive his decorations from the King.

Once he had left hospital he went home to Shrewsbury for a short leave, during which he received an eagle's feather from Chief Whirling Thunder of a Red Indian organisation in Chicago, for his great courage shown in combat. By the end of June, 1941, Lockie was completely fit again and went on a refresher course. He was soon throwing his Spitfire about the sky again and in July went back to operational flying as a Flight Commander with Number 611 Squadron. Within a few weeks he had shot down another four German aircraft to bring his total confirmed victories to twenty-six and then he was himself shot down. It happened on the 3rd August, after he had taken part in a sweep over Northern France. On the way back he saw some German soldiers on a road near Calais and dived to attack. No one seems to know what happened after that, for Lockie was never seen again. He was posted missing in action and a year later, when no further news of his disappearance had been received, it was officially announced that there was now no further hope and it must be presumed that he had been shot down and killed, either by enemy fighters or by anti-aircraft fire.

26

DYNAMIC SCOTSMAN

Squadron Leader A. A. McKellar
D.S.O., D.F.C. and Bar

THREE aircraft destroyed with one burst of fire, four shot down in less then ten minutes, five confirmed victories in one day, eight more destroyed in eight days – this was the fantastic, almost unbelievable record of dynamic, pocket-sized fighter ace Archie McKellar. In just one month of fast and furious fighting in the Battle of Britain, this five-foot-three-inch bundle of energy shot out of the skies seventeen of the Luftwaffe's aircraft and in the same period was awarded the D.S.O. and the D.F.C. and Bar.

Archibald Ashmore McKellar was born in Paisley, Scotland, in 1912, the only son of John McKellar, and educated at Shaw-lands Academy. On leaving school he went into a stockbroker's office, but this did not suit Archie, who preferred an open-air life. He moved very soon into his father's building and contract-ing business. The whole of his spare time was spent either on sport, or reading about the great fighter pilots of the First World War, and ultimately he became so interested in flying that he joined the Scottish Flying Club and in due course qualified as a pilot. In 1936 he joined the City of Glasgow Squadron of the Auxiliary Air Force, so that by the time war came in 1939 Archie was a very experienced pilot and it came as no great surprise when he was made a flight commander.

The Spitfires of the Glasgow Squadron were soon in action against the Luftwaffe, shooting down the first enemy aircraft over the British Isles in the Second World War on the 16th October, 1939, but McKellar on this occasion failed to make contact with the Germans. A few days later, however, Archie shot down the first enemy raider to crash on British soil. It was during an enemy raid on the Firth of Forth when McKellar, on patrol, found a solitary Heinkel 111. He made a stern attack on the bomber and with his first burst killed the German rear-gunner. He continued his attack down to tree-top height and the

Heinkel finally crash-landed on a hillside near Dalkeith in East Lothian.

A little over a month later, on November 29th, Archie helped to bring down another Heinkel. He found it flying near Tranent and chased it for several miles before getting in a burst of gunfire which set its port engine on fire. Several more Spitfires then joined in and the Heinkel was shot to pieces.

After these first successes against the early probing raids, Archie had to wait a long time before he again met the Luftwaffe. It was, in fact, August 15th, 1940, before he fought his next combat and in the meantime he had been promoted to Flight Lieutenant and posted to another squadron, Number 605, who were stationed at Drem in the north of England. He also changed his aircraft, for his new squadron was equipped with Hawker Hurricanes. He soon proved that his new fighter plane was just as good as, if not better than, his old Spitfire by destroying three Heinkel 111's and probably destroying a fourth in one combat.

He was leading his flight on patrol over the Newcastle area in the early afternoon of the 15th August when he spotted about ninety Heinkels heading towards Newcastle from the south-east. He led his flight down in a diving attack out of the sun and with his first burst sent one of the Heinkel's crashing down. Climbing into the sun he turned, and fired at another Heinkel from the side at a range of a hundred and fifty yards. As soon as smoke and flames shot out of the Heinkel's engine, he swerved to bring his guns to bear on another bomber, and opened fire from only twenty-five yards away. As he flashed over the rest of the German formation, he saw both Heinkels spiralling down engulfed in smoke and flames. He had a few rounds of ammunition left, so he resumed his attack on the remnants of the Heinkel formation, which by this time had scattered far and wide. He fired the last of his bullets into the fuselage and wings of another Heinkel, which he left with grey smoke pouring from its starboard engine.

The rest of his flight had downed five more Heinkels for certain and probably seven more, so it was a very jubilant band of Hurricane pilots who landed at Drem after this fight. Shortly after this, Archie McKellar was awarded the D.F.C. for displaying 'a great sense of leadership and tactics in launching his flight against ninety Heinkel 111's in his first large-scale encounter against enemy aircraft'.

In September, Archie was given the chance of further large-scale encounters with the Luftwaffe, when his squadron was

ordered south to Croydon. The next day, September 8th, Mc-
Kellar led his flight on their first patrol over Southern England,
but he failed to add to his own score, although his colleagues
claimed five enemy aircraft destroyed. The following day, however, he made up for it by destroying four Huns in a single fight.
His squadron sighted the Huns, seventeen Heinkel 111's, escorted by about sixty Messerschmitts, over Maidstone. The
Hurricanes attacked the fighters first and Archie after a three-
second burst sent one of the 109's down in flames. He then
closed on the Heinkels, attacking the leading trio from directly
in front. He opened fire at seven hundred yards and immediately the leading Heinkel blew up. At the same moment the
Heinkel on the leader's right rolled over on to its back and spiralled down in flames, apparently damaged by the explosion of the
first Heinkel. Archie kept his finger on the gun button and,
swinging to the right, directed his tracers at the last of the trio.
Its port wing snapped off at the wing root and it fell away. All
three Heinkels had been destroyed with one solitary twelve-
second burst of bullets!

On the 15th September, during two patrols in the afternoon,
Archie McKellar fought with such skill and tenacity that he
destroyed two Me. 109's over Croydon, a Dornier 17 over
Maidstone and probably destroyed a Heinkel 111 near Folkestone. Eight hours later he took off again and a few minutes after
midnight he brought down a Heinkel 111 night raider in flames
as it was about to unload its bombs on London. This led to the
award of a Bar to his D.F.C., the official citation concluding:
'He displays an excellent fighting spirit, is a particularly brilliant
tactician, and has led his squadron with skill and resource.'

Even though he had done so well already in air combat, Mc-
Kellar's most successful day of air fighting was yet to come. It
was the 7th October, when he shot down five Messerschmitt 109's,
four of them in less than ten minutes in one battle. On this day
he led Number 605 Squadron against fifteen 109's, which were all
carrying bombs, escorted by another fifty some distance behind
and at various heights. McKellar himself attacked the leading
Messerschmitt and after a short burst saw pieces fly off it. Then it
fell into a violent outside spin. He avoided an attack from another
109 and then lined up another fighter bomber in his sights. After
another short burst, the 109 burst into flames and crashed near
Biggin Hill airfield. Another 109 made an astern attack on Mc-
Kellar so he dived away and at 15,000 feet found yet another
Messerschmitt. He closed on it, pressed the gun button and this

Hun also burst into flames, before going down to crash into a wood near Maidstone. Archie caught sight of another 109 dodging in and out of the clouds, and again he closed in and fired. Again the enemy fighter caught fire, but this time its pilot managed to bale out before it dived into the ground. Returning to Croydon to refuel and rearm, McKellar was back on patrol ninety minutes later when he spotted another Me. 109. A few minutes later the 109 became his fifth victim for the day.

Soon after this amazing performance Squadron Leader McKellar was awarded the D.S.O. for his 'outstanding courage and determination' and 'his magnificent inspiration to his fellow pilots'.

Towards the end of October the dynamic Scotsman was again in action against the Luftwaffe. On the 20th during the morning patrol he destroyed one Me. 109 and damaged another, and six days later repeated the perfomance. The following day he scored his last official victory, an Me. 109 which crashed near Redhill to bring his bag to twenty-one destroyed, three probably destroyed and three damaged.

A few days later, on November 1st, 1940, Archie McKellar failed to return from the early morning patrol. No one seems to know how he met his death. His Hurricane was last seen as it dived out of some clouds and crashed into a garden. A Messerschmitt 109 also crashed nearby. Since no pilot of 605 Squadron entered a claim for this Hun, it could have been the Scotsman's last victim.

27

CANADIAN EAGLE

Squadron Leader H. W. Mcleod
D.S.O., D.F.C. and Bar

WALLY MCLEOD was another Canadian pilot who won special distinction on the Battle of Malta. In eighteen weeks while based on the George Cross Island, from June to October, 1942, he became the top-scoring Royal Canadian Air Force pilot with thirteen confirmed victories, despite the fact that his section was outnumbered on some occasions by as many as six enemy aircraft to one. During his short stay in the Mediterranean, Wally was shot down twice, shot up and damaged five times, managed to shoot down a German bomber when he had only one single cannon still firing, and shot down six Huns in five days. Over the same period he also lost twenty-five pounds in weight!

Henry Wallace Mcleod was born in Regina, Saskatchewan, on the 17th December, 1915, and joined the Royal Canadian Air Force exactly a year after the start of the Second World War. He carried out his flying training at Air Schools in Saskatoon and Ontario, and on completion of the course in April, 1941, was commissioned and after a brief embarkation leave was posted overseas to England, where he became a member of the famous 602 (Glasgow) Squadron. He served later with 411 (R.C.A.F.) Squadron, but during the whole of his stay in England from May, 1941, to April, 1942, he saw very little action and was unable to claim any victories at all. But in May, 1942, he landed in Malta and immediately things livened up. On his second day with his new unit, Number 603 (City of Edinburgh) Squadron, he was flying wingman to the Commanding Officer, Squadron Leader L. D. Hamilton, when he sighted and attacked a large formation of three-engined Italian bombers. In a combined movement Hamilton and Mcleod each managed to get in several bursts at one of the bombers which slowed down and began to smoke. Curbing his natural excitement at the prospect of his first kill, Wally concentrated his attention on the Cant 1007 to the exclusion of everything else about him – a mistake many an inexperienced fighter pilot had made before, but never made again. The inevitable happened – an unseen Italian fighter closed in behind Wally's Spitfire and the next moment shells were pouring into the fuselage of his fighter. Breaking away sharply, Wally thanked his lucky stars that the Italian pilot was a rotten shot, and then carefully nursed his damaged aircraft back to base. As he landed, he realised that he had already learned far more in half-an-hour over Malta, than he had in the previous twelve months in England. During the rest of his short stay in Malta, Wally's education in the art of aerial duelling progressed at the same rapid rate and within a few days he had destroyed his first victim, an Italian Macchi 202, which in Wally's own words 'went into the drink from sheer fright'. His second, a Messerschmitt 109, exploded in mid-air, so close to Wally's fighter that bits of wreckage from it embedded themselves in the wings of the Spitfire.

The pilot was thrown clear [Wally reported later] and his chute opened. After he had hit the water I circled him and he waved to me, apparently quite cheerfully. So I dropped my dinghy for him to show that I had no hard feelings either. He did not make any attempt to climb into the rubber dinghy and the reason became apparent when one of our rescue launches came out to pick him up. He had a cannon shell through his chest, and he died in the launch.

Shortly after this incident, Wally was transferred to a newly-formed Spitfire unit, Number 1435 Flight and soon became a Flight Commander. During one of his first actions with his new unit he was one of eight Spitfires who took on an armada of seventy enemy aircraft. After the initial attack, in which Mcleod scored hits on several bombers, the escorting fighters came down and the mainplane of Wally's Spitfire was holed, his flaps were blown off and all his guns except one were put out of action. But that one cannon was enough to account for one of the attackers, who carelessly overshot the Canadian and presented him with an easy target.

Awarded the Distinguished Flying Cross on the 29th September, 1942, Wally added a Bar to this decoration three weeks later, after shooting down six enemy aircraft in five days. Two of these he accounted for within minutes of each other after attacking a formation of six Junkers 88's. Although his Spitfire was damaged during the combat, he courageously attacked another formation of nine bombers and scored several hits before running out of ammunition. He then nursed his damaged Spitfire back to base and made a skilful landing without further trouble.

Towards the end of October, 1942, Wally flew his last mission from Malta and during the course of it managed to bag his thirteenth victim. The next day he left the island, flew to England, and before Christmas was repatriated to Canada for a period of instructional duty.

In the autumn of 1943, Wally Mcleod began his second tour of operations when he was appointed to command one of the Canadian Fighter Squadrons which were being sent overseas to join the Second Tactical Air Force. Renumbered 443, this squadron formed part of an R.C.A.F. Spitfire Wing under the leadership of Wing Commander 'Johnnie' Johnson, who very quickly recognised the talents of this daredevil ace from Regina.

'I'm pleased he's with me and not on the other side', he said of Mcleod in his autobiography *Wing Leader*.

Wally scored his first kill with the 'Hornet' Squadron – this, incidentally, was also the squadron's first victory in combat – on the 19th April, 1944, when the Canadian Spitfires were escorting Marauder bombers to attack a target north-east of Brussels. They flew at low level, and between Brussels and Louvain found a Dornier 217 at the same height. Wing Commander Johnson who was leading the Canadians told Wally to go in and finish the Hun, whilst the rest of the Spitfires hung back to get a grand-stand view of the duel. It was all over in less than a minute. Wally closed in from astern and fired one short burst of cannon shells from a hundred yards' range. The Dornier pulled up sharply, its starboard engine caught fire, debris flew of it, then it stalled and crashed into a field near a row of cottages.

On the 5th May in a running fight between Mons and Douai Johnson got his twenty-eighth kill and at the same time Mcleod chased a Focke-Wulf 190 eastward at low level in very bad weather. He finally shot it down after a very long chase, so long in fact that he did not have enough fuel left to fly back to his own base. He had to make a hurried landing at the first airfield he came to after crossing over the English coast.

Mcleod led the Hornets on an escort mission to Le Havre on the 14th June and found four Dornier 17's over the Channel. Two of them escaped, but Mcleod and another Canadian each crashed one into the Channel. The following day the Canadians moved to an airstrip in Normandy and on his first sortie from this tem-porary airfield the next day Wally shot down his seventeenth victim, a Messerschmitt 109. Exactly a week after this, Wally proved how good a marksman he really was by shooting down two F.W. 190's with only twenty-six shells from his cannons. It happened near Alençon when the Hornet Squadron engaged a group of about a dozen 190's. Wally shot down the first air-craft to fall with his opening burst, and a few seconds later with another very brief burst of gunfire, sent a second 190 down in flames. Later he discovered he had used only thirteen rounds of ammunition from each of his two cannons in disposing of the Hun fighters.

Not long after this, Wally did even better. He accounted for his twentieth victim without firing a single round of ammunition. The squadron had attacked thirty F.W. 190's over Bernay on the 20th July. Wally picked out an opponent, slowly closed in and was just about to open fire, when the German pilot pulled up in terror and baled out. Mcleod then went down and used up his ammunition during a strafing attack on a number of enemy road vehicles.

Wally's last success, an Me. 109 which crashed east of Alençon on the 30th July, brought his final score to twenty-one enemy aircraft destroyed and placed him at the top of the list of fighter pilots of the Royal Canadian Air Force. It also earned for him the award of the Distinguished Service Order on the 5th September. Wally's success, however, was short-lived and the brilliant career forecast for him was cut short when he was shot down and killed in aerial combat on the 27th September, 1944. Wing Commander Johnson was leading the Spitfires during the midday patrol over the Nijmegen-Venlo area when, twenty miles east of Nijmegen, they attacked nine Me. 109's. Wally was last seen climbing to attack a 109 which was several thousand feet higher and had all the advantages of speed, height, and the choice of when to make his attack. Several days later Wally was found dead in the wreckage of his Spitfire, which had crashed near the scene of the combat.

28

'SAILOR' MALAN

Group Captain A. G. Malan
D.S.O. and Bar, D.F.C. and Bar, *Croix de Guerre*, *Légion d'Honneur*,
Czech War Cross, *Croix de Guerre Belge*

THE eldest son of Willem and Evelyn Malan, Adolph Gysbert Malan was born in Wellington, South Africa in 1910. He was educated first at one of the farm schools near Slent, then at the local school at Stellenbosch, and finally at the Boys' High School in Wellington. He had already decided on a career at sea so in 1924 he joined the training ship *General Botha* as a cadet. He passed out with a clean record and a certificate in seamanship in 1927 and joined the Union Castle Steamship Line. Three years later he had passed his examinations for his Second Mate's Certificate. On his voyages between South Africa and New York, he began to think about flying and in 1935 he wrote a letter which was to lead to his acceptance by the Royal Air Force. A few months later he was at Filton Flying School near Bristol beginning his training as a fighter pilot. He won his wings and commission at Number 3 Flying School, Grantham, and earned special praise for his flying skill. At Grantham he was known as 'The Admiral' because of his seafaring associations, but later on when he joined Number 74 Squadron, he was promptly demoted to 'Sailor' by an ex-Royal Navy type and this is the name which has stuck ever since.

In the summer of 1938 Sailor's flying skill won him the *Sir Phillip Sassoon Trophy* for fighter combat tactics, and about the same time Malan was married to Miss Lynda Fraser at Ruislip. In the same year it was decided to re-equip 74 Squadron with Spitfires which were very new and already much discussed in flying circles. The squadron was very proud of its new weapon and felt that, should war come, it had a plane which would surely enable it to carry on the great traditions of the 'Tigers', established in the 1914–18 War by such redoubtable fighters as Micky Mannock and Taffy Jones.

When war did come the squadron carried out formation practice, fighter attacks, anti-aircraft co-operation flights dusk landings, night-flying training, in fact everything except operational missions. After eight months of this prolonged inactivity, the pilots had almost given up hope of flying their Spitfires against the Luftwaffe, when suddenly the Allied Armies in France and the Low Countries were overrun and Number 74 Squadron was ordered to patrol over the Dunkirk beaches.

Sailor led his flight on the 21st May, 1940, across the Channel and seeing the anti-aircraft shells bursting over Calais headed towards them through a great bank of puffy white cumulus cloud. A few seconds later Sailor sped out of the cloud and almost collided with a Heinkel 111. Instantly he did a quick swerve and then opened fire as he banked steeply to come in behind the German bomber. The bullets ripped into it, tearing large pieces out of its fuselage, and thick white smoke belched out. Then its wheels flopped down and it fell away into the clouds. Malan flew on and a few minutes later found a solitary Junkers 88. He came in behind it, opened fire at five hundred yards' range and saw his tracers spattering along the side of the bomber. Closing rapidly to a hundred and fifty yards and still firing he saw the 88 roll over into a dive with flames and smoke pouring out. Sailor had scored his first victories in his first combat.

The next day, just after dawn, Sailor shot down another 88 into the Channel, but the following day, although he was in the midst of fierce fighting, he had a bad day and failed to score. On the 24th he found his best form again disposing of an Heinkel 111 on his first sortie and a Dornier 17 on a later patrol. Soon after sending the Heinkel down in flames, his own Spitfire was hit by an anti-aircraft shell in the starboard wing and almost in the same instant bullets smashed into his plane, one of them breaking his ring reflector sight and another tearing a piece out of his flying boot. Climbing steeply into the sun to avoid his attacker, Malan decided there and then to fit the spare ring and bead sight which he carried in his locker. He quickly slipped it into place and then turned back to join in the battle, but by this time the dog-fight had moved on, so Malan broke away to return to his base.

After a week of this continuous action over and around Dunkirk, Malan and his fellow pilots were exhausted and consequently on the 27th May, 1940, Number 74 Squadron was taken out of the line, having destroyed thirty Huns in seven days for the loss of three pilots. Sailor's share was five and led to the award of the Distinguished Flying Cross a few days later.

By June 6th the squadron was operational again, but the Luftwaffe took a breather during the rest of the month, in an effort to build up sufficient forces to give a knockout punch later on. Most of their activity was confined to night raids so, although Number 74 Squadron was a day-fighter unit, many of its pilots volunteered to go up at night in an effort to intercept the night raiders. The distinction of destroying for the first time two bombers in one night fell to Sailor Malan.

During an air raid on Southend on the night of June 18th, Malan volunteered to try to intercept the raiders. His request being granted he took off and headed for the searchlight beams. Soon he spotted a Heinkel 111 caught by a searchlight and slowly he crept up behind the bomber; the crew had evidently been blinded by the light, for they did not appear to notice the Spitfire until Malan had got within range and had opened up with his eight Browning machine guns. Sailor saw his tracers entering the fuselage of the Hun and then his windscreen became covered in oil. Breaking away, he wiped away the oil and prepared to make another attack, but he need not have bothered, for already the Heinkel was spinning down out of control and a few seconds later crashed into the sea off Foulness. Malan continued his patrol and a few minutes later spotted another He. 111 held by searchlights. He fired five two-second bursts and immediately the Heinkel began to smoke and one of its crew baled out. Then it went down in flames and crashed near Chelmsford. At 12.30 a.m., only ten minutes after taking off, Sailor was back on the ground again.

During the first phase of the Battle of Britain in July, 1940, Sailor added a Heinkel 111, two Dornier 17's, and an Me. 109 to his bag, and before the end of the month had also added a Bar to his D.F.C. The official citation spoke of 'his magnificent leadership, skill and courage which have been largely responsible for the many successes obtained by his squadron'.

Shortly afterwards Malan took command of 'The Tigers'. On the first day on which he led the squadron into battle as their commanding officer, August 11th, his pilots enjoyed their greatest victory. In four combats between 7.45 a.m. and 4 p.m., the Tigers accounted for thirteen Me. 109's and ten Me. 110's destroyed, one Me. 110 probably destroyed, and nine Me. 109's and five Me. 110's damaged. Sailor's own share of this formidable score was two Me. 109's destroyed and two more damaged.

During the first fight near Dover shortly before 8 o'clock, the squadron surprised eight Me. 109's and Malan chased one of them across the Channel before finally sending it down to crash about a mile north-east of Cap Gris Nez. Two hours later on his second sortie Sailor attacked and severely damaged a pair of 109's near Dover, before he was set upon by eight more 109's and had to break off the combat. He missed the third patrol, during which the rest of the squadron chalked up sixteen victories, but on his own third sortie in mid-afternoon he led the Tigers to attack ten Junkers 87's escorted by about twenty Me. 109's. Sailor engaged one of the fighters and after three short bursts had the satisfaction of seeing the 109 burst into flames and go down into the sea off Margate.

August 12th found the Tigers grounded whilst their hard-worked ground crews patched up the bullet holes in their Spit-fires, but the following day they were again in action. They encountered forty-five Dornier 17's over the Thames Estuary and Malan led his pilots with great gusto. He attacked one Dornier from astern and after four short bursts the bomber was set on fire and dived towards the sea. Sailor closed in on a second Dornier, and within a few seconds this was also spiralling down. The South African used up the rest of his ammunition on a third Dornier, but saw no obvious results, so he turned away towards his base.

The Tigers were now sent to Kirton-in-Lindsay for re-equip-ping and training new pilots, and to rest those who had fought so hard. Whilst here Malan wrote his *Ten Rules for Air Fighting*, which later became famous throughout Fighter Command when the Air Ministry printed them on posters and had them pasted up in all fighter stations.

Malan led his squadron back to Biggin Hill, the most heavily bombed aerodrome in Fighter Command, in the middle of October and before long was adding to his already lengthy list of victories. Before the end of November his squadron had destroyed over eighty Huns, of which Sailor himself had accounted for eighteen; soon Malan was awarded the Distinguished Service Order for 'commanding his squadron with outstanding success over an intensive period of operations, and by his brilliant leadership, skill and determination has contributed largely to the successes achieved'.

Early in 1941, the Royal Air Force went over to the offensive and Sailor began leading his squadron as part of the Biggin Hill Spitfire Wing, on sweeps over Northern France, with the object of making the Germans come up to fight. During one of these he scored his twentieth kill. German fighters rose to meet the Spitfires as they roared over the French countryside, and Sailor picked out an Me. 109 and manoeuvred on to its tail. Even as he gave it a burst from close range his cockpit began to fill with smoke. Nevertheless he carried on. The Hun made two sharp turns, but Sailor hung on grimly and caught him with several bursts that sent the 109 plunging down to crash at over 400 m.p.h. When Malan returned to Biggin Hill, he found that the smoke alarm had been caused by a slight engine defect.

In May, 1941, Malan was promoted to command the Biggin Hill Wing, which included Numbers 92 and 609 Squadrons, and which at this time was probably the best Spitfire Wing in the whole of Fighter Command. On one of his first missions as Commanding Officer, Malan led fourteen Spitfires to cover the Kenley Wing who were returning from a mission to Gravelines. They engaged a number of enemy fighters and in a running dogfight Sailor added another Me. 109 to his tally.

On another occasion whilst leading his wing, Malan sighted twenty 109's flying in a large 'V' formation near Paris. The Spitfires dived on them, and Sailor singled out the right-hand flank Hun and closed to fifty yards before he opened up with his cannons. The 109 exploded and large pieces of it fell on to Sailor's Spitfire as he broke away; he narrowly missed the fuselage, which was hurtling through the air. Looking round the South African saw two more 109's spinning down in flames and then he attacked another 109 which was climbing into the sun. He fired, the tail of the Hun came off, and the 109 went down in a steep dive at terrific speed. Sailor followed not realising that he was wasting ammunition and saw the wings tear off the 109, which plunged into the earth with a terrific explosion.

Early in June, Sailor started a dogfight over Calais, settled into position astern of a 109 and kept up a constant peppering with his cannons until the 109 finally crashed into the sea a quarter of a mile from the French coast. A few days later he was ambushed by three 109's but by skilful flying evaded their attacks, eventually shot down one, and chased off the other two. On a sweep soon after this he again took on three Messerschmitts, but this time he did not have it all his own way. He shot down two of them all right, but the third got in a good burst of cannon shells which damaged the wings and cockpit of the Spitfire and wounded Sailor in the wrist and thigh. He escaped into some neighbouring clouds, coaxed his Spitfire home and landed at Biggin Hill with his wheels still retracted. He climbed out, walked to the sick quarters to have his wounds attended to and, a couple of days later, was in action again. This time six 109's attacked him, but even odds such as this were not too great for this brilliant air fighter and, after he had caused one of them to explode in mid-air, the other five gave up the fight.

During the month of June, 1941, Malan shot down nine Me. 109's, six of these within one week, and during the first week of July he put his score up to thirty-two destroyed, six probably destroyed, and twenty damaged. This was the record score for a Royal Air Force pilot which was to stand for nearly three years. He was awarded a Bar to his D.S.O. in July, 1941, for 'displaying the greatest courage and disdain of the enemy whilst leading his wing on numerous recent operations over Northern France'. The official citation paid tribute to his 'cool judgement, exceptional determination, and ability', and ended: 'His record and behaviour have earned for him the greatest admiration and devotion of his comrades in the wing'.

In August, 1941, after taking part in over two hundred fights, Sailor was taken off operations, and a few weeks later was on his way to the U.S.A., with five other well-known pilots to give a series of lectures and to make a tour of U.S.A.A.F. squadrons. He returned to Britain in November, 1941, and was posted to the Central Gunnery School at Sutton Bridge as a Gunnery Instructor. He was promoted to Group Captain in October, 1942, and in January, 1943, took command of the Biggin Hill Fighter Station. He remained here, although his duties prevented him from doing any operational flying until January, 1944, when he was given the task of training Number Twenty Fighter Wing for the forthcoming invasion of the continent. He became operational again and flew with his wing over the Normandy beaches whenever circumstances permitted. In July, 1944, he was given command of an Advanced Gunnery School at Catfoss, where crack fighter pilots of many nationalities, including Dick Bong, 'Screwball' Beurling, Stanislaw Skalski, Pierre Clostermann, and Don Kingaby were called in to pool ideas, try out new weapons and evolve new combat techniques. In 1945, Group Captain Malan took a six months' course at the R.A.F. College and then early in 1946 retired from the Royal Air Force.

He returned to his native South Africa to become secretary to Harry Openheimer, the diamond millionaire, but in 1950 he struck out on his own as a sheep farmer near Kimberley. He had become increasingly interested in politics since his return to South Africa and in May, 1951, suddenly appeared at the head of an 8,000 strong procession of ex-servicemen who protested against the Coloured Voting Bill. He was eventually elected National President of the Torch Commando, destined to bring about the defeat of the Dr Malan Government and the re-establishment of respect for the constitution of South Africa.

29

THE UNKNOWN ACE

Squadron Leader M. T. St J. Pattle
D.F.C. and Bar

THERE was some consternation in the tents which passed for the Officers' Mess of Number 80 Squadron, Royal Air Force at Sidi Barrani on the evening of August 4th, 1940. 'B' Flight Commander, Flight Lieutenant Marmaduke Thomas St John Pattle, had failed to return from a brush with Fiat C.R. 42's and Breda Ba 65's. Reluctantly, the Adjutant crossed his name from the Squadron lists.

It was not just that 'Pat' Pattle was a well-loved pilot. During the comparatively short time Number 80 Squadron had been in action with the outdated Gladiators, Pattle had proved that he was a brilliant tactician, and unerring shot and as brave a man as ever stepped into a cockpit. Those who flew and fought with him in the desert were convinced that one day soon, he would become one of Britain's leading aces.

For two days he was mourned as dead and then, without warning, he turned up again after a long walk across the desert. He was a little tired after his adventures, but otherwise unharmed. Those who had forecast a brilliant career for this pilot were able to sit back and watch their prophecies come true.

Although Pattle was relatively unknown to fighter pilots in the British Isles his eventual score put him right at the top of the list of aces. That he has never been officially acknowledged as the R.A.F.'s leading ace is due to the fact that the Ministry of Defence were never in a position to confirm his victories. All official records were destroyed when Greece was evacuated by the British forces towards the end of April, 1941. Semi-official records written from memory and intelligence summaries confirm that he destroyed many enemy aircraft during the few weeks that he commanded 33 Squadron yet Pattle's official records give no indication that he ever served with this squadron.

Pattle's exact score must remain a mystery. The last official score credited to him was 23, when he was awarded a Bar to his D.F.C. in March, 1941. Log-books, diaries, operations summaries and semi-official records confirm that he shot down at least 40 enemy aircraft. Pilots who survived the Greek campaign consider his true score to be nearer 60. There is no doubt that he was the highest scoring pilot of the Royal Air Force.

Born in Butterworth, Cape Province, South Africa, in 1913, Pattle was descended from a family with strong military connections – his grandfather was the first military magistrate of the Transkei, his father a drummer boy at Queen Victoria's Jubilee – and Pat himself naturally decided on a military career as soon as he had finished his education at Graemian College, Grahamstown. He joined the South African Air Force as a cadet, but in 1936 decided to transfer to the Royal Air Force. He came to England and began his training as a pilot. A born flyer, he excelled at aerobatics and markmanship, completed his training with honours, and subsequently was commissioned and posted to one of the Royal Air Force's most famous fighter squadrons, Number 80, who were renowned in pre-war days for their close-formation aerobatic displays. Pattle soon grew to love Service life and was extremely proud of his squadron, with whom he served for all but one month of his active-service life. When the war broke out in 1939 the squadron was stationed in the Middle East and Pattle was the flight commander of 'B' Flight.

The Gladiator biplane fighters with which the squadron was equipped were out of date compared with the modern monoplane fighters, the Spitfires and Hurricanes used by squadrons of Fighter Command in Britain, but during the first year of the war, the pilots of 80 Squadron flew their obsolete biplanes with such skill and tenacity that they were more than a match for the faster Messerschmitts, Fiats and Reggianes of the enemy. The South African worked out his own special methods of attacking the faster enemy fighters and so successful were they that he soon became the ace pilot of 80 Squadron.

At first the squadron was very successful, but then it seemed to hit a bad patch and a number of pilots were posted missing. It was at this early stage that Pattle worried his comrades by failing to turn up after a sortie.

He had taken off to lead his flight on an offensive patrol over the Western Desert. All was going well until they met a formation of Fiat C.R. 42's and Breda 65's. The Fiats dived out of the sun on to the tails of the four Gladiators and, as bullets thudded into the wings and fuselage of his aircraft, Pattle swung round into a climbing turn, hoping that the Fiats would be going too fast to keep him in their sights.

His hopes were realised. The Italians roared past and then split up as they wheeled to face the pilots of the Gladiators. Pattle was not a little annoyed at being jumped in this fashion and there was grim determination on his face as he picked out a dark green Breda and gently slid into position to make his attack.

The Italian bomber filled his sights as he opened fire with his four Browning guns. Within a few seconds thick smoke was pouring out behind the enemy aircraft. Slowly it flicked over, dived towards the ground and then made a heavy forced landing.

Shunning the urge to fly down and shoot up the crashed aircraft, Pattle returned to the thick of the fight. A Fiat C.R. 42 conveniently crossed his path and, with a well-aimed deflection shot, it fell away with smoke streaming from it. Pattle followed it down, but immediately heard bullets ripping through his aircraft. The stick went lifeless in his hands and the South African suddenly realised that he was spinning down in an uncontrollable aeroplane.

There was nothing else to do except push back the canopy and take a headlong dive over the side. As soon as he had caught his breath after the unfamiliar falling sensation, Pattle pulled the rip cord and the roar of the wind and the battle seemed suddenly shut off as he floated gently down. He made a mental note never to make the mistake of following an enemy down again. He landed lightly and then, taking his bearings by the hot, burning sun, headed east towards the British lines.

Several times he narrowly escaped capture by German patrols and, twenty-four hours after being shot down, he was picked up by a bunch of British soldiers. Some hours later he was back with 80 Squadron.

In November, 1940, the Greeks were slowly being forced out of their country, and it was decided that several R.A.F. fighter and bomber squadrons should be sent to help, among them Number 80 Squadron. Although still only equipped with their old biplane fighters, the squadron soon made its presence felt, and until the Germans sent reinforcements of Messerschmitts in the spring of 1941, were equal to the occasion, shooting down Italian planes by the score.

In January, 1941, the squadron was split into two separate units, one under the command of Squadron Leader 'Tap' Jones, the other led by Pattle. The South African immediately celebrated this move by shooting down three enemy planes in one day, the first of many triple victories. This brought his personal bag of Huns up to thirteen and won for him the Distinguished Flying Cross, one of the first decorations to be won by the R.A.F. in the Greek Campaign.

On February 7th, six Hurricanes arrived in Greece and were immediately despatched to Eleusis to replace the Gladiators used by Pattle and his flight. Three days later the Hurricanes went into action for the first time in Greece when Pattle's flight escorted thirty Blenheims on a bombing mission. A squadron of Fiat G. 50's attacked the Blenheims, but soon made off losing four of their number to the Hurricanes in the space of a few minutes, Pat himself setting the example by shooting down their leader.

The battle for air supremacy in Greece was now approaching its climax and on February 28th, 1941, the R.A.F. had its greatest victory of the campaign. In a little over one-and-a-half hours, the two British fighter squadrons, 80 and 33, massacred the enemy, shooting down twenty-seven Italian aircraft. Flight Lieutenant Pattle was in the thick of fighting from the start of the battle, shooting down two Fiat C.R. 42 fighters before being forced to leave the fight to refuel and rearm. The ground crew swarmed over his Hurricane as it came to a standstill and fuel began to pour into the petrol tanks as the South African jumped out to snatch a few puffs of a cigarette. The refuelling and re-arming was finished quickly and Pat was in the cockpit again heading back towards the main battle. He saw three specks near Valona and made a wide climbing turn in order to approach the formation out of the sun. As he swung round towards them, he recognised them as Fiat C.R. 42's, Italian fighters of a similar appearance and performance to the Gloster Gladiator. They could not have seen the lone Hurricane yet for they continued on their patrol, even as Pat closed in quickly from the rear and lined them up in his sights.

He opened fire from about two hundred yards, and kept his finger on the firing button as he poured a stream of bullets into first one, then another, and finally the last of the trio. The leading C.R. 42 went into a vertical dive and Pat poured another burst into it before it finally dived into the sea. As he swung his Hurri-cane round to engage the other Fiats, they both spun down leav-ing a trail of black smoke and flames behind them to be followed a few seconds later by two parachutes. His first burst must have found a vital spot in each.

The whole thing had taken only a few minutes, in fact it was still only thirty minutes since he had taken off from Paramythia, so he decided to have another look around for more victims. But the Italians had apparently decided they had lost enough planes for one day and after a fruitless search Pattle headed for Paramythia to celebrate his most successful day.

A few days later there was another big dogfight over Himara, when Pattle's flight of Hurricanes encountered a large formation of Italian fighters. With his first burst Pattle hit the fuel tank of a Fiat G. 50, which exploded and fell to earth in pieces. He flicked over to come up behind a pair of C.R. 42's, one of which pulled up towards the right. Pat followed and as the Fiat filled his gun sight, fired another burst. The little Italian fighter rolled over on its back and then fell away with flames and smoke streaming out behind. A black dot separated itself from the flam-ing wreck and a few seconds later a parachute opened. Mean-while, Pattle had sighted another C.R. 42 which had left the main dogfight and was now heading for the front line. The South African pushed the throttle wide open and in a few minutes had caught the biplane, which immediately dived down to tree-top height, in an effort to elude the Hurricane.

Pattle followed and opened fire in short bursts each time the

Fiat dipped into his gunsight. This went on for about two minutes until a final burst found its target, and the Italian fighter dived into the ground with a terrific explosion, the force of which turned the Hurricane completely over and rocked it about like a cork on a rough sea. He eventually regained control of his plane and turned to head back toward Himara, where the main battle had ended in another smashing victory for the R.A.F. This last triple victory in March, 1941, now brought Pattle's total bag to twenty-three and led to the award of a Bar to his D.F.C. a few days later.

Promotion soon followed, too, for early in April, the Commanding Officer of 33, another Hurricane squadron based at Larissa, was shot down and killed and Pattle took over the command. He quickly dispelled any doubts its pilots may have had about his ability to lead the squadron for on his first patrol as their Commanding Officer, he led them so skilfully that they attacked and outfought a group of some thirty Messerschmitt 109's, shooting down five of the enemy without getting even one bullet hole in their Hurricanes. He continued to lead the squadron with such skill and cunning that during the next few weeks, despite its inevitable losses against the vastly superior numbers of German and Italian fighters, the squadron scored on an average five enemy planes for every Hurricane it lost.

Gradually, however, with no replacement aircraft or pilots available, the Hurricanes were whittled down under the sheer weight of numbers and the squadron fell back to Eleusis. Pattle was exceptionally fatigued by almost non-stop operational flying by this time. He had lost a great deal of weight, had a high temperature, and was suffering from influenza. The Medical Officer advised him to give up flying for a few days, but Pattle knew that this would have lowered the squadron's morale – he determined to carry on.

During the early morning of the 19th April, Pattle shared in the destruction of a Henschel 126 and shot down two Me. 109's. He was mentally and physically tired and the Medical Officer refused to let him fly again. But there was an air raid and Pattle sick and tired as he was, flew yet again and shot down a Ju. 88.

On Sunday, 20th April, 1941, he still had a high temperature and was undoubtedly a very sick man. Despite this he insisted on taking off with the remaining 15 Hurricanes of 80 and 33 Squadrons, the only fighters left in Greece, to take on a great armada of Junkers 88 bombers heading for Piraeus Harbour, and escorted by a swarm of Messerschmitt fighters. After his first attack,

Pattle saw a single Hurricane climbing towards a defensive circle of Me. 110's. A lone German peeled off to dive at the Hurricane, and Pattle swooped to the rescue, knowing that in doing so he would expose his own tail. He pulled up under the first 110 and shot it down in flames. A second Messerschmitt exploded in mid-air, but the odds were too great even for Pattle. Seconds later his Hurricane, with Pattle slumped over the controls, fell away to plunge into the depths of Eleusis Bay.

30

'JAMIE'

Air Commodore J. E. Rankin
D.S.O. and Bar, D.F.C. and Bar,
Croix de Guerre Belge

ON a frosty February morning in 1941 a twenty-eight-year-old stocky, dark-haired Scotsman by the name of James Rankin pulled up outside the Station Commander's Office at an airfield south of London. If he was feeling a little nervous he might have been excused. He had just been promoted Commanding Officer of one of the roughest, toughest and finest squadrons in the Royal Air Force, who were stationed at the best-known fighter airfield in Britain, commanded by one of the R.A.F.'s greatest fighter aces. The Wing Commander was 'Sailor' Malan, who with over twenty victories was one of Fighter Command's top-scoring aces; the station – Biggin Hill, the top-scoring station in Fighter Command; the squadron – Number 92, the top-scoring squadron in Fighter Command. And Rankin had not one Hun to his credit; in fact, he had not even met the Luftwaffe in combat, although he had for some time been a flight commander with Number 64 Squadron. But Rankin need not have had any misgivings over his new position, for within a few weeks he proved he had all the qualities of a first-class fighter leader – wonderful eyesight, brilliant marksmanship, excellent flying skill and an ability to seek out and turn to advantage the slightest weakness of the enemy. He had also a quality which eluded many aces, an uncanny sixth sense which enabled him to control an air battle against a number of enemy fighters and yet at the same time be able to shoot down an enemy aircraft himself – and still have time to guard his own tail and be on the look-out for any other pilot of his squadron who might have run into trouble.

Born in Portobello, Edinburgh, in 1913, James Rankin was educated at Portobello School and the Royal High School, Edinburgh. He joined the Fleet Air Arm, but in July, 1939, transferred to the Royal Air Force as an instructor with Training Command. He did no operational flying until early in 1941 when he was given command of the East India Spitfire Squadron.

His first encounter with the Luftwaffe was on the 11th April when he destroyed a Heinkel 59 just off the French coast. A few minutes later a bunch of Me. 109's appeared and Jamie was able to see his bullets striking the cockpit of one of them before he was set upon by three more Messerschmitts. He avoided their attacks and returned to base without further incident. A fortnight later whilst patrolling over Dungeness with Flight Lieutenant Brunier, a Netherland fighter pilot, Rankin shot down a 109 in flames.

June, 1941, was 'Messerschmitt Month' for Rankin. Between the 12th and the 26th he destroyed eight of these enemy fighters in addition to claiming another as probably destroyed. Two of these he shot down during two sorties on the 21st June. The squadron was covering the withdrawal of bombers from France soon after lunch when Rankin dived on a lone Me. 109 flying about 2,000 feet below him. He fired both cannons and machine guns from directly astern of the 109 and had the satisfaction of seeing the tail of the enemy fighter break off and the pilot bale out. Two hours later whilst leading the squadron on a sweep to Gravelines and Boulogne, he attacked three Messerschmitts just off the French coast near Boulogne. He fired one short burst and one of the 109's rolled over on to its back and then dived into the sea.

Two days later during an afternoon sweep Jamie shot down two Messerschmitts in less than a minute. The Biggin Hill Spitfires were just turning between Béthune and Lille when several aircraft were sighted and the wing leader ordered Number 92 Squadron to investigate. Jamie led his squadron towards the enemy formation from the rear and on identifying them as Me. 109's set fire to one of them with a no-deflection shot from short range. The remaining 109's began to take violent evasive action, but Jamie got in a two-second burst at one which was climbing hard to the right. Black-and-white smoke shot out behind the Messerschmitt, and then Jamie had to swing away himself as another Messerschmitt came in behind him. On looking down a few seconds later Jamie saw the first 109 blazing furiously, and the second just beginning to burn and the pilot baling out.

In July, he shot down the squadron's 150th Hun, and by the middle of August his personal score had risen to thirteen confirmed victories and he was awarded a Bar to his D.F.C. Jamie shot down his thirteenth victim on the 9th August and during the same mission also damaged two more Messerschmitts.

On this occasion he was leading the wing on a sweep when they sighted and engaged a number of 109's near Le Touquet. Rankin chased and caught two of these, and in both cases scored hits with cannon shells. Later at Cap Gris Nez whilst dogfighting with three more Me. 109's, Jamie sighted another dozen approaching, and ordered his section to break away and return to base. One of the Messerschmitts followed the Spitfires down at over 450 m.p.h., but Jamie pulled up to the right and as the 109 overshot fired a burst with his machine guns only. The enemy fighter tried to turn whilst pulling out from his dive at less than five hundred feet, but failed to do so and crashed into the sea sending up a splash over a hundred feet high.

'Sailor' Malan finished his tour of operations in September, 1941, and Rankin took over from him as the Biggin Hill Wing Leader. The added responsibility of leading a large number of Spitfires gave Jamie a chance to show his qualities as a fighter leader, and time after time he gave his wing all the tactical advantages of height, surprise and so on, when they encountered the German fighters over Northern France. After twenty-one sorties as Wing Leader, Jamie was awarded the Distinguished Service Order. The citation credited him with eighteen confirmed victories and ended with the following words: 'Wing Commander Rankin is an outstanding wing leader who has displayed exceptional ability, determination and courage on all occasions.'

In December, 1941, Rankin handed over the Biggin Hill Wing to Bob Tuck and received a temporary rest from operations. He became Wing Commander Training at Number Eleven Group Headquarters. Whilst still occupying this position, the Belgian authorities honoured him by awarding him the Belgian *Croix de Guerre* for his brilliant leading of the Biggin Hill Wing, which included Number 609 Squadron; this squadron had several Belgian pilots flying its Spitfires.

Rankin resumed command of the Biggin Hill Wing in April, 1942, and during the following summer led the wing on over fifty operational missions. The Biggin Hill Spitfires shot down twenty-seven German aircraft on these missions and Wing Commander Rankin helped himself to three of these. He also succeeded in damaging at least eight more enemy fighters.

Jamie completed his second tour of operations in July, 1942, by which time he had a total of twenty-one confirmed kills. He was awarded a Bar to his D.S.O. for 'displaying great tactical skill, courage, and leadership combined with a great determination to seek and engage the enemy'.

Promoted to Group Captain in 1944, Jamie began a third tour of operations as leader of a Spitfire Wing during the invasion of Normandy. He flew numerous patrols over the Normandy beaches, but failed to add to his successes in air combat. By the time the war ended in 1945, Jamie had received further promotion to the rank of Air Commodore.

31

'LAST TRIP' SCHERF

Squadron Leader C. C. Scherf
D.S.O., D.F.C. and Bar

THE Mosquito fighter climbed gracefully into the cloudless sky on a sunny spring afternoon in April, 1944, and the pilot hummed contentedly to himself as he set a southerly course and headed for southern France at an altitude of less than a hundred feet. The pilot was happy because although he had finished one tour of operations and was now officially grounded, he had managed to persuade his old commanding officer to lend him an aircraft for one last trip against the enemy.

Nothing much happened until the Mozzie was approaching a place called Montereau near Tours, when the pilot spotted a Fieseler Storch flying low and very slowly. He pulled his throttle right back to fly as slowly as possible without stalling, but even so, he still approached the enemy plane at a fast rate. As he closed he pressed the button of his cine-camera and took pictures of the Hun until he was within range of his guns. He switched his trigger finger to the gun button, but nothing happened – the guns were not properly switched on. Cursing himself for his over-sight, the pilot quickly cocked his guns, but it was too late, his Mosquito had flown straight past the German army co-operation aircraft. As he swung his fighter round in a tight bank, the enemy aircraft landed in a small field and two Germans jumped out and headed for the woods. The Mosquito circled and the pilot pressed the gun-button. This time streams of cannon shells crashed into the Storch and immediately it blew up.

Feeling a little more satisfied the Mosquito pilot flew in and as he approached the German airfield at Lyons he caught sight of more enemy aircraft. He attacked a Messerschmitt 110 which went down in flames, and then closed in on a Potez 63, which soon went down to crash less than half a mile from the Messer-schmitt.

He was quite happy once more as he set course for home. On the way back he crossed the enemy aerodrome at St Yan. He fired the remainder of his ammunition into a row of Heinkel 111's parked around the airfield, and as he sped quickly away, his observer reported two of them blazing and a column of smoke rising from the airfield.

By the time he landed at base, the Mosquito pilot was feeling on top of the world and had already made up his mind that this certainly would not be his last trip if he could possibly help it.

The Mosquito pilot was an Australian by the name of Charles Curnow Scherf, who had been born at Emmaville, New South Wales, on the 17th May, 1917. A grazier in civil life he had en-listed in the Royal Australian Air Force in September, 1941, and a year later, after extensive training under the Empire Training Scheme, had received his commission and wings as fighter pilot. He embarked for the British Isles a month later, and on arrival was sent for a course at a Mosquito Operational Training Unit. On completion of this course in July, 1943, Charlie Scherf began his first operational tour with Number 418 (City of Edmonton) Squadron. This was a Canadian Mosquito night-fighter squadron and, although Scherf was the only Australian in the squadron, he quickly made friends with the Canadians. During his stay with 418 Squadron, Scherf took part in many 'intruder' operations over Europe, but he had to wait six months before he managed to bring down his first victim, a Focke-Wulf 200 which fell in flames at Bourges. Three weeks later he 'shot' down his second Hun without even firing a shot. It happened on the night of the 19th February, 1944, and Squadron Leader Scherf was on his way to Liepzig when he sighted and attacked a single-engined enemy

156

aircraft. He chased it round in such tight turns, that the enemy pilot eventually lost control of his aircraft, which spun away to crash into the ground near Florennes in Belgium.

Five days later the Australian, out on a patrol between Illesheim and Ansbach, set two Junkers 88's blazing furiously. Both went down to crash on the edge of their own airfield. On his next sortie on the 26th February, Scherf and a Canadian pilot visited the German airfield of St Yan. They destroyed three parked aircraft and then, whilst on their way to another airfield, came across a most peculiar procession of aircraft flying sedately along at 2,000 feet. In the lead was an enormous multi-engined Bi-Heinkel, a curious machine constructed from two Heinkel 111's joined together. Behind it, and being towed by it, were two giant Gotha gliders in line astern. The Canadian attacked the rear glider, whilst Scherf dealt with the other Gotha. Both fell seconds later in a shower of wreckage. The Mosquitoes then took it in turns to make a series of attacks on the Bi-Heinkel, which eventually dived to earth with all its engines put out of action and long tongues of flame leaping out behind it.

With a final score of seven and a half destroyed enemy aircraft to his credit, Squadron Leader Scherf completed his tour of operations in April, 1944, and was awarded the D.F.C. He was given the post of Intruder Controller and was thus grounded.

But one day he took off for 'one last trip' with the squadron and during that trip as already described, he destroyed two enemy aircraft in the air and three on the ground. They called him 'Last Trip' Scherf after that.

He was not finished yet, however, for he managed to get in two more day-off operations after this. And what incredible trips they turned out to be!

The first of these missions was on the 2nd May, when Scherf set out with another Canadian ace night-fighter, Johnny Caine, for North Germany and the Baltic area. Near to Rostock they found a number of flying boats moored on the water. Scherf got in a five-second burst and damaged a Heinkel 115, whilst Flying Officer Caine set two on fire and damaged two more. They flew on to Barth airfield and on their first strafing pass over the field Scherf destroyed one Junkers 52, and Caine blew up two more. Coming in from different directions for their second attack, this time the Australian destroyed a Dornier 217, and the Canadian two more enemy aircraft. The anti-aircraft fire was now so intense that they decided to go elsewhere, but not before Caine's Mosquito had been badly hit and about two feet knocked off its tail. On the way to Griefswald aerodrome the two Mosquitos ran into a lot of rain and low cloud; then one of Caine's engines stopped and he had to turn and head for home. Scherf turned to escort Caine back, but could not find him because of the bad weather, and so the Aussie decided to attack Griefswald alone.

When he arrived over the airfield he found a Junkers 86 circling around. He gave it one short burst at three hundred yards' range and the Hun crashed in flames. The Mosquito turned sharply and the Aussie came down for a strafing run across the field. He gave a Heinkel 111 a short burst of cannon-fire and it blew up in flames about fifty feet in the air. Scherf then sped away to try to catch up Caine, who meanwhile had informed him over the radio-telephone that he was all right so far but was ready to bale out if the other engine packed up. Coming back over Rostock airfield Scherf used up all his ammunition in one more low-level attack during which he blew up another Heinkel 111. Caine called up again to say that he was afraid he would not be able to make it and not to worry about him.

Scherf eventually got home without any further action and was actually reporting his conversations with Caine, when it was announced that Caine was approaching the base. Hurrying outside, the Australian was overjoyed to see his friend approaching on one engine, then waggle his wings in triumph and make a beautiful three-point landing.

Flying Officer Caine went on flying with 418 Squadron for several months after this incident and then did another tour of operations with 406 Squadron in 1945; by the time the war ended he had shot down five enemy aircraft, destroyed another fifteen on the ground and been awarded the Distinguished Flying Cross and two Bars.

The third 'last trip' that Scherf managed was perhaps the most exciting of all and took place two weeks later on the 16th May. This time he had a new navigator, Flying Officer Finlayson, D.F.C., and as usual another Mosquito, piloted by Flying Officer Cleveland, went with them. Again they headed for North Germany and the Baltic. Over the Baltic they sighted a Heinkel 111 and gave chase. Black smoke poured from the Hun as the pilot opened his throttle wide in an effort to get away from the Mosquito. Scherf caught it with no trouble at all, fired one short burst from directly astern and the Heinkel went down in flames into the sea. Continuing the patrol the Australian found an F.W. 190 circling over Kubitzer. After a few seconds of sparring, Scherf finally got in a good burst of cannon shells. The 190 flipped over on its back, burst into flames and went straight into the ground.

Heading southward Scherf and Cleveland found a number of enemy aircraft flying around the airfield at Parrow. Scherf attacked a Heinkel 177 from underneath and in front; one short burst of fire was enough to send it down to crash into Kubitzer Bay. Cleveland was busy with a Junkers 88 so the Aussie came down for a strafing run across the airfield. He saw a Heinkel 111 silhouetted against the bay and after another touch on the gun saw it blow up.

Out of the corner of his eye Scherf then caught sight of an Ardo floatplane, gave chase, fired and watched it fall in flames. He came in for a second strafing run and scored hits on a Dornier 18 moored on the water. There was plenty of smoke from it, but no explosion, so Scherf only claimed this one as damaged. The anti-aircraft fire over the German base was now so intense – Scherf's Mosquito had already been hit in the tail plane and one of the drop tanks – that the Aussie decided to clear out. As he turned he sighted another enemy aircraft a few miles away. He opened the throttle, caught up with the German plane, a Junkers 86, and shot it down. He then set course for home, having shot down five Huns in fifteen minutes, four of them in the last five minutes. His last trip was by no means over yet, however, for on the way home he was shot at by a German convoy, but escaped without further damage. The worst damage came a few minutes later from a large flock of small birds. Just north of Heligoland the noise of his engine disturbed the birds who rose in a great swarm in front of the Mosquito. Before Scherf could do anything about it they tore holes in the wings and fuselage of the thin wooden fighter, but the resolute Mosquito flew on and made a safe landing at base.

This was really was Charlie Scherf's last trip, and brought his tally to twenty-three and a half enemy aircraft destroyed – fourteen and a half in the air and nine on the ground – and a further seven damaged. He was awarded a Bar to his D.F.C. in May, 1944, and the D.S.O. in July, 1944, when his 'great skill, enterprise and fearlessness' were noted in official citations.

In September, 1944, Squadron Leader Scherf returned to Australia to serve as a flying instructor at Number 5 O.T.U., Williamtown, New South Wales. He was released from the Royal Australian Air Force in April, 1945, to return to primary production. He was killed in an unfortunate motor accident at Emmaville, New South Wales, in July, 1949.

32

POLISH HAWK-EYE

Wing Commander S. Skalski
D.S.O., D.F.C. and Two Bars

ALTHOUGH he was born in Kodyma, Russia, on the 27th November, 1915, Stanislaw Skalski moved to Poland when he was still a baby and was educated at a Polish village school and later at Lubno College. He had decided long before he finished his schooling that he wanted to make his career in aviation and consequently on New Year's Day, 1936, he enlisted in the Polish Air Force. After a long period of training, he eventually qualified as a pilot and was overjoyed to find himself posted to Number 142 Squadron, the well-known 'Wild Ducks' Fighter Squadron.

When Germany invaded Poland, the P. 11 fighters of the Wild Ducks were instantly scrambled to meet the German onslaught. Ten years earlier the P. 11 had been hailed as a really first-class fighter aircraft, but in 1939 it was almost obsolete; its top speed of 200 m.p.h. meant that it was only about half as fast as Germany's Messerschmitts and that it could just about keep up with the Luftwaffe's bombers. Nevertheless, in the hands of Skalski and his comrades of 142 Squadron, the P. 11's at first proved themselves more than a match for the Luftwaffe, until eventually the sheet numerical superiority of the Germans began to take its toll.

On the 2nd September, 1939, the Wild Ducks met the Luftwaffe in combat for the first time. Pilot Officer Skalski was the first to see the Huns and waggling his wings, he banked sharply to port and led three P. 11's to attack a formation of seven Dornier 17's. Approaching the bombers head-on, in spite of the concentrated fire of the nose guns of the leading Huns, he held his fire until the very last moment and then as the leading Dornier filled his gun sight he pressed the trigger and fired a burst from his two machine guns, breaking away at the very last split second to avoid ramming the Dornier. As he pulled his little gull-like fighter round to make another attack he saw the leading bomber plunge into a field with a terrific explosion. There was no time to congratulate himself on his first victory, for already he was closing on another Dornier, the sun behind him blinding the German rear-gunners. At a hundred and fifty yards' range he opened fire again and flames spurted from the Dornier's starboard engine. As he closed to less than fifty yards Skalski fired two more short, sharp bursts and the Dornier fell away into a spin, which was only arrested when it crashed into the ground. The rest of the German formation were now too far away for Skalski to stand a chance to catching up with them, so he turned away to return to his base.

For the next fifteen days Skalski was in action continuously against the ever-increasing numbers of Messerschmitts, Junkers and Heinkels of the Luftwaffe, and before his gallant little fighter plane was put out of action by dive-bombers, Stanislaw had managed to shoot down three more enemy machines. With the defeat of Poland now imminent, the Polish ace made his way with a number of other airmen to the Mediterranean and was lucky enough to find a ship which brought him to London.

Enlisting in the Royal Air Force in January, 1940, Skalski was posted to a flying school for a conversion course on Hurricanes and Spitfires and on 27th August, 1940, joined Number 501 Hurricane Squadron. With his modern monoplane fighter Skalski was now able to meet the Luftwaffe on equal terms, at least as regards the types of aircraft flown, if not in numerical equality. On the morning of the 30th August he opened his score in England when he shot down a Heinkel 111 east of Dungeness, and the same afternoon he damaged another Heinkel near Southend. During the next few days his log book recorded an Me. 109 shot down near Gravesend on the 31st August, an Me. 110 damaged over Tunbridge Wells on the 1st September and two Me. 109's shot to pieces over South Ashford on the following day.

The next time he encountered the enemy it was Skalski's turn to be shot down. On the 5th September he was so badly shot up by bullets and cannon shell splinters that he had to spend several weeks in hospital, before he rejoined 501 Squadron.

In the spring of 1941 he was transferred as a Flying Officer to the all-Polish Hurricane Squadron, Number 303. Victories eluded him for a time, but on the 24th July he got a Messerschmitt 109 near Gravelines and a month later during another sweep over Northern France he shot down another 109.

In September, 1941, Skalski was given command of a flight and on the 17th led his flight in an encounter which took them from Lens to Dunkirk, during which Skalski himself accounted for two more Messerschmitt single-seaters. These were his last victories on this particular tour of operations and brought his score to thirteen enemy aircraft destroyed. They also led to the award of the Distinguished Flying Cross and further Polish decorations to add to his Silver Cross and Cross of Valour.

After a rest period as a flying instructor, Skalski was given command of Number 317 (Polish) Squadron in April, 1942, and immediately was back in the thick of the fighting, adding a Focke-Wulf 190 to his bag on the 10th April, and scoring hits on a Messerschmitt 109 a fortnight later. Skalski was by this time the top-scoring Polish pilot still on operational duty with the R.A.F. and as a result of this and his wide knowledge of air fighting he was awarded a Bar to his D.F.C. and then requested by the Polish authorities, with the co-operation of the Air Ministry, to form a unit of veteran Polish fighter pilots. He chose his pilots carefully, trained them skilfully and early in 1943 took his 'Polish Fighting Team', to the Middle East where they became attached to one of the R.A.F.'s top-scoring squadrons, Number 145, then under the command of the American ace, 'Wildcat' Wade.

Within a few weeks 'Skalski's Circus' had scored twenty-five confirmed victories over the Western Desert, Skalski personally having disposed of four of them during the month of April alone. On the 8th May, Skalski became the first Polish pilot to lead an English Squadron when he was given command of the well-known Number 601 Auxiliary Squadron, which he led throughout the final operations in North Africa and during the invasion of Italy.

Returning to England during the winter of 1943, Skalski received a second Bar to his D.F.C. and the Polish Gold Cross. He received further promotion to the acting rank of Wing Commander and in April, 1944, took command of Number Two (Polish) Fighter Wing.

For the next three months he led his P. 51 Mustangs on numerous long-range fighter operations deep into France and the Low countries, destroying four more enemy aircraft, thus bringing his total bag to twenty-two and a quarter confirmed victories and establishing himself as the leading Polish ace of the war.

His last two victories were most unusual because he never fired a single shot. It happened on the 30th June, when Wing Commander Skalski was leading twenty of his Mustangs on a dive-bombing mission to a target north-east of Paris. Just as they dived to release their bombs, the Poles were attacked by a group of sixty Me. 109's and F.W. 190's from several thousand feet above them. The enemy fighters were undoubtedly hoping to catch the Mustangs just as they began to pull out of their dives. Before the Luftwaffe fighters could reach them, however, the Poles released their bombs on the target and began to gain height, turning towards the Huns to meet them head-on. The enemy formation immediately broke up into small groups, and dogfights began all over the place. Two Focke-Wulf 190's, flying side by side, came in at Skalski with guns blazing, but he skilfully avoided them and then quickly slid his Mustang round to make his own attack. As he closed in and lined up the pair in his sights, he was suddenly amazed to see them converge on each other, collide and fall, locked together, twisting slowly and shedding pieces. Skalski watched, fascinated by the sight until the pair hit the ground with a terrific explosion, and then quickly realising he was in a very dangerous position beneath the other Huns, climbed to rejoin the fight.

By the time he had reached the main dogfight it was all over, the Poles had destroyed six of the enemy, damaged another four and put the rest to flight. Skalski's pair were later confirmed by several of his pilots and he was no doubt very thankful, for who would believe a man who claimed two destroyed without even firing a single shot.

This incredible flight occurred during one of Skalski's last operational missions for shortly afterwards he was posted to the Advanced Gunnery School at Catfoss where, in the company of such redoubtable fighters as 'Sailor' Malan, 'Screwball' Beurling, Pierre Clostermann and Don Kingaby, he helped to evolve new fighter tactics.

The award of his Distinguished Service Order was announced a few days before the war ended and then this great Polish fighter left the Royal Air Force to return to his native country, where he was put in prison by the Russians. He was released later on and began work on his autobiography, which was eventually published under the title of *Black Crosses over Poland*. It must be a most thrilling and exciting story and perhaps one day it will be translated into English, so that we can all enjoy the experiences of a Polish ace in the Royal Air Force.

33

EIGHT VICTORIES IN ONE DAY

Wing Commander H. M. Stephen
D.S.O., D.F.C. and Bar

THE only man to score eight victories in air combat in one day
and the first man in Britain to receive the immediate award in
the field of the Distinguished Service Order, Harbourne Mackay
Stephen was born on the 18th April, 1916, at Elgin in Scotland,
and educated at schools in Elgin, Edinburgh and Shrewsbury.
After leaving school he became a copy boy with Allied Newspapers in London, and later on joined the advertising staff of the
Evening Standard. He took an interest in flying and in 1937
joined the Royal Air Force Volunteer Reserve, learning to fly
during weekends at Maidenhead. He seemed to be a born flyer,
for after only nine hours' dual instruction he made his first solo
flight. He graduated later to Hawker Harts, training to be a
fighter pilot, and due to the foresight of Mr T. Blackburn – then
General Manager of the *Evening Standard* and now Chairman
of the *Daily Express* – he was given leave of absence to take a
course on Hawker Hurricanes. When the time came and he was
due to return to his office, war was so imminent that all trainees
were retained, so that at the declaration of war he was already
with a fighter squadron as an operational pilot.

Commissioned in April, 1940, he was posted to 605 Squadron,
but soon left to join 74 Squadron. He went into action immediately taking part in the intensive air operations over the
French coast during the evacuation from Dunkirk. Although he
took part in many air battles at this time he failed to shoot down
his first Hun until the end of July. On the 28th the squadron
attacked thirty-six Me. 109's at 18,000 feet over Dover, destroying seven of them; Stephen accounted for one of these. It
was the beginning of a brilliant period of air fighting for the
young Scot, for during the next fortnight he destroyed eleven
more enemy aircraft. The period culminated on the 11th August
with an astonishing day's fighting, during which Stephen destroyed three Me. 109's and two Me. 110's, probably destroyed

another 109, and damaged two more, thus establishing a record score of eight victories in a single day's fighting.

His first victories were scored in his first fight at about 8 o'clock when the squadron intercepted a number of Me. 109's approaching Dover. Stephen attacked one, which fell into the Channel, and closed on a second, which after a very short burst from close range exploded in mid-air. He then chased two more 109's, one of which fell away shedding pieces, but he did not see this one crash so he only claimed it as a probable. Later he used up the rest of his ammunition on another 109 which he claimed as damaged. After breakfast Stephen took off on his second sortie, but due to wireless trouble failed to make contact with the enemy, although other members of the squadron had a scrap.

On his third mission the squadron spotted about forty Me. 110's approaching a convoy about twelves miles east of Clacton. As they closed on the enemy formation, the German planes formed up into an enormous circle, presumably with the object of guarding each other's tails. The Spitfires dived into the middle of the circle and then swung up and round in a circle going in the opposite direction to the Me. 110's. Within a few seconds the Germans broke in all directions. Stephen caught one with a long burst which caused the 110 to spin down in flames, and then attacked another 110 which began violent evasive action. The young Scot followed every move it made, determined not to be put off by the Hun, and eventually, after several minutes of twisting and turning, got in a burst which caused the 110 to spiral down into the Channel. Stephen now attacked another Me. 110 and scored several hits on its fuselage before breaking away to refuel and rearm.

The day was not yet over for Stephen, however, for ninety minutes later he was following his Squadron Leader into another fight with ten Ju. 87's and twenty Me. 109's near Margate. Stephen was detailed to attack the fighters and after a few moments found himself on the tail of one of the 109's. He fired – the 109 slowed and then dived away. Stephen followed, firing in short bursts, and eventually the German pilot baled out and his machine crashed in flames.

Mainly because of his great feat on the 11th August, young Stephen was awarded the Distinguished Flying Cross. The citation to the award stated that he 'has always displayed great coolness and determination in pressing home his attacks against the enemy'.

The squadron was sent to Wittering a few days later for a rest period, but on September 11th when they returned to Duxford the handsome Scot won fresh honours. He attacked a Junkers 88 which he badly damaged, before he was forced to leave it when a 109 intervened.

In October, 74 Squadron moved south to Biggin Hill again and immediately were caught up in the thick of the fighting. Stephen and his flight commander, Flight Lieutenant J. C. Mungo-Park, D.F.C. and Bar, were airborne on the 20th October when they found about thirty Me. 109's near Maidstone. Stephen attacked a bunch of four who immediately dived away towards Dungeness. He finally caught up with the last of the four and opened fire. The cockpit hood flew off and the tail shot away, before Stephen had to swing away as the other three Messerschmitts were climbing to get above him. In the general mêlée that followed, he got on the tail of another 109 and, after several quick bursts, the enemy pilot baled out and the 109 crashed into a wood. The other two 109's made off in a hurry.

Stephen sent another 109 down in flames over Maidstone a week later, when he was leading 'A' Flight for the first time, and soon after this he received a Bar to his D.F.C. for his 'courage and skill as a fighter pilot which have been a great incentive to other pilots in his squadron'.

On November 14th, Stephen shot down three Ju. 87's in a few minutes when the squadron intercepted a mixed formation of Stukas and Me. 109's over Dover. The Scot attacked a section of three Stukas and after one short burst one of them swung over and smacked into the Stuka close to it. Both fell away locked together until they hit the sea with a tremendous explosion. Stephen meanwhile had attacked the last machine of the trio and, after several well-aimed bursts, this went down to join its companions in their watery grave. Three days later Stephen sent an Me. 109 into the waves near Brighton Pier.

By this time the station score-board at Biggin Hill was nearing the six hundred mark, and quite naturally every pilot on the station was hoping it would fall to his lot to shoot down the Station's 600th victim, especially as everyone on the aerodrome had subscribed for a handsome present to the lucky pilot. The honour, and the prize, were shared by Stephen and Mungo-Park. Many fantastic tales have been told about this particular engagement and the events leading up to it, but these are the true facts about it as told by Stephen himself.

Somewhere between 10 p.m. and 2 a.m. on the 30th November, in the midst of a typical mess party, the total number of German aeroplanes credited to the station was confirmed as 599. Much secrecy was being observed to prevent cheating and no one definitely knew what the real score stood at. However, Mungo-Park seemed to sense that the next flight was the important one and in spite of a terrible hangover next morning, common to both of us, insisted that we took off on the first sortie of the day.

When daylight came it was wonderful to find a thick fog, so all the 'early' pilots climbed back into their beds at the dispersal huts and continued to sleep. Somewhere around 8 a.m. the operations staff rang through to advise us that a small convoy in the Channel was being attacked by German fighter bombers. They added that they knew there was nothing we could do about it as Biggin Hill was covered by fog. What the operational staff did not know, as they were in their underground control room, was that the fog was only a few hundred feet thick, for above it we could see clear blue sky. The problem was not to get up into the air but how to get the aeroplanes down again in one piece. However, as the Operations Controller asked for two volunteers to go and give some moral support to the convoy, irrespective of whether we could do anything to help, it gave us an opportunity of going after our 600th German and the fog gave us a good excuse in case we broke our Spitfires trying to land in fog back at base.

Above the fog-blanketed countryside as we flew towards the enemy we saw coming from Northern France a whole German fighter wing. Once in the air we found a most beautiful autumn day, with crystal-clear visibility and deep blue sky – a most exhilarating sensation. We decided that with a little skill we ought to be able to get ourselves one German out of this particular sweep which they were making over the southern counties, if only because we were two alone and unexpected. With caution we flew below them across the Channel and over Northern France. Turning back and round near Ramsgate we found ourselves at long last in front of the returning Germans and above them. We carefully selected a 109 on the edge of one of the outside formations whilst flying at 34,000 feet. I opened fire with a short burst from the starboard beam. Then Mungo-Park fired and I swung round to come in from astern, pieces flying off the Hun as I opened fire. The Messerschmitt rolled over and I followed, closing to about twenty yards' range, when after another three-second burst, the 109 dived inverted into a cloud doing at least 450 m.p.h.

The Messerschmitt crash-landed near Dungeness and the pilot, who was still alive, was lifted out of his plane and taken to the local hospital where he died a few hours later.

At this particular time, to shoot down an aircraft at a height in excess of 30,000 feet was regarded as being pretty chancy and extremely lucky. There is no question that this particular engagement was fought at the highest altitude up to this time, and the two victorious pilots thoroughly deserved their prize and the congratulations of their comrades.

Early in December, 1940, Stephen received the first ever immediate award in the field of the Distinguished Service Order for 'his exceptional courage and skill'. Soon after this he brought his personal score to twenty-two and a half destroyed and was then posted to Turnhouse in Scotland to join Number 59 O.T.U. as a Flight Lieutenant and Chief Flying Instructor.

Stephen helped to form Number 130 Squadron in 1941, and towards the end of the year was given command of Number 234 Squadron, which he led to Burma in 1942. Subsequently, he was given command of Number One-six-six Fighter Wing at Jessore, in Bengal, and then served on Fighter Operations with Number Two-two-four Group in Arakan, before returning to England in 1945.

On resigning his commission in the Royal Air Force in 1946, he rejoined the staff of the *Scottish Sunday Express*. In 1959, after being on the staff of Beaverbrook Newspapers for over twenty years, he was invited by Mr. Roy Thomson to join Thomson Newspapers Limited and today is General Manager of this organisation.

34

'I AM NOT DEAD YET!'

Group Captain M. M. Stephens
D.S.O., D.F.C. and Two Bars

ON THE 17th May, 1961, one of Britain's well-known newspapers reported the death of a famous wartime fighter pilot and gave a brief obituary. Later in the day the News Editor picked up the telephone and, to his considerable surprise, a voice said:

'I wish to fault this news item on three counts – (a) I am *not* a Squadron Leader and have not been one for nineteen years; (b) I am not forty-two, but forty-one years old; and (c) I am not dead yet!'

The gentleman who telephoned the News Editor with this

interesting information was Group Captain M. M. Stephens, D.S.O., D.F.C. and Two Bars.

The youngest son of a retired army officer who had spent most of his service career in India, Maurice Michael Stephens was born in Ranchi, India, on the 20th October, 1919, but returned to England at an early age and was educated at Mayfield College in Sussex. His elder brothers, Richard and Jack, soon followed in the military footsteps of their father, by joining the Royal Air Force, and consequently Michael was keen to join them. Just before his nineteenth birthday in 1938, young Mike was accepted for the Royal Air Force College at Cranwell. But the outbreak of war a year later meant that the tempo of training had to be speeded up, and so it was just fifteen months later, Christmas, 1939, that together with the other cadets of his entry, he emerged from Cranwell as a fully trained Pilot Officer.

His elder brother, Jack, had already flown Blenheims in the earliest raids of the war on Wilhelmshaven, Kiel and Heligoland, and was awarded the D.F.C. and Bar before being shot down, wounded and taken prisoner in June, 1940. Richard had also gone to Bomber Command as a Navigator/Bomb Aimer. But for once Michael had no desire to follow the ways of his brothers. He wanted to be a fighter pilot. His wish was granted, for soon after leaving Cranwell he was on his way to Kenley aerodrome to join Number 3 Fighter Squadron, where he took possession of a brand new Hawker Hurricane. Within a few weeks he had mastered the intricacies of the Hurricane and was throwing it about the sky as if he and the machine had been moulded together. The eagerness, common to all the fighter pilots based in England during the so-called 'phoney war', to get to grips with the enemy had to be contained for several months. It was in fact on the 10th May, 1940, the day that the 'phoney war' became the 'blitzkrieg' with the invasion of France and the Low Countries, that his squadron was ordered to France to provide air support for the hard-pressed British Expeditionary Force. Within minutes of landing at their new base at Merville in Northern France, the squadron's Hurricanes were refuelled and in action. Before the day had ended Number 3 Squadron had scored its first victories and suffered its first losses in men and machines. The squadron's list of victories grew rapidly during the next few days of continuous, hectic scrapping, but its casualties were also heavy, and after the first four days Mike Stephens found himself commanding a flight, and was made an Acting Flight Lieutenant.

By the time the German advance had forced the squadron's withdrawal from France on the 25th May, Mike Stephens was no longer a youthful pilot with dreams of meeting the Hun in the skies. He was now a tired, well-blooded veteran of air combat, with nine German aircraft to his credit and the ribbons of the Distinguished Flying Cross and Bar to testify to his courage, skill and fine leadership.

When Number 3 Squadron, or rather what was left of it, returned to England, it was ordered to a fighter station on the north to reorganise itself and to bring its quota of men and aircraft up to full strength again. Some of its seasoned fighter pilots, however, left the squadron in order to give the benefits of their experiences in France to other new squadrons which were being formed. It was in this capacity that Mike Stephens, newly promoted to Squadron Leader, went to Wick in August, 1940, to form and command a new Hurricane squadron, Number 232. When the squadron became operational, its activities were mainly limited to defensive patrols over Scotland and the North of England, and it was during one of these that Mike shot down his next victim, a German raider which had attempted to attack the British fleet in Scapa Flow.

In December, 1940, Mike Stephens volunteered to join the British Expeditionary Force in Greece. He left England later in the same month in the aircraft carrier *Furious* with a complement of Hurricanes. On arrival in the Middle East, the pilots from the carrier were diverted to the Western Desert, where they were used to reinforce existing squadrons. Mike joined Number 274 Squadron, with which he served for a time before being pulled out to go to Turkey, then under threat of invasion by the Germans. He flew for several months with Turkish Hurricane Squadrons near the Bulgarian frontier, before returning to the Western Desert in November, 1941, to take command of Number 80 Squadron.

He commanded the squadron for less than three weeks before he was shot down and wounded outside Tobruk. He had just led his squadron in a bombing and strafing attack on German transport near Acroma on the 9th December, when he noticed a dogfight in progress overhead, so he climbed up to join in the combat. Avoiding the attacks of two Me. 109's who dived on him, he spotted a Hurricane with a 109 on its tail. Speeding to the rescue, he opened fire, but had to break off as another 109 came in behind him. A cannon shell exploded in his starboard petrol tank, setting it on fire, and another blew out the starboard side

170

of his cockpit and at the same time Mike was wounded in both feet. Pushing back the cockpit hood he was just about to bale out, when the Messerschmitt overshot the Hurricane, and presented itself as an easy target. Scrambling back into his seat, in spite of the intense heat from his burning aircraft, Stephens lined up the Hun in his sights, pressed the gun button and shot down the 109 in flames. He then jumped over the side and, as he floated downwards, beat out the flames on his clothing. He landed within three hundred yards of the German lines, but for some unknown reason the enemy did not fire at him as he crawled and hobbled towards the Allied lines. After forty-five minutes he was met by a number of Polish soldiers who brought him safely back to friendly territory.

Squadron Leader Stephens was still in Tobruk hospital recovering from his wounds in January, 1942, when the news came through that he had been awarded an immediate Distinguished Service Order for the 'great courage and devotion to duty' displayed by him during this fight.

When he finally left the hospital, Mike was still temporarily unfit for flying so was given a staff appointment at R.A.F. Headquarters, East Africa, in Nairobi.

In the autumn of 1942 he returned to the Middle East and was attached for some time to the United States Fifty-seventh Pursuit Group, which had recently arrived from the United States and was training in Palestine. Anxious to get back on operations, Mike volunteered to go to Malta, was accepted and for the first time flew Spitfires on operations. He joined Number 249 Squadron at Takali, but had only been with the squadron three days when he was shot down into the sea midway between Malta and Sicily on the 12th October. Squadron Leader Stephens described the incident as follows:

We had been scrambled soon after first light to intercept an incoming raid, and had become tangled with a bunch of 109's. In the ensuing dogfight I shot down two 109's and as so often happened found myself alone. I saw a single Spitfire in the distance and headed towards it with the object of joining up and making a pair, when I was surprised by a single 109 which I saw just too late. He scored a hit on my engine, which started smoking and eventually came to a grinding halt. In the meantime the 109 had headed for home, as soon as I turned into his attack. After my engine cut I had plenty of time to transmit for a fix before baling out. I spent a long time in the water floundering around, as the air bottle of my dinghy was flat, but eventually managed to climb aboard and finish inflating it with the

171

bellows. I had a grandstand view of quite a number of combats during which I saw four aircraft shot down. I was quite confident throughout that I should be picked up by our Air/Sea Rescue Service, which was quite magnificent. Eventually I was rescued by a seaplane tender, since all the Air/Sea Rescue boats were already out. There was quite a heavy sea swell and I was as sick as a dog after I had been picked up by the boat.

The following day Squadron Leader Stephens must have made a complete recovery, for during an engagement in the afternoon south-east of Kalafrana he sent down a Junkers 88 in flames and then caused the pilot of a Macchi 202 to bale out.

After four days with Number 249 Squadron, during which he had destroyed four enemy aircraft, probably destroyed one and damaged several more, Stephens was given command of Number 229, another Spitfire squadron which was also stationed on the same airfield at Takali.

During the afternoon of the day on which he took over the squadron, he led it into two battles against the Luftwaffe, in which he destroyed an Re. 2001, and damaged two Junkers 88's. The following day, October 15th, he had another exciting combat. Leading a section of Spitfires on the early morning patrol, he had attacked a pair of Junkers 88's, causing one of them to fall into the sea. He was then attacked by six Me. 109's and an unlucky hit put his radio out of action. In an effort to evade the Messerschmitts, Stephens flew flat out at an altitude of less than ten feet, but the 109's persisted with their attacks and Mike had to continually break into them, firing whenever the opportunity occurred. In this way he was able not only to avoid most of the enemy's fire, but also to send one of the Messerschmitts into the sea. When he crossed Grand Harbour with its tremendous barrage of anti-aircraft fire, the Messerschmitts finally left him and Mike thankfully brought in his badly battered Spitfire for a belly landing at Takali.

A few days later Mike was awarded his fourth 'gong', a second Bar to his D.F.C. The official citation to the decoration had this to say of Squadron Leader Stephens: 'This officer has greatly enhanced the gallant reputation he so worthily holds'. At the same time the *Malta Times* described him as 'an exceptional pilot and leader, who has no hesitation in attacking the enemy whatever the odds'.

Squadron Leader Stephens continued to lead Number 229 Squadron for several months until after the siege of Malta had finally been raised and plans were afoot for the invasion of

Sicily. He was then promoted Wing Commander Flying at Halfar, Malta, until June, 1943, when he completed his final tour of operations. He had flown a total of 350 hours on operations and during this time had destroyed twenty-two aircraft, and probably destroyed a further seventeen.

On his return to the United Kingdom, Wing Commander Stephens attended the Empire Central Flying School at Hullavington and after a flying instructor's course became Chief Flying Instructor at Number 3 Operational Training Unit Flying Instructors' School in January, 1944. Here he remained, despite many attempts to get back on operations, until just before the end of the war when he was posted to the United States for liaison duties with the U.S.A.A.F. He returned to Britain soon after the war with Japan finished in August, 1945, and went to the Royal Air Force Staff College. Mike Stephens remained in the R.A.F. after the war and had reached the rank of Group Captain when he retired in November, 1960, to take up an appointment with Rolls-Royce (Aero-Engine Division) in Europe.

35

'TUCKIE'

Wing Commander R. R. S. Tuck
D.S.O., D.F.C. and Two Bars, D.F.C. (U.S.A.)

ROBERT ROLAND STANFORD TUCK was born in Catford, London, on the 1st July, 1916, the son of Stanley Lewis Tuck and Ethel Constance Tuck. He was educated at St Dunstan's Preparatory School, Reading, and later at St Dunstan's College. On leaving school in 1932, having already decided to go to sea, he joined the Lamport and Holt Line as a cadet. He was happy for a time until he became interested in flying, and then in September, 1935, he forsook the sea and joined the Royal Air Force.

By August, 1936, he had qualified as a pilot and was posted to Number 65 (East India) Squadron at Hornchurch as a newly commissioned Pilot Officer. In 1938 he was promoted to Flying Officer and, soon after the war broke out, was made a Flight

Commander. He was a Flight Commander with Number 92 Squadron when he first went into action against the Germans early in May, 1940. The squadron was patrolling over the coast of North Belgium when they encountered a large formation of Me. 109's. They tore into the German fighter pack and in a few minutes had shot down five Me. 109's for the loss of one pilot. Bob Tuck shot down one of them, his first confirmed victory, into a field near St Omer.

On a second patrol on the same day in the same area, the squadron attacked a number of Junkers 87's, who were escorted by about thirty Me. 110's. Tuck was detailed to engage the fighters and in a few minutes had positioned himself for a stern attack on a 110. He opened fire and the Messerschmitt plunged vertically down with flames leaping from its engines and wings. The Spitfire had followed the Hun down to tree-top height and now Tuck found another 110. After a chase lasting several minutes, Tuck put the German rear-gunner out of action and then the Messerschmitt crash-landed in a field. Tuck was just circling about fifty feet over the wreck when suddenly the German pilot jumped out of the cockpit, apparently unhurt, and fired at the Spitfire with a pistol. He was either a magnificent shot or very lucky, for one bullet went through the windscreen of Tuck's Spitfire and passed within an inch or so of his head. Tuck viciously swung his Spitfire round in the tightest of turns and stabbed the trigger of his eight Browning guns; he very quickly had his revenge as the German collapsed at the side of his wrecked machine.

Three Huns in his first day in action was by any standard an exceptionally good start and whetted Tuck's appetite for more. Consequently he was out again on the following day patrolling over the same area, which had already proved so fruitful. This time, however, he was leading a squadron, for Squadron Leader Bushell had been shot down during the previous day's operations and Bob Tuck had immediately been given command of the squadron. The squadron had not been over the French coast very long before they spotted a formation of twenty Dornier 17's with an escort of Messerschmitt 110's. A Hurricane squadron conveniently took on the Messerschmitts, so Tuck ordered his own squadron to attack the bombers. He himself throttled right back and approached the Dorniers slowly from the rear, in order to give himself more time to adjust his aim. He opened fire at four hundred yards' range and immediately scored hits on the port engine, wing root and fuselage of one of the Dorniers. It left the enemy formation shedding bits and pieces. Tuck followed, but as he was about to open fire again he felt a sharp pain in his thigh. Disregarding this, Tuck closed in quickly and pressed the firing button once more. Black smoke poured from the bomber, two of its crew baled out and the next moment it was enveloped in flames. Tuck headed for the rest of the Dorniers and soon picked out another victim. As he closed in from the rear of the Dornier, it suddenly went into a shallow dive, closely followed by the relentless Tuck who kept up an incessant series of short bursts of gunfire. The Dornier never faltered. It kept on straight down at the same angle until it hit the beach and exploded. By this time Tuck was very low both on fuel and ammunition, so he broke away and headed for home. Although he had lost quite a large amount of blood from his wound, he landed safely, walked to the Medical Room where his injured thigh was attended to, and then walked away to carry on with his other duties as Commanding Officer. The following day he was leading the squadron into action again, this time helping his new Flight Commander, Brian Kingcombe, to shoot down yet another Dornier.

Towards the end of May, 1940, the squadron was moved to Duxford and, during one of his first missions from this airfield on the 2nd June, Tuck led Number 92 and two other squadrons on a morning patrol over the Calais area. They found a bunch of Heinkel 111's escorted by fifty Me. 109's. Tuck shot down one of the Heinkels in his first attack, but was then set upon by six of the 109's. He escaped into some clouds, however, and then after a few seconds came out into clear sky again. He found another 109 and shot it down into the sea, using up all his ammunition in the process. He then broke away, set course and finally arrived at Biggin Hill with only five gallons of petrol left and five shell holes in his Spitfire.

In the middle of June, 1940, Number 92 Squadron was taken out of the main battle zone on the south-west coast and transferred to Pembrey in South Wales to rest and reorganise. Soon after his arrival in Wales, Tuck was awarded the first of his many decorations, the Distinguished Flying Cross. Although the squadron was still classified as operational and had to keep up a standing patrol over the coast of South Wales, the pilots rarely saw any German raiders apart from the odd, elusive reconnaissance machine, which always seemed able to escape into the clouds before the Spitfires could catch up with it.

About the middle of August, however, the squadron was suddenly called on to intercept an enemy raid approaching Portsmouth. In the subsequent engagement Tuck added a Junkers 88 destroyed and another damaged to his score. The very next day Tuck was patrolling at 15,000 feet over Cardiff when he encountered three Junkers 88's heading towards Ireland. He made several stern attacks, which seemed to have no effect on the Huns, so he came round for a head-on attack. He did much better this time, destroying two of them, and hitting the third with several bursts before it finally escaped into some clouds.

Tuck was returning from a flying visit to Northolt aerodrome some few days later when he ran into two Junkers 88's off Beachy Head. He chased one of them about thirty-five miles out to sea before he eventually shot it down. By this time he was right down to sea level and as he turned to deal with the second 88, it opened fire with its cannons. Tuck's Spitfire was hit in oil and glycol tanks and part of the propeller was shot away, causing a violent vibration. Tuck pulled the stick back hard and climbed, pushing the engine flat out, and had got back sixty miles before the engine caught fire and he had to bale out. He was only five hundred feet up when he jumped and his parachute only just had time to open before he landed, spraining his ankle.

A week later he was operating again on the morning patrol. He found a Dornier bombing shipping about fifteen miles off the Welsh coast, and in a few minutes had shot it down. As it dived earthwards, the rear-gunner of the Dornier got in a burst which put two holes in the cylinders of the Rolls Royce engine of the Spitfire. Tuck pulled away into a shallow dive towards the coast and by means of some excellent flying he just managed to crash-land his damaged fighter on the very edge of the cliffs near Tenby.

This was Tuck's last victory with Number 92 Squadron for early in September, 1940, he was given command of the celebrated Number 257 Burma Hurricane Squadron. He led his new squadron into action for the first time on the 15th September, when they found a big bunch of mixed bombers, flying in formation of anything from thirty to sixty aircraft, with escorting fighters above them. The squadron attacked the Huns as they neared London, Squadron Leader Tuck leading one flight against the fighters. He shot down one Me. 110 which crashed near Barking, and had caused pieces to fly off an Me. 109 before the battle was over.

A week later Tuck shot down an Me. 109 into the Thames Estuary, and on the 4th October destroyed a lone raider. On this latter occasion he had only been in the air about ten minutes when he was informed over the radio-telephone that there was a hostile aircraft near him. He had not finished acknowledging the information when his Hurricane emerged from a cloud and there right in the middle of his sights, not a hundred yards away, was a Junkers 88. He pressed the gun button and the 88 crashed near Southwold.

Now that the Battle of Britain had almost been won, things were very quiet for a time, so Tuck one day decided to pay a visit to his old squadron, Number 92. While he was there, the alarm sounded and 92 took off in their Spitfires to intercept. Tuck went with them and shot down a 109, the only victory scored on this particular sortie.

Bob Tuck's confirmed victories had risen to eighteen by the end of the year, when he was awarded the Distinguished Service Order, which he received from His Majesty the King at a ceremony on a big Coastal Command Station in Norfolk on the 28th January, 1941. Soon after this Tuck's Spitfire was fitted with cannons, which he used against the Luftwaffe for the first time on the 19th March, when he chased a Dornier 17 far out to sea before finally destroying it. On the last day of the month he was awarded a second Bar to his D.F.C., for 'his conspicuous gallantry and initiative in searching for and attacking enemy raiders, often in adverse weather conditions'.

During April the squadron took to patrolling at night as well as in the daylight, mainly because there was a great deal of activity at night and there seemed far more chance of meeting the Luftwaffe than in the daylight hours when they very rarely saw a hostile aircraft. On one of these night patrols, on the 9th April, Tuck found a single Junkers 88 which he promptly shot down into the sea just off Lowestoft.

He ran into trouble on the 21st June. He was flying alone on a routine patrol along the East Coast when he was jumped by three yellow-nosed Messerschmitt 109's. He shot down two of them into the sea and badly damaged the third, but during the fierce fighting his own Hurricane was so badly damaged that he had to bale out into the North Sea. He was picked up two hours later by a dirty old coastal vessel and the same evening was in hospital having his wounds dressed. Whilst his wounds were healing, Tuck was transferred to the Royal Navy for liaison work, but in the middle of July he returned to operations when he was promoted to command the Duxford Wing. It felt good to be flying a Spitfire again, especially as he could now take his wing to meet the Luftwaffe over their own territory. During the first sweep on which he led his new wing, he set them a fine example by shooting down a Messerschmitt 109 and damaging another.

Wing Commander Tuck continued to lead the Duxford Wing until October, 1941, when he was taken off operations and sent to the United States of America to give a series of lectures on air fighting, and also to advise the American aircraft industry on R.A.F. requirements. He spent about six weeks altogether on this goodwill tour of America and Canada, and then returned to England in December, 1941, to take command of the Biggin Hill Spitfire Wing. He destroyed two more enemy aircraft in January, 1942, to bring his final total to twenty-nine aircraft destroyed, eight probably destroyed and six damaged. Then, during a fighter sweep on the 28th January, 1942, his Spitfire was hit by anti-aircraft fire and he had to make a crash-landing near Boulogne. He was captured by some German soldiers and spent the next few years languishing in a prisoner-of-war camp.

Tuck refused to accept defeat even after being captured and finally in January, 1945, escaped from his prison camp. He joined up with the advancing Russian armies and was subsequently repatriated to Britain. Later on he left the Royal Air Force to take up a position with Marconi's and now lives with his wife and two children in a small village in Kent.

36

'THE WILDCAT FROM TEXAS'

Wing Commander L. C. Wade
D.S.O., D.F.C. and Two Bars

'You are not capable of being a fighter pilot', said the American ace of the First World War to a Texan youth of seventeen, who had just taken off for his first solo flight.

But that same veteran pilot, if he had lived, would have regretted making such a statement, for the Texas youth did eventually become a fighter pilot, and a very good one too. So good, in fact, that by the end of 1943 he had become the top-scoring American fighter pilot in the Royal Air Force with twenty-five enemy aircraft to his credit. He had risen to the rank of Wing Commander and become the only American pilot ever to win a Distinguished Service Order and a Distinguished Flying Cross with two Bars. He had never been shot down by an enemy plane and during two tours of operations in the Middle East he had shot down practically every type of aircraft employed by the Germans and Italians in this area. Even official citations, which are noted for their understatements, referred to him as an 'outstanding pilot' and the men who flew with him in the desert thought so highly of his qualities as a fighter ace, that they affectionately dubbed him 'The Wildcat from Texas'.

Lance Wade, to give him his correct name, was born in Tucson, Texas, in 1915, the son of a pilot who flew in the first world was as a member of the legendary 'Lafayette Escadrille' which played such a large part in American aviation history. Because his father was a flyer, young Lance naturally became interested in flying and in 1933 he flew an aircraft for the first time. Three years later he had saved enough money to buy his own aircraft which he flew whenever the opportunity came. By the time the Second World War started Lance Wade was quite an experienced pilot and, following in his adventurous father's footsteps, he volunteered to go to war as a fighter pilot. In December, 1940, he arrived in England and joined the Royal Air Force, who at this particular time were sadly in need of experienced pilots.

A course in learning to fly the modern fighters of the R.A.F. followed, and then Wade found himself on a boat bound for the Middle East. He arrived in Egypt in September, 1941, and was immediately posted to Number 33 Squadron, which had made a reputation for itself in the campaign in Greece, but was now reforming after losing all its aircraft and many of its pilots during the furious fighting in Greece and Crete. By the autumn of 1941 the squadron was fully operational again and its Hurricanes took off in support of the Eighth Army in the Western Desert campaign.

On one of his first missions in October, 1941, Lance Wade shot down two Fiat C.R. 42's in one dogfight and after this victories came regularly to this unusually modest American. One day in November he took off with five other Hurricanes from 33 Squadron to defend a forward airfield which was being attacked by a dozen Junkers 88's. Within a short time the enemy formation had been routed and Pilot Officer Wade had added a Junkers 88 to his victories. On the 24th November, on his second sortie, Wade and another pilot intercepted a Savoia 79 bomber escorted by six C.R. 42's. The two Hurricanes went for the fighters first, but these soon disappeared after the two Hurricanes had put the fear of death into them by the fury of their first onslaught – and after Wade had damaged two of them with accurate bursts of fire. The Savoia was now helpless without its escort and a few seconds later was spinning down in flames.

On the 5th December, Wade himself was brought down. The squadron had made a strafing raid on the enemy airfield at Agedabia, during which Wade had set fire to three Caproni bombers on the ground. He then noticed a Savoia 79 bomber flying very low and closed in to make an attack from astern. As he fired the Italian bomber exploded in a blinding flash and the next moment Wade was struggling to regain control of his Hurricane which had been caught by the full force of the explosion.

When he finally straightened out and had time to inspect the damage to his plane, he quickly realised he would have to abandon it. He was too low to bale out and had not enough power to climb, so he struggled on in an effort to reach the British lines before his engine packed up altogether. But, too soon, the engine came to a grinding halt and Wade had to put the Hurricane down in a belly landing whilst still twenty-five miles from the British Army's forward positions. He set fire to his fighter and then settled down to walk home to his squadron, which he rejoined a little over twenty-four hours later, none the worse for his experience apart from a few blisters. He was not used to walking the marathon in flying boots!

On the 7th February, 1942, Pilot Officer Wade was awarded the Distinguished Flying Cross. He had by this time carried out fifty-four operational missions, and he had 'displayed outstanding courage' and had 'done much to maintain the excellent morale of the Squadron'.

The short rest from operations that followed proved a real tonic to the American and he began his second tour with a double victory on the 28th May, 1942, when he shot down a Junkers 87 and a Macchi 202. On June 9th he destroyed a Messerschmitt 109 over Bir Hakeim. Two days later his own Hurricane was hit by anti-aircraft fire and he had to make a forced-landing. Again he had to walk back to rejoin his squadron. The following month he shot down two Me. 109's and a Junkers 88, and for a short time acted as deputy commander of the squadron.

He got his twelfth kill, another Me. 109 (this, incidentally, was the 200th enemy aircraft to be shot down by members of Number 33 Squadron in the Second World War), on the 2nd September and soon after this had another narrow escape. He was returning from a lone reconnaissance mission during which he had sent down a Junkers 87 in flames when he was ambushed by eight Italian fighters. He avoided their attacks so skilfully, however, that after a running dogfight which lasted several minutes, but felt like an eternity to Wade, they finally gave up and the American was able to make a successful return.

By the middle of October, Wade had brought his total victories to fifteen, and he was awarded a Bar to his D.F.C. Shortly afterwards he was promoted to Squadron Leader and left 33 Squadron to take command of 145 Squadron, who for the next few months were continually on the move, as they chased after the rapidly retreating enemy. They finally caught up with them in March, 1943, when the squadron settled in at Medanine. In less than a month the squadron destroyed twenty-one enemy aircraft, of which Squadron Leader Wade personally accounted for four. This led to the award of a second Bar to his D.F.C.

During April, 1943, Wade shot down two Huns without much trouble and during May accounted for two more, but during both of these fights his own Spitfire was damaged. On the first occasion he was leading 145 Squadron, who were acting as top-cover for Kittyhawks raiding shipping in the Gulf of Tunis, when they were attacked by Me. 109's. He shot down one of the Messerschmitts before his own Spitfire was hit several times by cannon shells.

'It was a gamble whether I baled out or tried to fly the aircraft back,' Wade said later.

He eventually decided on the latter course and made a successful landing at base thirty minutes later.

A few days later he was again leading his squadron providing top-cover for fighter bombers, looking for enemy shipping off the Tunisian coast near Cap Bon. They sighted a dozen Me. 109's about ten miles to the west and immediately Wade led half of his squadron to engage them. He shot down a 109, his twenty-third kill, before his Spitfire was again hit. His aileron was torn to pieces by a cannon shell, the glycol tank perforated and his engine began to smoke, but again Wade elected to remain in his fighter and again he flew it safely back to base.

In July, 1943, Wade received further promotion to Wing Commander and took charge of a Spitfire Wing which he led during operations over Sicily and Italy. He flew his last operational mission on the 3rd November when, whilst flying with only one other pilot, Wade attacked a score of Me. 109's and F.W. 190's over the Eighth Army lines in Italy. The American damaged three of the enemy fighters and his companion destroyed one before having to break off the engagement. At one time in the fight Wade had seven enemy aircraft attacking him. Pulling out every trick he knew he led the Huns at deck level along a valley and saw their fire spatter the rocks on either side of him. At every opportunity he got in a burst as he forced them to overshoot and in this way scored hits on three of the fighters.

The next day Wing Commander Wade completed his final tour of operations, having destroyed twenty-five enemy aircraft in air combat, and was posted to the Staff of Air Vice-Marshal Harry Broadhurst.

Less than two months later this fearless, charming American ace was dead, the victim of a tragic air accident. He was making a routine flight in an Auster light aircraft well behind the British lines in Italy, on the 12th January, 1944, when his aircraft went into an uncontrollable spin. It crashed before Wade had a chance to bale out, and its gallant pilot was killed instantly when it hit the ground and exploded. He was posthumously awarded the Distinguished Service Order, the citation to which summed up his career in the following words: 'An outstanding leader and fighter pilot, Wing Commander Wade's great skill, courage and devotion to duty have largely contributed to the high efficiency attained by his squadron.'

37

THE IMPERTURBABLE 'WOODY'

Wing Commander V. C. Woodward
D.F.C. and Bar

ONE of the main objectives of the Italian Forces, in the early days of the war in the Middle East, was to take possession of the Suez Canal and thereby cut off a very valuable means of communication and transport for the Allied armies. Against the might of the Regia Aeronautica, the Royal Air Force in the Canal Zone had just three squadrons of fighters and these fighters were obsolete compared to the modern monoplane fighters of the enemy. The three squadrons, Numbers 80, 33, and 112 were all equipped with Gladiator biplanes and their task was to defend an area of many thousands of square miles. In order to perform this formidable operation the squadrons had to be split up into flights which were detached to various parts of Egypt and ordered to keep up a standing patrol over their particular zone. This in turn meant that each flight could only afford to send up aircraft in sections of two or three, and inevitably these small forces had to intercept much larger numbers of Italian fighters and bombers. One of the forgotten pilots of the desert who carried out their allotted tasks so successfully during 1940 was a Canadian pilot of Number 33 Squadron, who was known to the rest of his squadron as 'the imperturbable "Woody" '.

Vernon Crompton Woodward, to give him his correct name, was born in Victoria, British Columbia, Canada on the 22nd December, 1916. He was educated at St Michael's Public School, Victoria, and on leaving school tried to join the Royal Canadian Air Force, but in pre-war days it was necessary to have the equivalent of a degree in order to become a pilot in the R.C.A.F. Since he did not possess this, young Woodward decided to come to England to join the Royal Air Force. He was sent to a civil flying school for a short course to see if he was suitable for training as a pilot and at the conclusion of the course passed all the examinations with flying colours and was accepted on a short-service commission as a pilot trainee. He spent the next eight months at Number 6 Flying Training School and on completion of his flying training was posted to the Middle East, where he joined Number 33 Squadron, stationed at Amriya.

Although he was operational from the day war broke out, he had no chance of showing his quality as a fighter pilot until June 1940, when the first campaign in Libya began with an Allied offensive. Within a few days 'Woody', flying in an old but robust Gloster Gladiator, was showing the cool, calm judgement which was to earn him the nickname of 'Imperturbable' and which was also to help him to become one of the leading aces of the first campaign in the desert. On the 14th June, Woody was in the Desert Air Forces' first action against the Italians, who had just entered the war. He took part in a strafing raid on an aerodrome at Sidi Azeiz early in the morning, machine-gunning and disabling a large silvery civil airliner, which was later captured by the Army. During another patrol later in the day, his flight intercepted a number of Italian C.A. 310 bombers, escorted by Fiat

C.R. 32's, over Fort Capuzzo and in the resulting dog-fight, Woody shot down a bomber in flames, his first confirmed kill, and then scored hits on a Fiat C.R. 32, which he last saw diving towards the ground with smoke streaming out behind it.

A fortnight later in another dogfight over Bardia, Woody shot down two Fiat C.R. 32's, one of them falling in flames. He claimed his fourth victim, a Fiat C.R. 42 this time, on the 24th July and on the same day also probably destroyed another of these Italian fighters. The following day, July 25th, provided Woody with an experience he would remember for the rest of his life. He was patrolling with Sergeant Slater, when they were attacked out of the sun by a squadron of C.R. 42's. If the Italians had been a little less excited at the prospect of two easy victories, they would probably have shot down both Gladiators in their first attack, but fortunately for Woodward and Slater they missed, and the Gladiators were able to start their own attack on level terms, at least in respect of height if not in numbers. In a short time the Gladiators had shot down three of the Fiats, one each and the other shared between them. Then Sergeant Slater was shot down and Woody was left alone to face the concerted attacks of the seven remaining C.R. 42's. A less 'imperturbable' man than Woody would undoubtedly have lost his head and tried to dive out of the fight, but the cool, calm Canadian quickly realised that it would be suicide to attempt such an action; he decided there and then that his only chance of survival was to turn into the enemy planes, meeting them head-on as they came at him with guns blazing. For what seemed an eternity to the Canadian but in actual fact lasted only seven or eight minutes, the unequal contest went on and then suddenly the sky was clear. The Italian fighters disappeared, presumably either because they had run out of ammunition or because they were short of fuel. Woody breathed a sigh of relief and then flew back to his base, where he made an excellent landing.

He climbed out of his Gladiator and sat down on the ground, to recall the thrilling events of the last half hour. The terrific nervous tension of the battle had drained every drop of saliva from his mouth and his tongue literally stuck to the roof of his mouth, but a cigarette brought a welcome relief, and he got up to survey the damage to his fighter. He counted just three bullet holes! Could anyone doubt his flying skill after this display?

It was December, 1940, before Woody shot down his next victim, and then in a period of three weeks from the 9th to the 20th he destroyed five C.R. 42's, probably destroyed another

184

fighter of the same type, and damaged four more enemy aircraft.

The squadron was re-equipped with Hurricanes early in 1941, and moved to Greece where under the command of Squadron Leader 'Pat' Pattle it was to win fresh honours. The pace of air-fighting had quickened with the arrival of the Hurricanes and Woody and his colleagues had to change their tactics to suit their new planes. They learned quickly, however, mainly due to the brilliant teaching, and leadership of their South African Commanding Officer who must surely be classed as one of the greatest fighter leaders of the war. One of the squadron's first missions with their new Commanding Officer was on the 5th April, 1941, when they were detailed to escort Blenheims, after which they were to strafe a target at Berat. Just as they were peeling off to make their attack, a number of Fiat G. 50's engaged them and only Pattle and Woodward were able to make a run over the airfield. Pattle destroyed two aircraft on the ground and Woody got another, before they both climbed to join in the dogfight going on overhead. In a few minutes Woody turned in behind a G. 50, shot it down with a well-aimed burst, and so was able to claim his first confirmed air victory in Greece.

One of the most famous of Italian bomber squadrons in Greece at this time was the celebrated 'Greenmice' Squadron, who were commanded by Mussolini's son. On April 6th, five Cant 1007's from this squadron made a raid on Volos and were intercepted over the target by Flight Lieutenant Littler, and Pilot Officer Kirkpatrick, who shot down one of the five before breaking away to refuel.

The remaining four bombers turned for home and were inter-cepted by Woody, who was the only member of 33 Squadron still in the air. Actually he had taken off late because his ground crew were still working in his Hurricane when the rest of the squadron became airborne. He chased them along the Gulf of Corinth, making a series of attacks from the side and rear and eventually shot down two of them in flames. He left a third diving into some clouds with smoke pouring from it, only break-ing off the engagement because he had run out of ammunition. When he landed at Larissa thirty minutes later he found that only four of his eight guns had fired, and therefore he had actually only used up half of his ammunition. He also found that the third Cant had been seen to fall into the sea just off the western mouth of the Gulf of Corinth, thus giving him three confirmed victories in one fight.

A week later Woody was carrying out a lone reconnaissance

flight between Monastir and Vive, when he was engaged by three Me. 109's. Cleverly out-manoeuvring the three Messerschmitts, he shot down one, the pilot of which baled out, and damaged a second, after which the 109's made off and Woody was able to complete his mission in peace and quiet.

Woody and Flight Lieutenant Dean were patrolling over our forward troops the following day, when they noticed a formation of Junkers 87's escorted by Me. 109's approaching. As soon as the two Hurricanes turned towards the enemy planes the Messerschmitts disappeared into some clouds and left the Stukas to defend themselves. They were no match for the Hurricanes, who tore the enemy formation to shreds. Woody destroyed two Stukas, and damaged two more, and 'Dixie' Dean got one confirmed and one damaged. The British and Greek troops had a grandstand view of the whole of the combat and were able to confirm the destruction of all three 87's.

On the 19th April, Woody helped his Commanding Officer to shoot down a Henschel 126 and later in the day destroyed an Me. 109. The next day all the remaining Hurricanes that were left in Greece, were assembled together and a sweep was planned for the late afternoon. Just as they were taking off a large enemy raid was plotted heading towards the airfield, causing the Hurricanes to take off hurriedly in ones and twos. They encountered a large formation of Junkers 88's, escorted by over a hundred Me. 110's and Me. 109's west of Piraeus. In the enormous battle that followed Squadron Leader Pattle shot down three enemy planes before he was himself shot down and killed; Flight Sergeant Cottingham also destroyed three before he was shot down and wounded; and Woody got one Me. 110 down in flames, three more damaged and one Junkers 88 probable, before he had to break away because he had no ammunition left.

The four Hurricanes that were still able to fly and fight after this tremendous battle, flew to Crete and for the next fortnight carried out patrols over ships evacuating troops from Greece. It was during one of these patrols over Suda Bay that Woody was wounded in the leg by cannon-shell splinters, during an attack by Messerschmitts. He managed to bring his damaged Hurricane safely back to Maleme airfield, however, where he discovered two more cannon shells exploded behind the armour at the back of his seat.

By the 18th May, all the Hurricanes had been wrecked, most of them on the ground by the constant strafing of the Luftwaffe, and for a fortnight or so the squadron's pilots and ground crews fought side by side with the Army, in fierce hand-to-hand fighting with the German paratroops. The seven pilots who were fit for flying duties were then evacuated to Amriya, where they joined Number 30 Squadron, and soon after arrival Flight Lieutenant Woodward learned that he had been awarded the Distinguished Flying Cross. The citation credited him with at least eleven enemy aircraft destroyed (actually he had nineteen confirmed victories at the time) and paid tribute to his 'outstanding courage, determination and vigour' and 'his fighting spirit and keenness which have set a splendid example'.

On the 13th June, Woody and his fellow pilots of 33 Squadron collected seven new Hurricanes from the base at Abu Suweir and flew them to Gerawla, where they were attached to Number 274 Squadron. Four days later Woody led six of the Hurricanes to strafe transport columns near Sidi Omar and was just about to dive on the objective when he sighted nine Ju. 87's escorted by six Me. 109's and six Fiat G. 50's at the same height. Immediately he took his flight into the attack and in the ensuing fight he personally destroyed one G. 50 and damaged another.

Woody scored his last air victory on the 12th July. He and Flying Officer Crockett had been scrambled to intercept a lone raider over Alexandria soon after lunch, and had been vectored for over an hour before they saw a Junkers 88 near Amriya. After Woody's first attack the 88 rolled and dived vertically towards the ground, closely followed by the resolute Canadian, who was determined this 88 should never get back to its base. After a long chase at ground level, Woody got in a burst, which caused the 88 to catch fire and then dive into the ground about forty miles south-west of Amriya. He saw two of the crew scramble out of the wreckage apparently unhurt, but both died later in hospital.

This last victory brought Woody's final score to twenty-one enemy aircraft destroyed, five probably destroyed and eleven damaged in air combat, plus another two aircraft destroyed on the ground. He was at this time the top-scoring Canadian ace, and his total was not exceeded until over twelve months later by the incredible 'Screwball' Beurling.

Flight Lieutenant Woodward completed his first tour of operations in September, 1941, and he was posted to Number 20 Service Flying Training School in Rhodesia as a Flying Instructor. He remained in Rhodesia until January, 1943, when he returned to the Middle East as the Commanding Officer of Number 213 Squadron, who were flying Hurricanes with the Desert Air Force. They were based well behind the main fighter force and their allotted task was the guarding of convoys along the North African coast. Their main objective was to keep away the Junkers 87 dive bombers and they were ordered not to engage any aircraft unless the convoys were attacked. Although they invited the Luftwaffe to attack them in numerous ways, the enemy fighters always kept their distance and so although Woody was fully operational for nine months on this convoy patrolling he was unable to engage in any more air fighting. His fine record of achievement was, however, recognised by the Authorities in August, 1943, when he was awarded a Bar to his D.F.C. for his 'outstanding courage and devotion to duty'.

In September, 1943, Woody relinquished command of Number 213 Squadron, and was posted to the Headquarters Staff of the Middle East Air Force, where he remained until April, 1945, when he was given command of the communications squadron flying Lodestars and Dakotas. Woody returned to England in 1946 and after accepting a permanent commission in the Royal Air Force in 1948, commanded Number 19 Squadron, flying Hornets. He became wing leader of a fighter wing in Germany comprising four squadrons of Hunters and later commanded a squadron of Canberras first in Germany and then in Malta. To-day he is a Wing Commander and still serving in the Royal Air Force.

38

MORE AIR FIGHTERS

MANY Royal Air Force fighter pilots went into action for the first time in the Battle of Britain, and the majority of pilots who survived the battle became the nucleus of the new fighter squadrons which were formed later in the war. These veterans were then able to pass on to newly trained pilots their vast knowledge of air fighting and at the same time were able to add to their own personal list of victories.

Finlay Boyd, a young Auxiliary Air Force pilot, was a flight commander in the renowned Number 602 (City of Glasgow)

Squadron when the Battle of Britain began. He went into action for the first time in August, 1940, and very quickly his accurate shooting, cool judgement, and expert flying skill brought him success against the Luftwaffe.

One of his first victories on the 16th August took less than a minute from take-off to landing. A score of Stukas came in for a dive-bombing attack on Tangmere aerodrome just as Boyd was taking off. He hardly had time to retract his undercarriage when he saw a Stuka screaming across his nose. He pressed the gun button and the Junkers 87 went straight into the ground. Boyd banked sharply, completed one circuit of the airfield and then landed to rearm.

By the end of September, 1940, the young fair-haired Scotsman had shot down nine enemy aircraft and been awarded the Distinguished Flying Cross for showing 'a keen desire to engage the enemy irrespective of the odds against him'. A month later when the squadron moved back to Scotland for a rest from operations Flight Lieutenant Boyd was awarded a Bar to his D.F.C. His score was then twelve confirmed victories and a share in the destruction of another enemy aircraft.

In 1941 Boyd was given command of Number 54 Squadron and a year later became leader of the Kenley Spitfire Wing. When he completed his tour of operations in the summer of 1942 he was awarded the Distinguished Service Order. He had been flying almost continuously against the enemy for over two years and was credited with a total of twenty-two and a half enemy aircraft destroyed.

Another Scottish Auxiliary pilot who fought alongside Boyd in 1940 was Pilot Officer George Gilroy, known to his comrades as 'Sheep' because he had been a sheep farmer in Scotland before the war began. Born in Edinburgh in 1915 he was commissioned in Number 603 (City of Edinburgh) Squadron in 1938 and first encountered the Luftwaffe in October, 1939, during the early German raids on Scotland. He shot down three Huns in the first few days of the Battle of Britain and before the end of July, 1940, had been awarded the Distinguished Flying Cross. He added a Bar to this decoration in June, 1942, after twelve months as commanding Officer of Number 609 Squadron, which he led on numerous escort missions, fighter sweeps and offensive patrols. He had ten confirmed kills to his credit when he was sent to the Middle East to take command of a Spitfire Wing in Tunisia. By February, 1943, when he was awarded the Distinguished Service

Order, he had shot down fifteen enemy aircraft and been wounded three times in action. From North Africa he took his wing to Malta, Sicily and Salerno, where having brought his final tally to twenty-one victories he was awarded the American D.F.C. He returned to England in November, 1943, and after a rest from operations was promoted to Group Captain.

Many Polish pilots took part in the Battle of Britain either with British squadrons or in their own Polish Kosciusko Squadron and the ace pilot of all these Poles was Squadron Leader Witold Urbanowicz, who kept seventeen German aircraft from returning to their native shores. He was born in 1906 and had joined the Polish Air Force on his eighteenth birthday. When the Nazis invaded Poland thirteen years later Urbanowicz was an experienced pilot in charge of an Air Training School at Deblin. He escaped together with fifty cadets to Rumania, made his way to the Balkans and found a ship to take his class and himself to France.

Eventually after many adventures Urbanowicz arrived in England and was immediately accepted by the Royal Air Force as a fighter pilot. A brief refresher course on Spitfires and Hurricanes followed and then he was posted to a Hurricane squadron in August, 1940.

On the 15th August he scored his first victory. He was patrolling over the sea near Portsmouth when he spotted four Messerschmitts behind him. He turned and charged headlong into the Huns who scattered in all directions. Witold pursued one of them many miles out over the Channel before finally getting in a burst of gunfire which sent the Messerschmitt into the sea.

The first Polish fighter squadron in the Royal Air Force was formed towards the end of August and Urbanowizc, because of his long experience as a fighter pilot, was given command of 'A' Flight. He led his flight so successfully that when the commanding officer of Number 303 Squadron was killed, Urbanowicz was promoted to succeed him.

He led the squadron for the first time two days later when they intercepted a number of German bombers over the East End of London. They quickly put the Huns to flight and Witold personally disposed of a Dornier 215. On a similar interception patrol a few days later he destroyed an Me. 109 and an Me. 110. After this Urbanowiczs' personal score rose rapidly – in three days he shot down nine German machines.

His last combat during the Battle of Britain occurred on the

30th September, when he led the Poles against thirty bombers over South Kent. He himself engaged a Dornier 215 which soon fell in flames and then he closed on two Me. 109's which did not see him until it was too late. Two short bursts from thirty yards' range sent both of them crashing into the Channel. These last three victories now brought the Polish ace's tally to seventeen and led to the award of the *Virtuti Militari*, the Cross of Valour, and the Distinguished Flying Cross.

Urbanowicz spent the next few months at Fighter Command Headquarters, but in April, 1941, began his second tour of operations as Commanding Officer of the first Polish fighter wing in the R.A.F. He was able to fly only on a very few missions, however, before he was sent to Washington as an Assistant Air Attaché. He remained in the United States until December, 1943, having made numerous requests to be allowed to return to active service in Britain. Finally he volunteered to go to China to fight with the American 14th Air Force. He was accepted and in the early part of 1944 was in action against the Japanese Zeros. At the ripe old age for a fighter pilot of thirty-eight he got the better of several Zeros whilst in the Far East and the Americans thought so highly of him as a fighter pilot that they gave him the Air Medal for his efforts. Witold Urbanowicz returned to the U.S.A. in 1944 and on leaving the Air Force in 1946 took out American citizenship papers.

Jim Hallowes fought his first battles with the Luftwaffe in France before the Battle of Britain had started. An ex-Halton aircraft apprentice, he was a Sergeant Pilot in a Hurricane Squadron when he was awarded the Distinguished Flying Medal for an action which occurred in June, 1940. His squadron had intercepted a formation of enemy aircraft, and Hallowes was concentrating his fire on an Me. 109, when he himself was attacked and hit by another fighter. His propeller stopped spinning as his engine cut out, but he regained control of his Hurricane and began to glide back to friendly territory. Realising that his aircraft would never make it, he prepared to abandon his plane by parachute, but before he could do so, the Messerschmitt came in for a second attack. Hallowes dropped back into his seat, kicked on the rudder bar to slow down his plane, and as the 109 overshot the damaged Hurricane, Sergeant Hallowes lined up the Hun in his sights and then pressed the gun button. The eight Browning guns spat defiantly and the next moment the 109 exploded. A few seconds later Jim Hallowes was floating down beneath his parachute, as his burning Hurricane fell in flames.

Posted to Number 43 Squadron when he returned to England, Jim Hallowes won a Bar to his D.F.M. during the Battle of Britain and in November, 1940, was commissioned and posted to Number 65 Squadron. During 1941 he flew on fighter sweeps with Number 122 Squadron and the following year was given command of Number 165 Squadron. He was awarded the Distinguished Flying Cross in 1942 for his fine leadership of this squadron. The official citation to the award credited him with the destruction of nineteen enemy aircraft, one of which he had shot down at night. By the time the war ended Hallowes was a Wing Commander and his score was reported unofficially as twenty-one enemy aircraft destroyed.

'Chris' Le Roux, who was born in South Africa in 1920, was another veteran of the fighting in France and the Battle of Britain, during which period he baled out of burning and badly damaged Hurricanes on at least twelve occasions. When the Royal Air Force went over to the offensive in 1941, Le Roux was posted to Number 91 Squadron as a flight commander and during the next fifteen months carried out over two hundred operational sorties, which included shipping reconnaissances, strafing raids on enemy aerodromes and ground installations, escort missions and fighter sweeps. He destroyed at least nine enemy aircraft in the air and several more on the ground and by the end of 1942 was wearing the ribbons of the Distinguished Flying Cross and Bar.

In 1943 he was sent to Algeria where he took command of Number 111 Squadron, which he led for three months during which time he added another five Huns to his bag. Whilst he was commanding this squadron he found a tortoise, which was soon adopted as the squadron's mascot. For many months the tortoise walked around, gaily decorated with the name *Oscar* painted on one end of its shell; '111' daubed on the other side; and its rear end displaying a red, white and blue roundel. The squadron operations book also claimed the best line-shoot of the campaign as having been made by this gay South African during his stay with the squadron. It records that Le Roux was telling of a landing he made in some particularly bad weather:

'You know,' he claimed, 'I didn't realise I was down until I heard the ground crew clapping.'

Le Roux won a second Bar to his D.F.C. while he was in Tunisia and then in 1944 returned to the United Kingdom to assume command of Number 602 Squadron, which he led throughout the fierce fighting that went on during the invasion of Normandy. He had shot down a total of twenty-three and a half enemy aircraft and was almost at the end of his third tour of operations, when he was killed in an unfortunate aircraft accident on the 19th September, 1944.

39

NIGHT FIGHTERS

NIGHT fighting had been a purely defensive operation for the first part of the war; Beaufighters, Hurricanes and Defiants had waited over and around the coasts of England for the German bombers and over the years had managed to curb the menace of the night raiders. When the Mosquito fighter aircraft arrived, and with them the latest radar equipment, things had changed and the night fighters now known as 'intruders' had gone over to the offensive. They flew out to France and Germany and surprised the Luftwaffe over their own aerodromes. German night fighters had countered this by concentrating their attacks on R.A.F. night bombers and by 1944 our bomber losses were rising rapidly. The R.A.F.'s reply was to use Mosquitos as long-range escort fighters, seeking out and destroying the Luftwaffe night fighters as they attempted to intercept the British bombers.

Branse Burbridge was the pilot of one of these Mosquito escort fighters and he, with the aid of his navigator 'Bill' Skelton, established a record night-fighting score for any one crew of twenty enemy aircraft destroyed.

Burbridge and Skelton had teamed up together when posted to Number 85 Squadron early in 1944 and from the beginning worked together with perfect understanding. Skelton would sight the image of the enemy aircraft on his radar screen, lead the Mosquito until Burbridge could pick out the darkened outline of the enemy machine, and then Branse's deadly marksmanship would do the rest.

In ten months from March, 1944, these two fearless fliers

carried out over a hundred operational sorties together and shot down twenty enemy planes. Each of them in the same period won the D.S.O. and Bar, and the D.F.C. and Bar. Sixteen of their victories were scored the hard way, during thirty escort missions deep into the heart of enemy territory. Five times they had to fly back to base on one engine, and on one occasion their Mosquito was hit and caught fire over Hamburg, but Burbridge, by means of some expert flying skill and a little luck, managed to put out the fire and limp home across the North Sea. Four times they returned to their airfield to report the destruction of two enemy planes during a single patrol. On one occasion they claimed four victories during one patrol. This notable achievement occurred on the night of November 4th, 1944.

That night Burbridge and Skelton set out on an escort mission which involved over seven hundred bombers and fighters. Over the enemy coast Skelton got a contact on his radar screen and gave his instructions clearly and precisely to bring the Mosquito close behind the tail of a Junkers 88 night fighter. Burbridge opened fire and flames leaped from the port engine of the German plane. Another burst and the 88 went into a steep dive and exploded as it hit the ground.

Burbridge climbed back to rejoin the main bomber stream which carried on and attacked its target successfully. They were on their way home when Bill Skelton got another contact. It took some time before they finally closed with the Hun and recognised it as another Junkers 88. Five minutes later it was a blazing wreck on the ground.

The bomber force now being well ahead of the Mosquito, Burbridge decided to go down to look for German night fighters taking off from the aerodrome at Bonn-Hangelar. He found a Messerschmitt 110 with wheels and flaps down coming in for a landing. It landed – nose first in a river just short of the aerodrome – after a deadly burst of cannon shells from the Mosquito. A few seconds later Burbridge sighted a Junkers 88 nearing the same airfield. He fired straight into its belly and the 88 fell into the airfield in a blazing mass.

When the Mosquito landed at base that night it was soon discovered that Burbridge had used up only two hundred rounds of ammunition in destroying the four German night fighters. At that rate he would have had sufficient shells and bullets left to dispose of six more Huns!

Early in 1945 Branse Burbridge and Bill Skelton finished their tour of operations, although Branse managed to wangle one more intruder sortie on the 23rd April, 1945. He took with him as navigator Flight Lieutenant Boak, Bill Skelton having been posted to Hundred Group, and had a very successful trip to Denmark where he managed to shoot down a Junkers 88 to bring his own personal score to twenty-one confirmed kills, two probables and one damaged, thus making him the R.A.F.'s most successful night-fighter pilot. A few months later he left the Royal Air Force and became a lay preacher.

The record score by any night-fighter navigator was set up by Flight Lieutenant Douggie Oxby, D.S.O., D.F.C., D.F.M., and Bar. In just over three years of operational flying he produced thirty-six visual contacts on enemy aircraft, which resulted in twenty-six interceptions. During these actions twenty-two enemy aircraft were destroyed, two were probably destroyed, and two were damaged.

Oxby had begun his night-fighter career in 1941 as a Sergeant Radar Operator with Number 68 Squadron, which was then based in the Midlands, and had teamed up with an Australian pilot, Flight Lieutenant M. C. Shipard, who later on was awarded the D.F.C. and Bar. They scored their first victory in November, 1941, when the destroyed a Heinkel 111 over Anglesey during a raid on Liverpool; soon after this they were posted for service in the Middle East, where with Number 89 Squadron, they shot down seven enemy aircraft over the Western Desert in night battles. Oxby was awarded the D.F.M. in October, 1942, when the citation mentioned that he had taken part in five intruder patrols over Sicily and several convoy patrols. It also said that 'on one occasion in October, 1942, he took part in a successful interception at 22,000 feet without the aid of oxygen, in order that his pilot could obtain the benefit of the little that was left'.

A Bar to his D.F.M. and a commission followed after a period of service in Malta, by which time Oxby and Shipard had destroyed thirteen Huns, probably destroyed two more, and damaged a further two. In July, 1943, Oxby said goodbye to his Australian friend and returned to England for a rest period. In March, 1944, he began his second tour of operations when he was posted to Number 219 Squadron. Shortly before the squadron moved to France, he became navigator to the Commanding Officer, Wing Commander Peter Green, and very quickly they set up a thriving partnership. On one of their first missions together they shot down three Junkers 87's.

They were patrolling over Nijmegen at about 8.30 p.m. on the

2nd October, when the Ground Controller informed them of the presence of a number of Huns, Oxby got a contact a few minutes later, well above and at a range of about two miles. Giving his instructions clearly and concisely to his pilot, Oxby led the Mosquito towards the Hun, until Green caught a glimpse of a plane at a distance of 3,000 feet, flying very slowly at around 140 m.p.h. Putting down all his flaps in an effort to slow down to the speed of the enemy, Green closed in and soon identified the plane as a Junkers 87, this being verified by Oxby with the aid of his night glasses. He opened fire from slightly below the Hun and saw strikes on the fuselage. The Stuka turned to the right and Green fired again. Immediately the 87 disintegrated and some of the wreckage hit the Mosquito, but no great damage was done, so they continued their patrol.

Five minutes later Oxby got another contact and soon Green was closing on another Junkers 87. This was more troublesome than the first, taking violent evasive action, and for a time Green lost sight of it. But Oxby quickly led him back towards the 87, and this time Green made no mistake, the German falling in flames about seven miles east of Nijmegen. Turning back towards the town, Oxby within a few minutes had found another Hun, which again proved to be a Junkers 87, when they were near enough to identify it. After two bursts of cannon shells it blew up and the remains fell burning to the ground. Green was then ordered to return to base, but even as he turned to head for home, Oxby got another contact, so they decided to investigate. They found yet another Stuka and were almost in position to open fire when the 87 fired a cluster of eight white recognition colours, which momentarily blinded Green and forced him to break away. They failed to make any more contacts after this, so flew back to their base at Brussels Melsbrook where they landed at 9.30 p.m.

Awarded the D.F.C. soon after this remarkable success, Oxby continued to fly with Wing Commander Green until February, 1945, by which time they had shot down a further five enemy planes at night. Then Peter Green was killed whilst testing a Mosquito and Douggie Oxby had to finish the war with a new pilot. He was awarded the D.S.O. in February, 1945, by which time he had helped in the destruction of twenty-one aircraft and he just had time to help his new pilot to destroy one more plane before the war ended.

Another successful night fighter who fought right through the war was Desmond Hughes, who was born in Northern Ireland in 1919. He joined the Cambridge University Air Squadron when he was nineteen years old, and he was still an undergraduate at Pembroke College when the Second World War broke out. Within a month he had been commissioned and in June, 1940, was posted to Number 264, the Madras Presidency Squadron, who were equipped with Defiant two-seater turret fighters. The first time the squadron encountered the enemy was on the 29th May, 1940, over Dunkirk, and immediately they scored a tremendous success. The Luftwaffe pilots mistook them for Hurricanes, and thereupon made attacks from the rear of the Defiants, right in the face of the rear-firing four-gun turrets of the English aircraft.

In two fierce battles, the Madras squadron claimed seventeen Messerschmitts, and twelve Junkers 88's and Stukas without loss. Des Hughes accounted for two Huns in operations over the Thames Estuary and Kent in August, 1940, and then the squadron was withdrawn from daylight operations, the Defiants being too slow and vulnerable for the Messerschmitts; instead they began to fly on night fighting missions. Hughes with the help of his rear gunner, Sergeant Fred Gash, soon shot down two bombers over London and in April, 1941, was awarded the Distinguished Flying Cross for his efforts. A month later he added a Junkers 88 to his score.

In 1942 Hughes was posted to 125 Squadron and, soon after joining it, he shot down the first enemy plane to be destroyed by this squadron. Later on he shared in the destruction of a Junkers 88 before leaving England to take up the position of flight commander in Number 600 (City of London) Beaufighter Squadron in North Africa in 1943. Now teamed up with Flight Lieutenant Laurie Dixon, he shot down two Ju. 88's in one night, destroyed a Cant bomber a few weeks later, and in March, 1943, received a Bar to his D.F.C. During the next five months he shot down seven more enemy machines, including three Ju. 88's in one patrol, and in September, 1943, he was awarded a second Bar to his D.F.C. He returned to England to take up a post at Fighter Command Headquarters and later on was promoted to Wing Commander in charge of night operations at Headquarters Number Eighty-five Group in the Second Tactical Air Force.

In July, 1944, he began his second tour of operations when he took command of 604 Squadron, a Mosquito night-fighter unit of the Second Tactical Air Force in France. Again teamed with Dixon, he shot down another two enemy aircraft to bring his final score to eighteen and a half, and at the end of March, 1945, was awarded the Distinguished Service Order. The citation stated that he 'had displayed the highest standard of devotion to duty throughout a long period of operational flying'. It also paid tribute to 'his outstanding keenness, great skill, and unsurpassed determination'.

When the war ended Des Hughes decided to remain in the R.A.F. and shortly afterwards he was offered, and accepted, a permanent commission in the Royal Air Force. Today he is a Group Captain and has added the C.B.E., and A.F.C. to his other decorations.

With a final score of eleven enemy aircraft and nineteen flying bombs destroyed and several more aircraft damaged, Wing Commander Russell Bannock, D.S.O., D.F.C. and Bar, was the leading night-fighter ace of the Royal Canadian Air Force. Born in Edmonton, Alberta, on November 1st 1919, he was already an experienced pilot when he joined the R.C.A.F. in September, 1939, and consequently he was kept in Canada as a flying instructor for the first four years of the war. He arrived in England in February, 1944, went to a Mosquito Operational Training Unit in Salop, and finally began his tour of operations when he was posted to Number 418 Squadron in June, 1944. A week later he destroyed an Me. 110 in flames whilst on an intruding patrol. Following this during a period of eight weeks between 19th June and 12th August, 1944, Bannock and his navigator, Flying Officer Bob Bruce, D.F.C. and Bar, shot down nineteen flying bombs. One night, on July 5th, these two destroyed four 'doodle bugs', another night they brought down three and on four other occasions they destroyed a pair of these V-1's. During this same period Bannock had added another aircraft destroyed to his bag.

Towards the end of August the squadron went back full-time to intruder operations and on the 30th of the same month Bannock made an intruding raid on an airfield near Copenhagen, during which he set fire to a Junkers 88 and blew up an Me. 110. A fortnight later he shot down his fifth enemy aircraft and before the end of September had been promoted to take command of 418 Squadron and had been awarded the Distinguished Flying Cross and Bar.

On the 27th September, Bannock shot down two Me. 108's near Parow airfield. In the second combat his Mosquito was damaged by flying debris and his port engine set on fire. Nevertheless, he managed to put out the fire and then flew over 600 miles back to his base at tree-top height with one propeller feathered.

In November, 1944, Wing Commander Bannock was given command of 406 Squadron, another Canadian Mosquito intruder unit, and during the next six months led it so successfully that by the time the war ended, the Lynx Squadron had become the top-scoring intruder squadron in Fighter Command. During the same period Wing Commander Bannock destroyed four more Huns to put himself at the top of the list of Royal Canadian Air Force night fighters.

When the war ended, Bannock became Director of Operations, R.C.A.F. Headquarters, in London. He attended a Royal Air Force Staff College course from September, 1945, to May, 1946, when he returned to his native country. Subsequently he retired from the R.C.A.F. and joined the de Havilland Aircraft Company of Canada.

BIBLIOGRAPHY

AIR ACES	Gordon Anthony	*Home & Van Thal*
FLAMES IN THE SKY	P. H. Clostermann	*Chatto & Windus*
R.A.F. BIGGIN HILL	Graham Wallace	*Putnam & Co.*
FIGHTER PILOT	Paul Richey	*Hutchinson & Co.*
SO FEW	David Masters	*Eyre & Spottiswoode*
SAILOR MALAN	Oliver Walker	*Cassell*
WING LEADER	J. E. Johnson	*Chatto & Windus*
NINE LIVES	Alan Deere	*Hodder & Stoughton*
THE BIG SHOW	P. H. Clostermann	*Chatto & Windus*
WINGS OVER OLYMPUS	T. H. Wisdom	*Allen & Unwin*
COMBAT REPORT	Hector Bolitho	*Batsford*
DESTINY CAN WAIT	Polish A.F.A.	*Wm. Heinemann*
TIGER SQUADRON	J. I. T. Jones	*W. H. Allen*
TEST PILOT	N. F. Duke	*Wingate*
FLY FOR YOUR LIFE	Larry Forrester	*Muller*
REACH FOR THE SKY	Paul Brickhill	*Collins*
NIGHT FIGHTER	Rawnsley & Wright	*Collins*
NEW ZEALANDERS IN THE AIR WAR	Alan W. Mitchell	*Harrap*
PILOTS OF FIGHTER COMMAND	Capt. Cuthbert Orde	*Harrap*
DRAWING THE R.A.F.	Eric Kennington	*Oxford Univ. Press*
303 SQUADRON	Arkady Fiedler	*Peter Davies*
MALTA SPITFIRE	Beurling & Roberts	*Farrar & Reinhart, N.Y.*
BORN TO FLY	Georges Blond	*Souvenir Press*
FIGHTER COMMAND	A. B. Austin	*Gollancz*
R.A.A.F. OVER EUROPE	Frank Johnson	*Eyre & Spottiswoode*

R.C.A.F.		
OVERSEAS	——	*Oxford Univ. Press*
SPITFIRES OVER	Brennan, Hesselyn &	
MALTA	Bateson	*Jarrolds*
RAIDERS APPROACH	B. Sutton	*Gale & Polden*
GLASGOW'S FIGHTER		
SQUADRON	F. G. Nancarrow	*Collins*

Various issues of the following magazines:
R.A.F. FLYING REVIEW
FLIGHT
THE AEROPLANE
AERONAUTICS
AIR FORCE NEWS

HIGHEST SCORING FIGHTER PILOTS, ROYAL AIR FORCE, 1939–1945

					Enemy aircraft destroyed
JOHNSON, Air Commodore J. E.	.	.	.	.	38
PATTLE, Squadron Leader M. T. St. J.	.	.	.	.	34
CLOSTERMANN, Wing Commander P. H.	.	.	.	33
FINUCANE, Wing Commander B. E.	.	.	.	.	32
MALAN, Group Captain, A. G.	.	.	.	.	32
BEURLING, Squadron Leader G. F.	.	.	.	.	31½
BRAHAM, Wing Commander, J. R. D.	.	.	.	29
TUCK, Wing Commander R. R. S.	.	.	.	.	29
CALDWELL, Group Captain C.R.	.	.	.	.	28½
CAREY, Group Captain F. R.	.	.	.	.	28
DUKE, Squadron Leader N. F.	.	.	.	.	28
FRANTISEK, Sergeant J.	.	.	.	.	28
LACEY, Squadron Leader J. H.	.	.	.	.	28
GRAY, Wing Commander C. F.	.	.	.	.	27½
LOCK, Flight Lieutenant E. S.	.	.	.	.	26
WADE, Wing Commander L. C.	.	.	.	.	25
DRAKE, Group Captain B.	.	.	.	.	24
LE ROUX, Squadron Leader J. J.	.	.	.	.	23½
BADER, Group Captain, D. R. S.	.	.	.	.	22½
BOYD, Wing Commander R. F.	.	.	.	.	22½
KINGABY, Group Captain D. E.	.	.	.	.	22½
STEPHEN, Wing Commander H. M.	.	.	.	.	22⅓
SKALSKI, Wing Commander S.	.	.	.	.	22¼
CROSSLEY, Wing Commander M. N.	.	.	.	.	22
HUGO, Group Captain P. H.	.	.	.	.	22
STEPHENS, Group Captain M. M.	.	.	.	.	22
COMPTON, Group Captain W. V. C.	.	.	.	.	21½
DEERE, Group Captain A. C.	.	.	.	.	21½
HESSELYN, Squadron Leader R. B.	.	.	.	.	21½

HIGHEST SCORING NIGHT FIGHTERS,
ROYAL AIR FORCE, 1938–1945

		Enemy aircraft destroyed
OXBY, Wing Commander D.	Radar Operator	22
BURBRIDGE, Wing Commander B. A.	Pilot	21
SKELTON, Squadron Leader F. S.	Radar Operator	20
BRAHAM, Wing Commander J. R. D.	Pilot	19
CUNNINGHAM, Group Captain J.	Pilot	19
HUGHES, Group Captain F. D.	Pilot	16½
RAWNSLEY, Squadron Leader C. F.	Radar Operator	16
KUTTELWASCHER, Flight Lieutenant K.	Pilot	15

THE RED BERET

by
Hilary St. George Saunders

This is the story of Arnhem, Bruneval, the Ardennes, Normandy, the crossing of the Rhine. It is the story of the Red Devils, the most heroic band of daredevils any war has ever produced.

NEW ENGLISH LIBRARY

NEL BESTSELLERS

Crime

T013 332	CLOUDS OF WITNESS	*Dorothy L. Sayers* 40p
T016 307	THE UNPLEASANTNESS AT THE BELLONA CLUB	
		Dorothy L. Sayers 40p
T021 548	GAUDY NIGHT	*Dorothy L. Sayers* 40p
T026 698	THE NINE TAILORS	*Dorothy L. Sayers* 50p
T026 671	FIVE RED HERRINGS	*Dorothy L. Sayers* 50p
T015 556	MURDER MUST ADVERTISE	*Dorothy L. Sayers* 40p

Fiction

T018 520	HATTER'S CASTLE	*A. J. Cronin* 75p
T013 944	CRUSADER'S TOMB	*A. J. Cronin* 60p
T013 936	THE JUDAS TREE	*A. J. Cronin* 50p
T015 386	THE NORTHERN LIGHT	*A. J. Cronin* 50p
T026 213	THE CITADEL	*A. J. Cronin* 80p
T027 112	BEYOND THIS PLACE	*A. J. Cronin* 60p
T016 609	KEYS OF THE KINGDOM	*A. J. Cronin* 50p
T027 201	THE STARS LOOK DOWN	*A. J. Cronin* 90p
T018 539	A SONG OF SIXPENCE	*A. J. Cronin* 50p
T001 288	THE TROUBLE WITH LAZY ETHEL	*Ernest K. Gann* 30p
T003 922	IN THE COMPANY OF EAGLES	*Ernest K. Gann* 30p
T023 001	WILDERNESS BOY	*Stephen Harper* 35p
T017 524	MAGGIE D	*Adam Kennedy* 60p
T022 390	A HERO OF OUR TIME	*Mikhail Lermontov* 45p
T025 691	SIR, YOU BASTARD	*G. F. Newman* 40p
T022 536	THE HARRAD EXPERIMENT	*Robert H. Rimmer* 50p
T022 994	THE DREAM MERCHANTS	*Harold Robbins* 95p
T023 303	THE PIRATE	*Harold Robbins* 95p
T022 968	THE CARPETBAGGERS	*Harold Robbins* £1·00
T016 560	WHERE LOVE HAS GONE	*Harold Robbins* 75p
T023 958	THE ADVENTURERS	*Harold Robbins* £1·00
T025 241	THE INHERITORS	*Harold Robbins* 90p
T025 276	STILETTO	*Harold Robbins* 50p
T025 268	NEVER LEAVE ME	*Harold Robbins* 50p
T025 292	NEVER LOVE A STRANGER	*Harold Robbins* 90p
T022 226	A STONE FOR DANNY FISHER	*Harold Robbins* 80p
T025 284	79 PARK AVENUE	*Harold Robbins* 75p
T025 187	THE BETSY	*Harold Robbins* 80p
T020 894	RICH MAN, POOR MAN	*Irwin Shaw* 90p

Historical

T022 196	KNIGHT WITH ARMOUR	*Alfred Duggan* 50p
T022 250	THE LADY FOR RANSOM	*Alfred Duggan* 50p
T015 297	COUNT BOHEMOND	*Alfred Duggan* 50p
T017 958	FOUNDING FATHERS	*Alfred Duggan* 50p
T017 753	WINTER QUARTERS	*Alfred Duggan* 50p
T021 297	FAMILY FAVOURITES	*Alfred Duggan* 50p
T022 625	LEOPARDS AND LILIES	*Alfred Duggan* 60p
T019 624	THE LITTLE EMPERORS	*Alfred Duggan* 50p
T020 126	THREE'S COMPANY	*Alfred Duggan* 50p
T021 300	FOX 10: BOARDERS AWAY	*Adam Hardy* 35p

Science Fiction

T016 900	STRANGER IN A STRANGE LAND	*Robert Heinlein* 75p
T020 797	STAR BEAST	*Robert Heinlein* 35p
T017 451	I WILL FEAR NO EVIL	*Robert Heinlein* 80p
T026 817	THE HEAVEN MAKERS	*Frank Herbert* 35p
T027 279	DUNE	*Frank Herbert* 90p
T022 854	DUNE MESSIAH	*Frank Herbert* 60p
T023 974	THE GREEN BRAIN	*Frank Herbert* 35p
T012 859	QUEST FOR THE FUTURE	*A. E. Van Vogt* 35p
T015 270	THE WEAPON MAKERS	*A. E. Van Vogt* 30p
T023 265	EMPIRE OF THE ATOM	*A. E. Van Vogt* 40p
T017 354	THE FAR-OUT WORLDS OF A. E. VAN VOGT	*A. E. Van Vogt* 40p

War

Western

General

Mad

....

NEL P.O. BOX 11, FALMOUTH, CORNWALL

For U.K. & Eire: customers should include to cover postage, 15p for the first book plus 5p per copy for each additional book ordered, up to a maximum charge of 50p.
For Overseas customers & B.F.P.O.: customers should include to cover postage, 20p for the first book and 10p per copy for each additional book.

Name ....

Address...

....

Title ....
(MAY)